Children's Voices

Talk, Knowledge and Identity

Janet Maybin
The Open University, UK

palgrave
macmillan

First published in hardback 2006
This paperback edition published 2007 by
PALGRAVE MACMILLAN
Houndmills, Basingstoke, Hampshire RG21 6XS and
175 Fifth Avenue, New York, N. Y. 10010
Companies and representatives throughout the world

PALGRAVE MACMILLAN is the global academic imprint of the Palgrave
Macmillan division of St. Martin's Press, LLC and of Palgrave Macmillan Ltd.
Macmillan® is a registered trademark in the United States, United Kingdom
and other countries. Palgrave is a registered trademark in the European
Union and other countries.

ISBN-13: 978–1–4039–3330–0   hardback
ISBN-10: 1–4039–3330–8   hardback
ISBN-13: 978–1–4039–3331–7   paperback
ISBN-10: 1–4039–3331–6   paperback

This book is printed on paper suitable for recycling and made from fully
managed and sustained forest sources. Logging, pulping and manufacturing
processes are expected to conform to the environmental regulations of the
country of origin.

A catalogue record for this book is available from the British Library.

Library of Congress Cataloging-in-Publication Data
Maybin, Janet, 1950–
    Children's voices : talk, knowledge, and identity / Janet Maybin.
        p. cm.
    Includes bibliographical references and index.
    ISBN 1–4039–3330–8 (cloth) 1–4039–3331–6 (pbk)
        1. Communicative competence in children. 2. Verbal ability in children.
3. Children–Language–Social aspects. 4. Dialogue analysis. 5. Identity
(Psychology) 6. Oral communication. 7. Anthropological linguistics. I. Title.

P118.4.M39 2005   2005049566
306.44–dc22

10   9   8   7   6   5   4   3   2   1
16 15 14 13 12 11 10 09 08 07

Printed and bound in Great Britain by
CPI Antony Rowe, Chippenham and Eastbourne

For Jo, Simon, Seth and Zareen

Contents

Acknowledgements

I am deeply grateful to the children whose recorded conversations form the basis of this book. They welcomed me generously into their lives and I have returned again and again to the data they provided. In reproducing their voices here, I hope I have done justice to the liveliness and complexity of their language use. I also want to express my thanks to the headteachers and staff of the two schools where I carried out my research; I could not have done the work without their support.

I have had many conversations about this research with colleagues and friends over the years and these dialogues lie behind and have helped to structure my account in the book. I would like to thank the following people, all of whom have provided encouragement and commented on book chapters or on previous papers: Richard Barwell, David Bloome, Ron Carter, Angela Creese, Jennifer Coates, Sharon Goodman, David Graddol, Martyn Hammersley, Mary Lea, Theresa Lillis, Deidre Martin, Neil Mercer, Gemma Moss, Sarah North, Kieran O'Halloran, Ben Rampton, Alison Sealey, Brian Street, Joan Swann, Karin Tusting and Margie Wetherell. I want particularly to acknowledge my intellectual debt to Brian Street, who has been a generous and inspiring teacher and friend. Responding to comments and suggestions from others has led me to new insights and understanding. Of course, all responsibility for shortcomings in the final manuscript lies with myself. I would also like to thank photographer John Hunt and the school children models (not in the research) who posed for the photograph on the front cover, and Pam Burns for her help with formatting the manuscript. I owe Seth an enormous debt of gratitude for his forebearance and support while I was working on numerous drafts. Finally I would like to thank Shirley Tan of EXPO for her meticulous editing and Chris Candlin and Palgrave, especially Jill Lake, who gave me the opportunity to draw my work on children's meaning-making together, within this book.

Transcription Conventions

In representing children's voices in the transcripts, I have recorded their non-standard grammatical expressions as accurately as possible, but not their non-standard pronunciation of particular words. In order to make the transcripts more readable, I have added some written punctuation. The names of people and places have been changed, to protect anonymity.

Comments in italics and parentheses clarify what's happening, or indicate non-verbal features e.g. *(points to snail)*, *(laughter)*.

(...) indicates words on the tape which I can't make out,

/ indicates where another speaker interrupts or cuts in,

⌈ indicates simultaneous talk. The overlapping talk is also lined up
⌊ vertically on the page.

Ages of children

Camdean

Julie (10 years)
Kirsty (10 years)
Sharon (10 years)
David (10 years)

Lakeside (main research site school)

Darren (12 years)
Karlie (12 years)
Simon (12 years)
Keith (12 years)
Sherri (almost 12)
Tina (almost 12)
Alan (11 years)
Karen (11 years)
Kevin (11 years)
Kieran (11 years)

Martie (11 years)
Michelle (11 years)
Terry (11 years)
Lee (11 years)
Geoffrey (10 years)
Helen (10 years)
Melissa (10 years)
Nicole (10 years)
Sam (10 years)

Introduction

> The word in language is always half someone else's. It becomes 'one's own' only when the speaker populates it with his own intention, his own accent, when he appropriates the word, adapting it to his own semantic and expressive intention. Prior to this moment of appropriation, the word does not exist in a neutral and impersonal language (it is not, after all, out of a dictionary, that the speaker gets their words!), but rather it exists in other peoples' mouths, in other peoples' concrete contexts, serving other people's intentions: it is from there that one must take the word, and make it one's own.
>
> (Bakhtin, 1981, pp. 293–94)

> The ideological becoming of a human being ... is the process of selectively assimilating the words of others.
>
> (*op cit.*, p. 341)

In this Introduction I explain the focus of the book, introduce my theoretical approach to analysing children's talk and provide an outline of the individual chapters.

Focussing on the margins

This book is about a part of children's language experience which lies outside the scope of mainstream accounts. I focus on how 10–12 year-old school children use talk to construct knowledge and identity, particularly through their use of other people's voices, and especially in 'off-task' conversations among themselves. While there is a long history of research on talk and learning in school, this has tended to concentrate on children's curriculum-orientated talk. Findings are usually framed in terms of what could be termed an 'educational gaze', that is, educational definitions of knowledge and skills and psychological measurements of child development. In this book, I construct a different kind of lens through which to examine what is happening in children's talk. First, while my recorded data includes children's dialogues with teachers and talk among themselves as they work through classroom tasks, it also covers the whole range of children's other talk in school: 'off-task' talk in the classroom, at break time, as they pass through the school corridors, get changed for swimming or sit together at lunchtime. I take my cue for what children can do in talk not from their rather muted role in dialogue with the teacher, but from their undirected conversations elsewhere where they pursue their own questions and preoccupations. Secondly, I draw on linguistic ethnography and poststructuralist theory to construct an analytic framework which is orientated towards a much broader conception of knowledge and learning than is usual in traditional educational research, and incorporates a more dynamic conception of communication. I use this framework to capture some of the ongoing collaborative processes of meaning-making in children's talk, both inside and outside the classroom, right across the school day.

The children in my study are at the point of negotiating the transition between childhood and adolescence and are starting to explore new kinds of knowledge, relationships and identities. Attending two nearby Middle Schools in Southern England which I used as my pilot and main research site, they could be seen as a fairly homogenous group in terms of age, ethnicity, social background and locality. The schools served largely white working-class public housing estates, situated at the edge of a new city and abutting on to more rural farm-land. However, as I shall explain in the course of the book, this apparent homogeneity is deceptive. I was to discover an enormous range of diversity in children's personal experience, and in the different ways in which they inhabited the same nominal categories of age, gender and class. While there is now a rich literature documenting cultural and linguistic diversity in classrooms, I provide an account of the diversity of the individual experience of 10–12 year-olds who seemed, on the face of it, to come from a very similar social and ethnic background.

Conceptualising voice and meaning-making

Like many people of my generation working in language and education, I have been strongly influenced by the Russian psychologist

Vygotsky's ideas[1] about how children learn through dialogue and how this learning then feeds into individual conceptual development. However, while most neo-Vygotskian work has focussed on dialogues between teachers and pupils, adopting the educational gaze I mentioned above, I am applying his ideas about language and thought more broadly. Vygotsky makes it clear that the dialogues through which children learn have strong cultural-historical dimensions. They are vehicles of socialisation as well as of conceptual development and the two processes are closely intertwined. As he puts it, 'The history of the process of the internalisation of social speech is also the history of the socialisation of children's practical intellect.' (Vygotsky, 1978, p. 27). My approach in this book is to view children's dialogue as an important vehicle for constructing knowledge about their social world as well as more formalised educational knowledge, and as fulfilling a number of simultaneous individual and social functions. Talk is referential, in the sense of referring to and representing the world, evaluative in making some kind of comment on experience, interpersonal in its contribution to children's construction of relationships with others and emotive in presenting children's inner feelings. These meanings are always co-present and always interrelated, in teacher-pupil dialogues as well as in children's talk among themselves.

Alongside my exploration of children's talk in the book, I build up an analytic framework, a language of description, which can capture the multifunctional, dynamic nature of their ongoing meaning-making. Treating culture as a verb rather than a noun,[2] in other words, seeing culture as emerging through processes within social practice rather than consisting of set patterns and products, I examine how ideas about contextual cues in talk, dialogue and evaluation can be used to unravel the intricate dynamics of meaning in children's talk. There is a tension here between the essentially processual nature of social practice and the fact that people orientate towards relatively stable social categories, beliefs and values. In the context of the different timescales of change at different levels of social life, I focus mainly on change at the micro level, in the course of children's social activity in everyday life. These moment-by-moment negotiations of identity and knowledge will feed into children's personal change over a number of years, as they make the transition from childhood into adolescence. And both these different kinds of change, with their different timescales, intersect with broader, slower-acting cultural change in social beliefs and values.

The book suggests ways of operationalising a number of concepts from the writings of Bakhtin and Volosinov[3] and applying them within a detailed linguistic ethnographic analysis of children's communicative practices. I use the Russian language philosopher Mikhail Bakhtin's concept of speech genre, together with ideas from linguistic anthropology about context cues in language, in order to look at how children draw on the contexts of their lives for meaning-making within talk. Bakhtin (1986) sees all language as patterned into a large and changing variety of speech genres (spoken and written), from informal everyday conversations, bureaucratic language, business documents, political speeches, to all manner of literary genres. A speech genre includes the language forms and use, content themes and evaluative perspectives which emerge in a specific sphere of human activity. Speech genres are an integral part of social practices, which include what people do as well as their use of language. Social practices in their turn both reflect and help to produce the macro-level complexes of language, knowledge and power (sometimes referred to as discourses[4]), which organise how people think and act.

I see the Bakhtinian concept of evaluation as central to the 'ideological becoming of a human being'. 'Evaluation' refers to the way in which we can never talk about anything without making some kind of judgement reflecting an assumed evaluative framework and signalling our own position in relation to it. Children, as I discovered, are constantly evaluating their social experience in the course of talk and this evaluative activity reveals how they are becoming conscious of their positioning in the world, acting on their environment and developing a sense of themselves as a particular kind of person. At the same time as expressing individual agency, the evaluation in children's talk reflects their social background and the beliefs and values of their community. The social parameters of evaluation reflect the macro level discourses I referred to above. In this sense it is part of their socialisation into particular kinds of culturally authorised evaluative perspectives and judgements about how to be in and act on the world. I see children's ongoing identification as individuals and their continuing socialisation as two sides of the same process, with evaluation as a double-edged driving force.

The arguments of Bakhtin and his colleague Volosinov about the multi-voiced nature of language lie at the heart of this book. Bakhtin and Volosinov see language as full of the voices of different genres, and what Bakhtin calls the social languages of different age groups, generations, professions and classes. More profoundly, they see words as always carrying the intentions of previous speakers and the connotations of their former contexts of use. This emerges most clearly in the ways in which children, quite literally, take their words from other people's mouths. When I first listened to the recordings, I was struck by how often children referred to or quoted the voices of teachers, parents, friends, textbooks and pop songs, and also how they reproduced their own voice in anecdotes and in other references to previous experience. The voices children reconstruct seem to provide them with an extraordinarily rich resource for meaning-making. Reproduced speech was the main means used by the 10–12 year-olds in my study to invoke previous experience and bring it to bear on what was happening in the present. In particular, the children evaluated people, relationships and events through the ways in which they rephrased and reframed reported speech and through their orchestration of dialogues in anecdotes and longer narratives. This evaluation was negotiated and reconfigured through the ongoing dialogue between children and other people so that individual impressions and reactions became socially forged.

In summary, this book is about what 10–12 year-olds talk about and how they do it, especially when they are away from adults, focussing in particular in the role of contextualisation, dialogue and evaluation in children's developing construction of knowledge and identity, especially through their use of reproduced speech. This construction of knowledge and identity feeds into the longer term processes of socialisation and identification, which continue in various ways throughout life. The book is also about a linguistic ethnographic approach to investigating children's language practices, and what this can deliver in terms of insights about children's meaning-making. I use linguistic ethnography to find ways of conceptualising identity not through labels like class, gender or age or in terms of fixed personal attributes but as emerging through the flow of social practice. I also use it to locate and describe the unofficial knowledge which children are generating through talk together, beyond the official school curriculum.

The anthropological perspective has always worked in two directions, making the familiar strange as well as making the strange familiar. In the research I had to shift away from the familiar educational gaze in order to defamiliarise what I saw in the classroom and to move towards the children's perspective. In the account in this book, I develop an analytical framework which reveals insights about children's (strange) private worlds and documents the relatively under-researched dynamic processes of meaning-making in their ongoing informal talk.

Outline of the chapters

In the book I interweave discussion of examples of children's talk with the development of my argument about how we can understand their meaning-making. In the first chapter I set the scene for the rest of the book. I give some flavour of collecting the recorded data and doing the research which laid the basis for my understanding of the children's social lives and their cultural world. I also develop the basis for my conceptual framework, which involved a shift towards more dynamic conceptions of context, dialogue and identity. First, I explain how I moved from a relatively static image of how different contexts influence children's talk to a more dynamic conception of how current and alternative contexts are reconfigured in children's talk, as part of their meaning-making. Secondly, I develop the idea of dialogue beyond the notion of the collaborative construction of knowledge in neo-Vygotskian work, through using Bakhtinian ideas about the patterning of dialogic links within and across conversations. Thirdly, I begin to explore Bakhtin and Volosinov's argument that language use is always evaluative, in relation to examples from the children's talk, and examine the role of evaluation in children's ongoing socialisation and construction of identity.

In Chapter 2, I develop my analysis of the contextual cues in talk. I suggest that children switch easily between the different speech genres in their lives and draw creatively and strategically on the generic resources of different contexts for meaning-making. I introduce Goffman's notion of framing to look at how relationships and identities are negotiated at a micro-level from moment to moment within speech genres. I suggest that contrasts between contextual cues and framing in teacher-dominated talk and in peer talk are associated with different kinds of knowledge construction, together with different opportunities for evaluation and identity.

Chapter 3 focusses on the patterns of collaboration that I found in children's conversations. I explore the multifunctional nature of children's talk and the ways in which utterances can be retrospectively refunctioned across the course of a conversation. I examine ideas about the relationship between language and gender, suggesting that while there are certain gendered patterns in the data, there is no simple correlation between children's gender and their language use. The expression of gender identity emerges partly through children's choices of personal style in language, within the context of their engagement in speech genres and associated social practice which are both a resource for, and a limitation to, children's creativity.

In Chapters 4–7, I develop my argument about the central importance of children's reproduction of other voices in the interrelated
processes of meaning-making, socialisation and the construction of
identity. I first look in Chapter 4 at how reproduced voices and
snatches of dialogue provide enormously powerful ways of recreating
and commenting on experience and drawing the listener in. Reported
speech particularly clearly illustrates Bakhtin's concept of 'double-
voicing', where the intentions of the original speaker and the intentions of the speaker reporting the voice are both represented within a
single utterance. I examine how children convey judgements about
people, relationships and events through the different ways in which
the voices are reported.

Chapters 5 focusses on how reproduced voices are orchestrated in
anecdotes in children's ongoing talk among themselves. I look at the
role of children's stories in representing and evaluating experience,
and in presenting and exploring identity. I examine three interrelated
levels of narrative meaning which are produced through the text of the
story, through its function at a particular point in a conversation and
through the contextual links it makes with children's experience. I use
the anecdotes of three individual children to look in particular at the
role of reproduced voices in conveying children's agency and their
negotiation and performance of gender identity.

The longer stories which children produced in my interviews with
friendship pairs are discussed in Chapter 6. I look at the way in which
children used these to present and explore personal experiences at
greater length, and to reflect on the moral issues which confronted
them in their lives, about justice, care and cruelty and adult relationships. Again, I look at the dialogical production of the stories, the
articulation of contextual links and the ways in which children's
orchestration of the dialogue between reported voices expresses and
drives the plot, and also the evaluative function of the story.

The way in which children's use of reported voices contributes to
their socialisation is explored from a slightly different angle in Chapter
7. While the previous three chapters focussed on reported speech
which was fairly clearly signalled as coming from a different speaker, in
this chapter I examine examples from the children's talk where the
boundary between the speaker's voice and the voice they are reproducing is less clear cut, and other voices appear to merge with the children's own. I adapt Bakhtin's taxonomy of different kinds of voice
reproduction (Bakhtin, 1984) to analyse the ways in which children
report, repeat, appropriate and stylise the voices of teachers and textbooks, both in teacher-pupils dialogues and in talk among themselves.

I then discuss how this contributes to their induction into educational speech genres and school procedures.

A considerable amount of the talk of the children I studied was focussed around literacy activities. The organisation of space and time in classroom life, the management and assessment of children and the production of schooled knowledge were all articulated through the reading and writing tasks which filled children's days. In Chapter 8, I draw on Foucault's account of institutional disciplining in addition to Bakhtinian theory, to analyse the emphasis on procedure and product in classroom talk and its role in children's induction into school literacy practices. I also, however, challenge the division often assumed in educational research between in-school and out-of-school literacy. I use examples from my data to argue that classrooms contain a mixture of official, unofficial and hybrid literacy activities, with varying possibilities for different kinds of knowledge production, relationship and identity.

Finally, in the Conclusion, I briefly draw the different threads of the book together.

1
Setting the Scene

each sphere in which language is used develops its own *relatively stable types* of ... utterances. These we may call *speech genres*.

... each sphere of activity contains an entire repertoire of speech genres that differentiate and grow as the particular sphere develops and becomes more complex.

(Bakhtin, 1986, p. 60)

Going into the school I am struck immediately by the amount of talk. Teacher-pupil dialogues in classrooms, the continual low murmur of talk of children carrying on with work. Children talking as they mix paints for art-work in the landing outside the classroom, children joking in the changing rooms before PE. Children chatting at lunchtime while eating their sandwiches ... a group of older, 11 year-old boys and girls bantering and teasing.

(Fieldnotes, 26.9.90)

In this chapter, I set the scene for the rest of the book in two ways. First, I give some flavour of the experience of researching children's talk across the school day: what it actually felt like observing and recording children and trying, as far as I could, to enter into their world. This was an extraordinarily vivid experience, which influenced my later work on the data and shaped my own development as a particular kind of researcher. Secondly, I set out my conceptual framework for the analysis of children's communicative practices, explaining my shift from initial rather static ideas about the relationships between talk, context and identity to more dynamic conceptualisations of dialogue, contextualisation and the emergence of identity through social practice.

These two processes – the experience of doing the research and the building up of a language of description – were closely interlinked. The study of language has long been dominated by an essentially structuralist set of conceptions about communication and the production of meaning, and the study of children's language by psychological and linguistic conceptions of individual development. What I was most interested in, however, was not children's individual linguistic or psychological competencies, but their involvement in the messy, contingent, collaborative process of language use in everyday life, and how this might be contributing to their construction of knowledge and identity. Within this process, language has multiple meanings and is often ambiguous; its referential, interactional and emotive functions are closely intertwined. It is also always on the move: elliptical, processual and recursive.

I wanted to find out how children use ordinary complex everyday talk to learn about their world and gain a sense of themselves, and how this language is involved in their socialisation into particular cultural practices and their development into particular kinds of people. I needed to find some way of describing the intensely interactive and fragmentary talk I was recording in school, my research lying somewhere at the junction of anthropology, social psychology and sociolinguistics. Searching for a more dynamic language of description grounded within everyday social activity involved me in a struggle between a more formalist framework from linguistics, with its powerfully precise procedures and terminology for describing patterns within communication, and the commitment within ethnography to particularity and participation, holistic accounts of social practice and openness to reinterpretations over time (Rampton *et al.*, 2004).

As I was carrying out my fieldwork in the early 1990s, poststructuralist and social constructivist ideas were beginning to shift the focus within social sciences away from rather unitary conceptions of individuals, language texts and culture towards what was happening *between* them, and the social processes through which individuals, texts and culture actually come into being. Researchers started looking for ways of capturing and describing how people negotiate aspects of identity and are identified by others, construct meanings and are inducted into and perform particular kinds of cultural practices. It is in relation to these more poststructuralist ideas about talk, knowledge and identity, and especially Bakhtinian[1] concepts of evaluation, dialogicality and genre, that I developed a framework for analysing children's situated communicative practices and their role in the double-edged process of socialisation and identification (i.e. how children identify themselves and are identified by others).

Shifting the lens

I start with a vignette from the first day at my main research site school. I am sitting next to my tape recorder taking notes at the side of the class, a mixed Year 6 and Year 7 group of around thirty 10–12 year-olds. The upstairs classroom is light and airy, with colourful displays of children's work on the walls. The tables are arranged in clusters, each designated for work in mathematics, science or English. Around me the children are working in small groups, apparently cheerfully, on the worksheets which organise their activity throughout most of the day. As I watch, the teacher moves around the class helping individuals amid a general low buzz of talk which is punctuated every now and then as she raises her voice to instruct or harangue an individual, or speak to the whole class. Some children are restless, getting up frequently to look for pencils and rulers and starting arguments over where they want to sit, while others get on with their work, talking now and then with children seated near them.

On that first day I had an overwhelming sense of the ordinariness of what I was seeing, an impression of 'business as usual' in the schooling of working class children. Having decided to set aside the lens of curriculum goals and educational competencies, I initially had no alternative way of reading what I was seeing, or of understanding its significance for the children themselves. In my pilot study in a nearby school, I had attached a radio microphone[2] to a 10 year-old girl, Julie, for three days and collected a considerable amount of data about her informal interactions with other children, picaresque anecdotes and rapid switches of style between different contexts. I now wondered if this had been beginner's luck and whether I would manage to collect any interesting data at all from this class where I was going to spend the next three weeks. My main reaction to being in the classroom that first day was an acute awareness of my inability to read beyond the surface of what I was seeing, a lack of meaning for my own presence, and a strong feeling of paralysing boredom.[3]

My misgivings about being able to collect the data I wanted were to radically change over the next three weeks. In order to record the children's talk I used a radio microphone, switched around different children in two friendship groups (three girls and three boys) whom the teacher had suggested were 'ordinary', fairly talkative children. I also collected copies of all the texts they were using and producing. In addition, I used two small tape recorders to record as much as possible of the other talk going on in the classroom, which also usefully deflected attention from the 'wired-up' child. I began to spend my time helping the children who weren't being recorded with their work, creating a role for myself within the classroom community and starting to build relationships with individual children. Break-times were spent checking equipment and notes and playing back tapes and chatting with children who wanted to hear recordings of themselves. Gradually I began to establish a regular set of working practices which carried me through the school day and gave me a sense of my own place and purpose in the classroom. As I spent more time among the children and started listening to the recordings, I began, slowly, to tune into their experience and perspectives.

This tuning in involved dislodging my initial perceptual framework, which had been organised around the official school timetable and curriculum. I began to realise that there was an alternative framework of time and space within the school which was equally, if not more, significant for the children themselves. The contexts where children expressed their own viewpoints and experience most vividly were not within the teacher-managed classroom activities, but in the gaps between the official curriculum spaces. During the minutes before the teacher entered the classroom after break-time, in a classroom corner away from the teacher's gaze, when the children lined up for lunch or chatted in the school coach on the way to the swimming pool, they pursued their own agendas and explorations through talk among themselves. I noticed that recurring themes and personal topics from conversations in these alternative spaces within the school day were fleetingly referred to in talk around a classroom activity, and off-the-cuff remarks in class which I had barely registered before acquired a new significance. My perceptions of the interstices between official spaces opened up and expanded, creating a new lens through which I read what was happening in the classroom.

I now saw Darren moving confidently around the classroom with his sharp haircut, Kim's hostile glance at the teacher and Kevin and Kieran working quietly together in a corner, in the light of my knowledge about their preoccupations and viewpoints expressed in unofficial talk elsewhere. This lens was strengthened, further laminated, as it were, (as when layers of glass are melded together to make a stronger pane) when I returned to Lakeside, my main school site, the next term after the observation and taping to interview the children in friendship pairs about the themes and topics which were cropping up in the continuous recordings. Sitting with a friend and myself in the relative discomfort of a corner of the school store room (the only available private space), children talked at length about different aspects of their out-of-school lives, questions over which they were puzzling and their feelings about particular events and relationships. In addition to providing further recorded data about the ways that children used language to express and reflect on experience, these interviews gave me another point of reference from which to interpret the other data I had collected.

My experience of fieldwork was not only crucial for collecting the recordings and observations, but also for establishing an ethnographically informed lens through which to read and interpret my data. In contrast to research which views children's language through what I have called the educational gaze, my shift into the children's viewpoints was accomplished, as I have explained, by focussing first on their meaning-making in unofficial spaces and then looking back, in the light of this, at their talk around classroom activities, shifting out again to the experience of the interviews and finally applying the laminated lens from these accumulated experiences in my subsequent work on the data.

The researcher in the data

The starting point for my research on children's talk was Martin Hammersley's (1990) definition of ethnography as social research gathering empirical data from real world natural contexts using a range of unstructured methods, particularly observation and informal conversation. The focus is usually a small scale setting or group and data analysis involves the interpretation of the insider meanings and functions of human actions.[4] In my own case, I immersed myself as far as I could in the children's worlds through my observations and contact with them in school. While I was familiar in general terms with the large working class housing estate where most of them lived (and I had carried out home interviews there with parents of young children for a previous research project), my knowledge about the out-of-school lives of the children I was recording was gathered from what they told me, and from references within their recorded talk. In contrast to traditional full-blown ethnographies written from long-term fulltime involvement in the field, Green and Bloome (1995) have suggested that more limited studies, like my own, could be described as employing 'an ethnographic perspective'.

The ways in which ethnographers construct and present knowledge from this personal experience of observation and involvement in particular situated 'realities' has always been contentious[5] and it has been argued that they can never fully share their data because of its autobiographical-epistemic dimension.[6] In other words, the ethnographer's personal experience in the field is at the core of their construction of ethnographic knowledge. One of the crucial aspects of ethnographic research is the building of relationships with other people involved in the research process, imbued as this is by all kinds of cultural, political, social and personal issues. My own access to the field, and the quality of the data I collected, depended on my relationships with the head teachers who negotiated parental permission in the pilot and main research site schools, with the teachers of the classes I recorded, and, most crucially, with the children themselves.

During my time in school, I tried to spend as much time as possible with the children. I ate lunch with them, I hung around with them at break-time and I stayed away from the staff room. Although there is a strong ethnographic tradition for researchers studying adolescents or children to become honorary in-group members themselves,[7] I was cautious about aligning myself too closely with the pupils. For a start, I was very obviously an adult and could by no stretch of the imagination have passed for under thirty. I was not a pupil, not working class and I did not live in the children's community. I felt that any sense that I was a kind of in-group member, seductive as this might seem, would have been based on false premises. There were also important methodological and ethical reasons for maintaining a distance from both children and staff. Methodologically, in order to have access to children's private conversations, I needed a certain closeness and trust with them, which involved separating myself from the staff and avoiding a 'teacher' identity. But I also wanted to maintain the privilege of an outsider to ask naive questions and I wanted to avoid being drawn into social alignments with some children which would have inhibited my relationships with others.

The researching of people's private conversations raises particular ethical issues, and more especially in the case of children because of the very asymmetrical relationship of power between the researcher and the researched. My relationship with the children followed its own trajectory, from my introduction to them by the class teacher as someone who had studied so hard that she was now approaching the highest possible qualification (not an introduction that I myself would have chosen), through my encounters with children who sought me out at break-time to ask what I was really doing and what I wanted to be, to my acceptance as a normal part of classroom life and a useful resource for extra help with their classroom 'jobs'. At the beginning of my research I tried to answer children's questions as honestly and clearly as possible, telling them that I was interested in their talk because it showed me how they were thinking about things. The children seemed to accept my assurance that no-one except myself would listen to the recordings I was collecting. After the first few days or so, most of them appeared to take the recording processes for granted and to lose interest in the precise purposes of the research.

I needed to respect the trust of the pupils and the confidentiality of their private talk and to avoid any disclosures about this to school staff.[8] On the other hand, I also needed to respect the trust of the head teacher and staff who were allowing me fairly free access to their pupils. In fact, the teachers' organisational and disciplinary management of pupils relieved me of adult responsibilities which would otherwise undoubtedly have interfered in my relations with the children. My role as a friendly approachable adult who was called by her first name, joined in circle games in Physical Education and spent all her free time around tapes or children, depended for its effectiveness on the very institutional practices which constrained and disciplined pupils. These practices constructed adult/child relationships in particular ways against which my interactions with individual children were different and this difference was a source of creativity, a potential for relationship which we could negotiate for ourselves. My anomalous position, as neither teacher nor pupil, neither trainee student nor crime prevention officer (the other kinds of people whom children had experienced spending time in their classroom), allowed me to sidestep potentially restrictive identity positionings and to engage with children in ways which facilitated my recordings and enabled them to talk more freely with me about their lives.

I found that I had to manage a continual double positioning, simultaneously inside and outside the data. I myself was part of the research setting, involved in the production of the data I was collecting through my interactions and conversations with the children, most clearly in the interviews where their accounts of personal experience were prompted by my questions and collaboratively shaped in conversation with myself and their accompanying friend. My observations emerged partly through my relationships with children and through my involvement in classroom practices, as I became a regular part of the classroom scene. On the other hand, I was also continually monitoring my own activities and relationships with the children and the staff, to ensure that these activities and relationships were not interfering with the purposes of the research. This fragile position often felt precarious and nerve wracking: losing the trust of either the children or the staff, or the children's parents, could have meant the end of the research at any point. Particularly anxious moments in the school included being left on my own with the class for twenty minutes when, to my relief, I was not called on to exert a disciplinary role. On another occasion Nicole, who was clandestinely chewing gum with a group of students sitting in the 'quiet area' screened off from the main classroom, noticed me watching them and, fixing me with her eye, remarked 'Janet won't split on us, will you, Janet?' I gave her what I hoped was a disarming but enigmatic smile, and the moment passed.

The interviews, which I carried out the term after making the recordings, marked the highpoint of the rapport and trust between myself and the children. Many of them talked freely and openly about diverse aspects of their lives. An incident towards the end of my time in the school, however, underlined the essentially tenuous and transitory nature of our relationship. The class teacher, Mrs. Kilbride, was launching a public diatribe at Karlie about her lack of cooperation and bad attitude and turned to me to enlist my support. I realised that to give that support would undermine and even deny my relationship with Karlie (and possibly my relationship with others). On the other hand, to speak up in support of Karlie would seem like a direct attack on the very institutional authority which had made my research possible. As I hesitated and then failed to respond, Karlie's sullen look in my direction left me in no doubt about her interpretation of my silence. In spite of Karlie trusting me with so many personal details about her life during the recording period and in our interview, the very fact that Mrs. Kilbride felt it her right to enlist me as a source of support positioned me, in the last analysis, on the side of the school institutional authority.

A few months after I had left the school I met one of the class, Helen, at an interschool sports event, which I was attending to watch one of my own (rather younger) children participate. Helen was friendly but slightly offhand and I realised that, in spite of the intensity which I had experienced and was still feeling in my relationships with the children, there was no longer any area of ongoing shared experience to sustain that relationship. Without shared social practice, there could be no interpersonal connection. In retrospect, perhaps my own feelings about my relationships within the field had been heightened in particular ways because they were tied up with my construction of ethnographic knowledge, and with my developing identity and personal investment as a researcher. In fact, our lives had only overlapped for a couple of months, offering me a brief, transitory glimpse into the children's world. While I would remain immersed in my recordings over many months and years to come, revisiting children's talk with peers and our conversations in the interviews again and again in relation to different intellectual frameworks for understanding the data, the children's own lives had already moved on and the fragile connection that I had established with them was gone.

From context to contextualisation

How could I begin to make sense of the interactive, chaotic and sometimes incomprehensible recordings which I was collecting? I started out with an interest in how children might be using language differently in various contexts across the school day: the differences in the structure and content of their talk in a private conversation in the cloakroom, for instance, as opposed to when they were talking in the classroom with their teacher about a mathematics problem. I guessed that children might present, and develop, contrasting kinds of knowledge and alternative aspects of their identity within these different settings.

At the beginning I had a kind of tableau image of what the anthropologist Bronislaw Malinowski (1923, 1935) called the 'context of situation', which involves a setting and participants. Within the Trobriand Islands where Malinowski did his anthropological research, the setting could be a tropical beach where men are talking as they mend their fishing nets. In order to make sense of what the men are saying, the researcher needs all kinds of cultural understandings about local beliefs, practices and idioms, without which a literal translation of the men's talk is meaningless. Similarly, in the classroom, one can envisage a kind of tableau where the teacher is bent over a desk helping a child and other children are carrying on with activities at nearby desks; we (and the participants) interpret what the teacher and children say in the context of knowledge about institutional rules, roles and relationships and classroom procedures. For instance, the children know that when the teacher addresses the class and says

'I want all this work put over the back', she is referring to an established classroom procedure for what they should do with their finished
pieces of writing, that she has the right to direct their activities in this
way and that they will be scolded if they don't comply.

I could, then, represent the children's use of language in different
settings across the school day in a series of such tableaux, each involving different participants and different kinds of social practices. There
was the classroom tableau, the sitting-at-lunch tableau, the getting-
changed-for-swimming tableau, and so on. I saw the meaning of talk as
shaped through a series of contextual layers within each of these
settings, with the classroom or other context shaping the meaning and
significance of a particular conversation, which in its turn shaped
the meaning of particular utterances.[9] There was plenty of evidence
that the children were highly sensitive to context, and varied their language use accordingly. I was finding differences, both in the kinds of
knowledge which emerged as significant in the different contexts and
in the ways in which children presented themselves and negotiated
relationships with others through talk. There was, however, a rather
static quality to this view of the relationship between talk and setting.
In focussing on vignette-like scenes, I was failing to fully address
the dynamic communicative processes that were running through
them. In addition to dissecting specific language events, I realised that
I needed some way of capturing and describing the ongoing, communicative processes which underpinned them and also the ways
in which children made links and connections across the different
settings within their lives.

One way of looking at language use in more dynamic terms is by
using Bakhtin's concept of speech genre, that is, the relatively stable
patterning in language use (spoken or written), content themes and
evaluative perspectives which emerge in different spheres of human
activity (Bakhtin, 1986). Within the genre of teacher-pupil dialogue,
for instance, there is usually an initiation-response-feedback structure
where the teacher questions children, they respond and she evaluates
their response. The content is focussed on classroom procedures and
curriculum content, and the authoritative reference points for evaluating people and their actions are the school institutional practices. In
the speech genre of unsupervised peer group talk, on the other hand,
talk ranges over a variety of personal topics and dialogues are much
more loosely structured, with many interruptions and switches of
topic. The notion of a genre emerging from social activity switches the
focus from a more static tableau-like notion of setting (for example,

a classroom), to the various different social activities, involving different kinds of speech genres, which may be going on within it.

This focus on dynamic social activity also switches attention from the ways in which contexts affect how people speak, to the ways in which speakers orientate towards and invoke specific aspects of context, within talk, as part of ongoing social practice. Speech genres, through their patterning of themes, language use and evaluative frames of reference, shape the ways in which particular aspects of the current context are assumed by speakers, marked, made relevant and then intricately involved in meaning-making. Within linguistic anthropology, the ways in which speakers make links with and invoke particular aspects of social context against which they intended their words to be interpreted, has been termed 'contextualisation' (Duranti, 2001).

Contextualisation can, of course, involve specific references to some aspect of the immediate physical surroundings, but it can also involve references to particular kinds of social practices. For instance, when Nicole accused Melissa of writing graffiti about Laura on the mirror in the girls' toilet and Melissa protested 'Why? Why did I get Laura?', the meaning of 'get' here refers to peer group practices of attacking another child, often in retaliation, and the values about individual rights and justice encoded within these practices are invoked as the evaluative frame of reference for Melissa's remark. And when Sam complained about a boy who had escaped punishment: 'he was lucky that Mr. Perry didn't do him', the meaning of 'do' refers to chastisement of children by teachers which could include a strong telling off, or worse. Here, Sam invokes the school institution as his evaluative reference point: he may feel that justice hasn't been done, but doesn't question the authority of the school to administer it. Volosinov (1973) uses the term 'evaluation' to refer to the way in which people's use of language always expresses some kind of position and value judgement, in relation to what they are talking about. There is always an assumed evaluative framework behind what they are saying, which is invoked within their talk.[10] Within any one setting in school, there can be a range of such conventions and reference points for evaluation, linking in with school, peer group and wider community practices.

In addition to making links with some aspect of social practice in their current context in this way, children also frequently referred to genres and practices in other contexts, often through reproducing a detail or a snatch of reported dialogue (as I shall explore in Chapter 4), which indexes (links with) a speech genre which in its turn indexes a recognisable social activity. The terms 'indexicality' and 'deixis' are both used to refer to the way in which words point to some aspect of context. This includes the grammatical use of tense (for example to indicate a switch to a past context), pronouns pointing to people within a particular context and demonstratives like 'this' or 'then' which fix specific objects and events in particular places and times. Indexicality is now also used more broadly to indicate the ways in which a range of aspects of language, including style, are linked with the sociocultural context. In every case, the word or aspect of language makes a link not symbolically, but through a contiguous link (as when smoke indicates a fire).[11]

Meaning in language works through a combination of indexical as well as symbolic signs. There may be indexical chains linking specific uses of language to stances and speech genres which in turn link to scenarios. For instance, when Darren is telling other children about his confrontation with a man, he uses snatches of dialogue to index the stances, the verbal idiom and the interactive pattern which indexes an aggressive standoff:

Darren   This man called me a fucking bastard, right,
          I go 'back to you', he goes 'come here', I go 'come on, then'
          and he's got about size ten trainers and he chased me, right,
          and then when he got, he catched me, right, like that, and
          he goes 'who's fucking saying?' And I goes 'fuck off', I says
          'fuck off' and he goes, he goes, 'Do you want a fight?'

Again, when Karen explained to me how she first met her boyfriend when she was at the swimming pool with her friend Helen, she did this through reproducing their dialogue:

Karen   Because he started talking to us and she stood still and
         I stood still and didn't move and he goes 'Do you two ever
         move?' and she goes 'Well we've just walked all the way from
         Scotland to get down here, so we've got to walk all the way
         back, now'. He goes 'God, why, don't you like swimming up
         there? Oh yeh, the water's dirty, isn't it, so you come down
         here'.

The humorous stance and sparring, inventive banter Karen uses to invoke the interaction index the speech genre associated with boy-girl playful flirtation in group contexts. In the data more generally, I found that brief pieces of reported dialogue could invoke a rich array of associations and were used to represent people, relationships and whole scenarios. The children's accumulating social experience of different speech genres provided a set of mediating schemas through which they could connect a piece of reported speech with the particular content themes, interactive patterns and evaluative positions which were generically associated with this way of talking.[12] These evaluative positions, in fact, are central to the point which the child is intending to make: children's use of contextualisation is always connected in some way with taking up an evaluative perspective. It is also connected with presenting themselves as a particular kind of person. Thus Melissa presents herself as someone who doesn't 'get' other people unless there is a good reason and Sam presents himself as looking to the school to regulate children's behaviour. Darren's aggressive swearing is presented as justified and admirable in the context of the fight and Karen presents her boyfriend as quick-witted and humorous. In this way, contextualisation, and the evaluative positioning it involves, is closely tied up with children's performance of identity.

In an important sense, rather than producing words which then have particular meanings because of the context in which they were spoken, the children are creating contexts themselves in order to produce particular meanings within their talk. They are construing the semiotic resources of their current context in particular ways, and also invoking and reproducing social activities from other contexts and from a particular perspective. Some aspects of these contextualisation processes can be traced within the linguistic features of children's talk, but, as Malinowski showed, it is not possible to interpret the points children are making, or the meaning of the social experiences they are invoking in order to make these points, without an ethnographic understanding of their social practice. In particular, we can only understand the evaluative frames children are invoking, and the evaluative positions they take up, in the light of knowledge about the values and beliefs which are part of their social world. The evaluative significance of contextualisation within children's talk, in relation to socialisation and identification, also emerges through the interactive patterns within their dialogues, as I shall explain in the next section below.

From dialogue to dialogicality

The more dynamic concept of contextualisation reconfigures the analytical distinction between text and context (that is, treating texts as separate from and occurring within contexts), by focussing on the processes through which they are interdependent, each involved in the creation and interpretation of the other. There has been a parallel shift of interest in social psychology and sociolinguistics, away from a focus on individuals with fixed attributes and on to more interactive, social conceptions of learning and identity.[13] Rather than looking at what an individual child's use of language might reveal about their stage of development, psychologists have become more interested in how the interactive processes within children's situated dialogues might facilitate collaborative thinking.[14] And rather than seeing individual language use as signalling some aspect of social identity such as gender, race, or class, sociolinguists are now researching how aspects of identity are performed and negotiated through ongoing interactions and relationships, within the flow of social practice.[15]

Many of the negotiations of meaning between children in my recordings appeared highly interactive, part of ongoing collaborative activities and fluid, provisional explorations of ideas and experience. I was initially intrigued about how the children's dialogues might function, in a Vygotskian sense, as a kind of social thinking, supporting collaborative learning about personal experience and addressing specific questions arising in their lives. Here, for instance, are Julie, Kirsty and Sharon, who have been anxiously discussing the amount of swearing on the tapes I was collecting. The girls are sitting together while they finish off some work in the classroom:

Table 1.1

Julie	Children aren't meant to swear
Kirsty	If people swear at them, they can swear back
	(brief pause)
Julie	I swore at my mum the other day because she started, she hit me
Kirsty	What did you do?
Julie	I swore at my mum, I says 'I'm packing my cases and I don't care what you say' and she goes 'Ooh?' and *(I go)* 'Yea!' I'm really cheeky to my mother.

Julie and Kirsty seem to be collaboratively engaged in working out what is appropriate speech behaviour for children, as opposed to adults. The invoking of voices for the characters in children's anecdotes, as I shall explore in more detail in Chapters 5 and 6, provides them with a way of animating and briefly exploring alternative viewpoints and the relationship between them. Julie uses a snatch of reported dialogue to conjure up the familiar experience for Kirsty and Sharon of arguments with parents, spiced up by the references to violence and swearing. Julie seems to be offering the account of her mother hitting her as a possible example of an occasion when it might be appropriate for a child to swear. She is also providing Kirsty and Sharon with a glimpse of her relations with her mother, which they can compare with their own relationships at home. The anecdote acts as a kind of fleeting shared reflection on social experience. The presenting of different evaluative positions in it, and within the conversation preceding it, is an important part of the girls' developing social knowledge. The accumulation of children's exchanges of perspectives and experience will be internalised, according to Vygotsky, and used to guide their future actions. So this might be termed 'learning through collaborative talk'.

If we look more closely at this talk, however, we can also identify some more intricate dialogic processes involved in exploring the question of swearing. While I use the term 'dialogue' to refer in general terms to children's conversation, 'dialogic' refers to the way in which speakers' utterances are always simultaneously orientated, in terms of their structure and context, in two directions: backwards towards previous utterances, both within the current conversation and through memory in past conversations, and forwards, towards an audience (and possibly future audiences). For instance, within the anecdote itself, Julie's 'I'm packing my cases and I don't care what you say' is a response to 'she hit me', and also an anticipation of how her mother might respond ('I don't care what you say'). Her mother's 'Oh?' is then both a response to Julie's initial defiant statement and also a question, requesting a further answer. This dialogic chain[16] of utterances between Julie and her mother provides most of the content of the anecdote, creating the drama and driving the action.

There is also a dialogic chain, within which the anecdote forms one link, made up of the give and take of turns in the ongoing conversation between the girls. Within this chain, the anecdote creates a kind of discursive space with a range of possibilities for dialogic connections. Julie and Kirsty's positions expressed just before the anecdote could be summarised respectively as *Children shouldn't swear* and *Their swearing can sometimes be justified*. At first, Julie's anecdote seems to suggest that she is agreeing with Kirsty in providing an example where, perhaps, she is justified in 'swearing' (she avoids the actual reproduction of swear words themselves). This is followed immediately, however, by Julie's comment 'I'm really cheeky to my mother', which seems to undercut this initial agreement and shift back towards her original statement 'Children aren't meant to swear'. As Markova (1993) points out, the collaborative negotiation of meaning cuts across physical divisions between turns, so that the dialogical quality of speech is not concentrated at the boundaries of individual speakers' turns, but emerges in crisscrossing dialogic links within and across turns. The meaning and significance of Kirsty and Julie's initial comments are 'dialogised' as the evaluative positions they suggest are set against each other and reconfigured within the course of the anecdote. It is through these kind of responsive and addressive relationships, where children's utterances both answer previous voices and anticipate their own future answers, that meaning-making becomes collaborative, dynamic, and often ambiguous.

At the most basic level, I found that terms like 'speaker' and 'listener' were unwieldy and misleading in trying to understand the dialogic interweaving of voices within children's conversations. Rather than one speaker communicating a particular 'message' and another responding in the conventional notion of a dialogue, there was a constant ongoing process of interactive and recursive meaning-making among children. As I shall explore in more detail in Chapter 3, one child might start an utterance and another complete it, or retrospectively undermine a previous meaning. Meanings were often ambivalent, picked up and foregrounded in different ways by subsequent speakers. Meaning-making emerges as an ongoing dialogic process at a number of different, interrelated levels: dialogues within utterances and between utterances, dialogues between voices cutting across utterance boundaries and dialogues with other voices from the past.

For Volosinov and Bakhtin, these dialogic patterns are reflected within the structuring of individual consciousness. Thus Bakhtin suggests that 'to think about (someone) is to talk with them' (Bakhtin, 1984) and Volosinov argues that connections between thoughts are not organised on the basis of grammar, but on the basis of dialogue, as one thought calls forth an answering thought, and so on. Inner thoughts and sensations are always social and evaluative and even the most basic sensations, like hunger, are experienced as connected with personal feelings about social experience (Volosinov, 1973). Individual consciousness is in this sense an accumulation of social, dialogic experiences, each one interpreted and responded to in the light of previous dialogues, and simultaneously shifting and repatterning the accumulation of that previous experience. Since utterances and texts in the outer social world are a site of struggle, and are populated with the voices of others, then one must assume that an inner consciousness constituted from internalised dialogues is itself inherently multivoiced, dialogic and fragmented.

Evaluation, socialisation and identity

I have pointed out how the contextualisation and dialogic processes within talk involve the taking up and negotiating of evaluative stances towards what is being talked about. In a more fundamental sense, for Volosinov, all language use is evaluative, because it always emerges from a situated perspective within a particular material world. Only aspects of the social environment which have social meaning and value are codified within semiotic systems and so evaluation moulds referential meaning and determines what is referred to in the first place. Thus, 'every utterance is above all *an evaluative orientation.'* (Volosinov, 1986, p. 105). Volosinov calls this expression of evaluation the 'evaluative accent' of a word or phrase. Because of the intersection of differently orientated interests at all levels of social life, there is always a struggle between different evaluative perspectives, which can be visible even within individual utterances. This struggle is often represented and played out within the dialogues created by children within their anecdotes.

Much of children's informal talk could be characterised as what Bakhtin calls 'inwardly persuasive discourse', which he describes as contemporaneous, semantically open and intensely dialogic: 'it is not so much interpreted by us as it is further, that is, freely, developed, applied to new material, new conditions; it enters into interanimating relationships with new contexts. More than that, it enters into an intense interaction, a *struggle* with other internally persuasive discourses' (Bakhtin, 1981, pp. 345–346). Julie and Kirsty's conversation illustrates this kind of intense interaction between inwardly persuasive discourses. Knowledge building within this sort of talk tends to be provisional and fragmented. Bakhtin contrasts inwardly persuasive discourse with the authoritative discourse of textbooks, teachers, parents which is semantically fixed, associated with knowledge that can only be transmitted and received, not negotiated or transformed. He suggests that there is a tension between authoritative and inwardly persuasive discourse which is played out at every level of language, right down to the individual utterance, for instance the ambivalence within Julie's utterance between whether her swearing is justified or cheeky. There is also a tension, I would suggest, between what counts as authoritative discourse in different contexts.

The intrinsically evaluative aspect of language use (which is often masked in more formal textual analysis which abstracts talk from its dynamic social context) has particular significance for the role played by talk in children's socialisation into the beliefs, values and social practices of a particular community. Evaluation is individual, expressing a viewpoint taken by a child on the actions of someone else or on a more general state of affairs. It is also, however, simultaneously social because a child's viewpoint reflects more widespread cultural beliefs and values about what, for example, constitutes a good parent, or a good child and about how they are expected to behave, think and feel. For older children, who are engaging in an increasingly wide range of social practice, the ways in which they orientate towards, configure and problematise particular beliefs and values through their talk is central to their active engagement in their own socialisation, and also lies at the core of their ongoing realisation of themselves as a particular kind of person.

Anecdotes provide an especially good opportunity for the 'presentation of self' (Goffman, 1969) and in the argument with her mother Julie creates a particular kind of voice for her own role, conveying an image of herself as a feisty daughter who is morally justified in swearing at her mother. Children's self presentations may also of course be accepted, challenged or subverted by others, who in their turn may present an alternative view of the original speaker and a different evaluation of their actions. The relational aspects of identity are explored by children both through the give and take of ongoing dialogue, and through the relationships between the voices they invoke in their talk (like Julie and her mother). Often, as the hurly burly of classroom life moves rapidly on, evaluation remains unsettled and the participants in a particular interaction are left with a series of alternative interpretations and viewpoints.

The social anthropologist Richard Jenkins (1996) argues that identity can only be understood as process, as 'being' or 'becoming'. While there are obviously constraints on the possibilities of identity – the influence of very early childhood experience, differential access to external resources – he sees it as essentially a practical accomplishment, an ongoing dialectical process between internal definitions of the self as similar to or different from others, and external definitions offered by others through naming, categorising, responding to us, treating us, talking about us. Because a projected identity has to be perceived and accepted by others in order to have saliency, Jenkins suggests that identities are 'to be found and negotiated at their boundaries, where the internal and external meet (p. 24). Within Julie's anecdote, for instance, Julie represents this kind of boundary negotiation going on between her internal sense of herself and her mother's reaction. Julie's presentation of herself to Kirsty and Sharon emerges both through her production of the anecdote in the context of a particular dialogue, and through their responses to this presentation. The presentation and perception of the kind of person a child is, is thus to some extent an ongoing dialogic process, emerging provisionally and unstraightforwardly through the cut and thrust of dynamic interaction.

This negotiation between a child's identification of themselves, often through expressing how they are different from, or similar to others,[17] and their identification by others through talk is contextualised within the social practices which make up the children's world. The speech genres associated with these social practices are themselves connected with more macro level discourses (ideological complexes of knowledge and power) about education, childhood, gender, family and so on, which organise social life and position people in particular ways. Foucault (1981) suggests that these macro level discourses are circulated through powerful institutional processes within, for example, education, medicine and the law, which produce particular kinds of subjectivity within people, silencing areas of human experience which don't fit within a particular institutional context. In this book I treat identity not as a fixed set of attributes, but as a set of dispositions (some more open than others) which emerge through an interactive process between how children see and express their own position and meaning in the world, and how they are 'identified' by others, in the course of their engagement within speech genres and social practices which are connected with more macro level sets of ideas, in the different spheres of activity across their lives.

The process of the development of children's identity is therefore both social and individual. Through their social background and experience, their repeated exposure to, and positioning within, particular kinds of speech genres, the children become predisposed towards particular perceptions, actions and ways of reading the world and themselves. They draw on a range of socially authoritative evaluative frameworks for making judgements about people and events. As the linguistic anthropologist William Hanks (1996) points out, genres are a key part of habitus,[18] that is, individual dispositions to 'evaluate and act on the world in typical ways'. He suggests that 'Through habituation and infused with the authority of their agents, genres make certain ways of thinking and experiencing so routine as to appear natural.' (Hanks, 1996, p. 246). The concept of habitus includes both social habituation and individual agency (Bourdieu and Waquant, 1992): children exercise choice in expressing and presenting themselves in local activities and interactions, and in constructing representations of their social world and of their own place within it. They draw on the semiotic resources available and set up alternative evaluative reference points next to each other. Within the social and institutional constraints which shape experience and identity, the children are to a certain extent continually constructing themselves as particular kinds of people, through contextualisation, dialogicality and the evaluative processes within talk.

The problematic relationship between how we see ourselves and how others see us becomes a central concern and theme within the social lives of older children. These children are acquiring new skills of presentation and new ways of interacting with others, as the social world of peers becomes more important and friendship emerges as a significant affective domain in addition to the family. They are learning to manage interactions with adults outside their family, negotiating membership of formal institutional settings and acquiring a stronger sense of self. As they move from childhood into adolescence they do not simply take on a coherent body of values and beliefs from the older generation, but struggle to understand the inconsistent and conflicting experiences, accounts and evaluations around them, comparing their experiences and reflections with others, appropriating and contesting perspectives and judgements and trying out new aspects of identity in the context of various different social interactions among themselves and with adults.

This period of children's lives is particularly significant, not just in revealing the social processes involved in moving from childhood into adolescence, but in highlighting the cultural knowledge which children recognise as important and relevant to them, within the larger social context. Overlapping general themes which persistently emerged in the continuous recordings of children's talk over the school day, and which I explored further in the interviews, included questions around their changing relationships with parents and other authority figures, the imperatives, possibilities and boundaries of friendship and of new kinds of gendered relationships and identities, and moral issues of justice, care and cruelty. Often the knowledge generated and explored in relation to these themes is strategic: how to cope with a particular situation, how to get the better of a stronger opponent, how to safeguard one's own precarious sense of self. It is also frequently procedural: how to do the tasks in school they were required to complete and also how to 'do' being a girlfriend, being a teenage boy and so on. As well as reflection, there is a considerable amount of projection and planning in children's talk, as they rehearse new roles and situations.

While, as I shall discuss later in the book, knowledge appears more fixed and non-negotiable within the authoritative discourse of textbooks and worksheets, the knowledge negotiated between children was often dialogically open. They returned again and again in their talk to particular questions and themes. It is as if the exploration of a theme in a particular account, or through a particular interaction, functions at a metalevel as a turn in what might be called a 'long conversation', which is carried on between children in different places and at different times, about the various ways of knowing which are involved in moving from childhood into adolescence in their particular cultural setting.

Towards a more dynamic language of description

I started with some reflections on my own ethnographic experience of recording and observing children's talk, in order to explain how I came to focus on the dynamic, ongoing nature of their meaning-making and the importance of contextualisation, dialogicality and evaluation within their communicative practices. These communicative practices play a central role in children's socialisation and in their emerging sense of themselves and identification by others. In a parallel process, my own production of knowledge about these practices and my construction as a researcher emerged through my interactions and dialogues with the children, my familiarisation with the contexts of their lives and my entering, to a certain extent, into their evaluative perspectives.

I have struggled to find a language of description which can both identify the intricate linguistic features of children's talk, and acknowledge its dynamic nature within social practice. Basic terms like 'context', 'speaker', 'listener', 'meaning', and 'function' seem to imply a kind of fixity, a finalisability which does not fit with the more processual quality of the data I collected. I am then left with a choice of crude verbal forms like 'constructing', or 'developing' or 'emerging' to try and capture the dynamic aspects of children's dialogue and meaning-making. These verbs raise their own awkward questions about agency, with 'constructing' suggesting too much, 'emerging' too little and 'developing' trailing connotations of psychological developmentalism. 'Knowledge' and 'identity' also, of course, convey a sense of a fixed territory, with boundaries, and I am much more concerned with the construction, development and emergence of these over time, through children's collaborative communicative practice.

I have had to continue using many of these terms, and I have tried to organise them around ideas which acknowledge the processual, dynamic nature of what they are labelling. I draw on the notion of contextualisation, as it has been developed within linguistic anthropology, to capture how, in an important sense, speakers are continually invoking and creating the contexts against which they intend their words to have meaning. I have explained how I use Bakhtin's term 'speech genre' to conceptualise the dynamic patterns in language use, content themes and evaluative perspectives which emerge through different spheres of social activity. Children's engagement and positioning within speech genres is an important part of their socialisation, and of the emergence of their sense of themselves. Children also index speech genres through reported speech, as a way of indexing stances, relationships and social practices. I shall also use Bakhtinian ideas about dialogicality to capture some of the ongoing interactive processes within children's talk. One of my purposes in this book is to operationalise Bakhtin's notions of utterance, genre and dialogicality within an analysis of children's talk, and to explore whether these concepts can be brought together in an analytic framework which captures the dynamic, collaborative, contextualised nature of children's verbal meaning-making. Finally, I see what Volosinov terms 'evaluation' as playing a crucial role both in children's socialisation and within the processes of identification. In many ways it articulates the interaction between what Bauman and Sherzer (1989, p. xix) call 'the dynamic interplay between the social, conventional, readymade in social life and the individual, creative and emergent qualities of human existence'.

The points below, based on my research, summarise my own evaluative perspective on the role of children's talk in the construction of knowledge and identity and my evaluative accenting of the terms used in this book.

1. Children are actively involved in their own socialisation, especially through their talk and interaction with others. Socialisation is a

never ending process, mediated through social practice, i.e. through what people do and say, and what they think and believe.

2. Children's talk is simultaneously referential (representing the world), interpersonal (creating relations with others) and emotive (expressing inner states in the speaker). It is also always evaluative, expressing a position and making some kind of value judgement, explicitly or implicitly, on its subject matter.

3. An important aspect of social practice is the language genres which emerge within different spheres of human activity. These will be particularly significant in my analysis of children's intertextual referencing through reported speech, especially within their narratives.

4. In trying to capture social constructivism in action, as it were, the processes of contextualisation, dialogicality and evaluation are all interlinked within children's knowledge-making through talk.

5. These processes are also interlinked within children's ongoing performances, negotiations and exploration of identity. Identity has both social and individual aspects, emerging through children's habitual positioning and engagement within social practice, and at the same time through their own choices and agency at a micro level.

2
Context, Genre and Frames

Each word tastes of the context and contexts in which it has lived its socially charged life; all words and forms are populated by intentions. Contextual overtones (contextual, tendentious, individualistic) are inevitable in the word.

(Bakhtin, 1981, p. 293)

Miss P. What are your parents going to think, coming into a mess like this? Well they're not coming into a mess like this. Tough. You sit there and I'll clear up. And when I've finished, you can go home. okay?

Some   *(uncertain)* ⌈ yea
pupils   ⌊ no

Children slip easily in and out of the speech genres in different contexts. In the speech genre of teacher-pupil classroom dialogue, for instance, pupils are used to responding to their teacher's questions and then having their answers evaluated by her. The children I recorded were generally quick to spot cues pointing to the response that was required. Unusually, in the quotation above, Miss Potts' pupils were initially nonplussed by her final question because a *no*, would sound defiant, while a *yes* would suggest they expected her to clear up their mess.

In this chapter I start to look at the role of genre in children's talk: how they switch between the genres connected with different contexts and how they draw on the generic resources of their current context in making-meaning. As I explained in Chapter 1, I found Bakhtin's concept of speech genres (patterns of distinctive themes, evaluative perspectives and ways of using spoken or written language which emerge within different areas of human activity) useful for conceptualising the dynamic communicative processes within social practice, and for tracing contextualisation in children's talk. References to a current context are organised and interpreted within the frameworks of speech genres and references to other contexts are often made through a reported voice or reported dialogue which indexes a speech genre connected with that context.

Teacher-pupil classroom dialogue was one kind of speech genre which children regularly took part in. Across the various recordings of talk that I collected within the boundaries of the school day, other different speech genres emerged, for instance in the whole school assembly and when children talked informally among themselves. My interviews with the children in friendship pairs also developed their own recurring generic patterning, which included the longer narratives of personal experience that the children told me and their collaborative warranting (supporting and authenticating) of each others' accounts. Finally, a number of children asked me for tapes to record themselves talking with family and friends at home. While this did not provide a systematically collected data-set, I shall use one example from a home recording which I found particularly interesting in its generic implications, in the discussion later below.

I could identify broad patterns of themes, language use and evaluative reference points across these different genres, within which children could express different sorts of relationships and be rather different kinds of people. But the ongoing, dynamic and sometimes contested construction of themes and evaluative viewpoints in talk makes the Bakhtinian concept of a speech genre much less precise than a grammatical term like 'sentence'. In identifying speech genres, I have taken my cue from what the speakers themselves treat as a different genre, signalled through a change in their language use and in the themes and reference points for evaluation which they foreground. In this way I distinguished differences, for instance, between the genre of pupils' talk to each other focussed on classroom tasks, a genre orientated around teenage popular culture (using the term 'teenage' in a fairly loose sense) and a genre of imaginative role play at home with younger children.

In addition to these fairly broadly conceived genres, at a micro-level within talk there can also be switches between what Goffman (1974) calls 'frames'[1] which tell participants at any particular moment what's going on. Miss Potts' pupils, for instance, in the example at the beginning of the chapter, are used to her haranguing the class like this and they interpret what she is saying and doing in terms of a 'telling off' frame, within the genre of teacher-pupil dialogue. Contextualisation also operates through these micro-level interpretative frames which highlight particular identity positions for participants and specific social alignments between them, from the range of positions and alignments available within a genre. For example, Miss Potts here is an exasperated teacher who has the right to scold recalcitrant pupils and her words are interpreted by them within this particular frame. At a different time in the classroom and within a different frame she might be a satisfied teacher praising a diligent pupil. A change in frame always involves a change, at some level, in evaluative perspective. I use Goffman's concept of frame to look at these micro-level negotiations of meaning, relationship and positioning at particular points within different speech genres.

While there was usually sustained, consistent framing with relatively fixed positions, relationships and evaluative reference points within teacher-pupil dialogue, as there often is in strongly institutionally structured talk, in looser genres like informal conversation there tends to be much more frequent manipulation and transformation of frames. In talk among themselves, children often switched quite rapidly, transforming an argument into a joke or a flirtation into 'just playing'. This frame-switching can involve intertextual references to other speech genres, for instance when a child put on a teacher's voice to 'tell off' another child, or when a group of girls started quietly singing a popular song together in a corner of the class.

In this chapter, I shall look at contextualisation processes at the level of both genre and frame, and I will also begin to examine how the patterns of framing in the genres of teacher-pupil talk and informal pupil talk are linked with rather different ways of constructing knowledge.

Switching contexts

Children's sensitivity to context, and their ability to switch quite dramatically between different settings, was strikingly displayed in a tape which recorded a visit by 10 year-old Julie to the girls' toilet during a mathematics lesson. The transcript below starts in the classroom, where the students have been given a number of bills for imaginary cafe customers and have to work out how much each will pay. Julie has just added up Tom Ato's bill.

Table 2.1

Julie	Three pounds twelve I make Tom Ato. Back in a second. Miss, can I go to the toilet please?
Miss P	Yes alright *(sound of Julie's heels as she goes down the corridor. When she enters the toilets the acoustics on the tape change abruptly, with the tiled walls making the voices echo. Carol and Nicola are already there)*
Julie	Oh, hi. Where did you get your hair permed?
Nicola	*(...)*
Julie	You're not going out with Sasha, are you?
Nicola	Yea
Julie	Are you?
Nicola	Yea, I hope so *(laughs)*
Julie	You've got darker skin than me, I've got a sun tan. *(pause) (to Carol)* I should think so too, it's disgusting, that skirt is! Aii – don't! *(Nicola starts tapping her feet on the tiled floor)* Do you do tap dancing? *(both girls start tapping their feet and singing)*
J+N	'I just called to say I love you, and I mean it, from the bottom of my heart'
Julie	Caught you that time, Carol – ooh! What's the matter, Carol, don't show your tits! *(laughs) (to Nicola)* I went like this to Carol, I says, I pulls down her top, I went phtt 'don't show your tits!' *(Nicola laughs). (Julie leaves the toilets, walks down the corridor, re-enters the classroom, and sits down.)*
Julie	Turn over – six plates of chips – oh I've nearly finished my book. I've got one page to do.

In each of these two contexts, the classroom and the toilet, Julie is involved in a different speech genre, with contrasting ways of using language, content themes and evaluative perspectives. In the speech genre of 'doing mathematics' she is engaging with the language of the worksheet and orientating towards mathematical knowledge and school procedural conventions. She talks about a numerical calculation, asks her teacher politely for permission to go to the toilet and afterwards remarks about nearly finishing her exercise book. Personal activity in the classroom is evaluated in relation to the institutional authority of the teacher, worksheet and school. In this context, Julie and her friends are fairly docile pupils straining to interpret the teacher's instructions and produce neat, acceptable pieces of work to fill up their exercise books. Julie's initial comment 'Three pounds twelve I make Tom Ato' and her final remark 'Oh I've nearly finished my book. I've got one page to do' express her orientation, in this context, towards the identity of 'good pupil'.

In contrast, in the speech genre in the girls' toilets content themes revolve around issues of personal appearance and heterosexual romantic relationship and Julie talks about going out with boys, hairstyles, skin colour and sun tanning, tap dancing, a 'disgusting' skirt and showing tits (a word not normally used in the classroom). Personal worth in the toilets is determined not by how quickly and accurately sums can be completed, but by how attractive you are to the opposite sex and how much experience you have had in 'going out' with them. In this context, the girls are young adolescents trying out particular notions of femininity and checking out each other's experience with boys. The 'you' in 'I just called to say I love you, and I mean it, from the bottom of my heart' has a different kind of identity from the 'you' addressed in instructions on the worksheet. In displaying her knowledge of the song and singing it with Nicola, Julie signals the importance of this world of music, romance and desire as an important evaluative reference point for the kind of person she currently wants to be.

The conversation in the toilets seems to belong to a different world from the talk in the mathematics classroom, even though Julie moves easily between them and is talking informally with peers in both cases. Children's own sexuality was never referred to directly in any of the formal talk I recorded in classrooms, and only rarely in informal classroom talk, but it came more frequently to the fore in less regulated contexts. Children's sexuality was, in Foucault's terms, an area of silence in classroom discourse. Of course, the talk in the cloakroom has its own preferred positionings and areas of silence. Children's prowess at school work was often ignored or stigmatised in talk with peers about non-curriculum topics, for instance through the labelling of successful pupils as 'boffins' (a disparaging term for studious children). Some children, like Julie, managed to combine a 'good-enough' pupil identity with being an active player in the speech genres of teenage popular culture.

The generic production of meaning

For Bakhtin, whatever we have to say is always shaped within a generic form and our generic knowledge also guides our interpretation of the words of others. Individual words and phrases are not neutral, but 'taste' of the contexts in which they are habitually used. They contain echoes of their generic whole and a single reference to a text book, or a brief snatch of song, can invoke very different kinds of identities, relationships, social practices and evaluative perspectives. Bakhtin suggests that children learn to participate in the speech genres (including both oral and literate forms) of different spheres of human activity in the course of learning language itself. Speech genres can also become hybridised and simple primary genres like everyday conversation and brief informal notes are absorbed into more complex secondary genres like novels and speeches. While relatively experienced in some genres, the 10–12 year-olds I recorded were also continually learning: they observed how the teacher reacted to contributions from their peers, they stood at the periphery of group conversations at break time and they listened to other children's personal anecdotes while waiting in line in the corridor.

The two linked narratives which I examine below further illustrate how different sites in children's lives at home and at school provide different generic resources, and how, in this case, they are appropriated within a child's imaginative stories. In contrast to the example of Julie's talk in the toilets, where she is projecting herself into teenage social practices, Michelle's imaginative storytelling shifts her and her friends into a more childly[2] world of fairy tales and playacting. While the children I recorded varied in physiological maturity and in their degree of orientation towards more childly or more adolescent activities, many children shifted regularly between the two. The same child would discuss boyfriends on one occasion, and dolls on another. Through their talk, children could try out new kinds of scenarios, identities and relationships, and they could also revisit and fall back into familiar practices.

Michelle was a slight, retiring 11 year-old girl whom I had not noticed in the classroom until I ended up helping her and Kim with their work one afternoon and got into chatting with them about what they liked to do outside school. Michelle said she often made up stories with friends and offered to tape one of these for me. The first two extracts below comes from Michelle's recording of herself, her 4 year-old cousin, Natalie, and a 10 year-old friend, Sharon, who are all playing together in Michelle's bedroom. They construct a long, imaginary story which starts with Michelle announcing the title and invoking the genre: 'Once upon a time there was a little girl called Cinderella'. However, in the very first sentence of the story, Cinderella's 'playing out the front' locates the scene not in a fairytale world, but within the children's own lives, where they often played together in the road running outside their houses. Michelle models what she wants the other characters to say:

Table 2.2

Michelle	The friendly dragon, which is called Frederick. Once upon a time there was a little girl called Cinderella and she – she was playing out the front *(sound of soft humming)*. And then she bumped into a dragon *(Natalie laughs)* and the Dragon said 'hallo',
Sharon *(as dragon)*	Hallo
Michelle	And the little girl said 'hallo'
Natalie *(as girl)*	Hallo
Michelle	'what's your name?'
Natalie	What's your name?

The story which ensues is constructed of linked domestic scenarios: giving visitors cups of tea, washing up, playing shop and mothering. Michelle continues to heavily cue Natalie, but Sharon occasionally adds a personal touch to her role as dragon. Later on, the dragon has a stomach ache, breaks the bed, keeps the mother and daughter awake with his snoring and gets pushed over in the garden by Natalie and hurts his head. He gradually changes, as the story proceeds, from an awkward visitor into, in effect, another child in the home. The extract in Table 2.3, from fairly early on, is typical of the mixture of individual improvisation around domestic activities and Michelle's continuing intermittent narrator-scaffolding. There is also a brief reference to an alternative, non-domestic world 'out in the black dark forest'. On the tape, the strained and slightly gravelly voice Sharon puts on to portray the dragon stands out from the other two voices:

Table 2.3

Michelle	Oh no!
Natalie	What?
Michelle	You've dirtied all my cups and I ain't got none for my cup a tea.
Sharon	I know what, I can clean them up for you
Michelle	What?
Sharon	Oh, my paws are dirty aaw
Michelle	*(to Natalie, in high voice)* Can you wash up for me please, darling?
Natalie	Yes *(sound of crockery)*. Where's the cloth to do it? *(pause and continuing sound of crockery)*

Table 2.3 – *continued*

Michelle	You washed up yet?
Natalie	Yes
Michelle	Good girl! We've got enough. Oh for a cup of tea! Do you want a cup of tea?
Sharon	No thank you, it's time I must be going
Michelle	'Where do you live'
Sharon	/Out in
Michelle	/the little girl said
Natalie	Where do you live?
Sharon	Out in the black dark forest
Michelle	The little girl said 'Do you like living out there?'
Natalie	Do you like living out there?
Sharon	No, it's cold and I have to suffer.

Finally, after further domestic incidents, Michelle ends the story by announcing that the dragon was 'allowed to live with us again. And we were all one good happy family'. In this narrative Michelle, Sharon and Natalie draw on their shared domestic experience to produce a genre of activity which is very close to 'playing house'. Questions like 'Can you wash up for me please, darling?', 'Good girl!' and 'Oh for a cup of tea!' sound as if they are directly appropriated from Michelle's observations of daily life at home. While the dragon is gradually absorbed into this domestic world, however, he also brings the traces with him of a rather different fairy tale landscape and sometimes uses language reflecting his own generic origins ('the black dark forest', 'it's cold and I have to suffer'). The cosy domestic life which dominates most of the plot, characterisation and use of language is briefly recontextualised and thrown into relief as the 'inside' against the dragon's starkly contrasting 'out there'.

While Frederick is rendered docile within the framework of familiar everyday activities in the bedroom story, Michelle produced a rather different kind of ending in a second story about dragons which she told at school the next day. This second story, performed by Michelle at break time with her friend Josie, in some ways follows up the darker themes raised by Sharon in her brief account of 'out there' in the first bedroom story. It also starts with 'Once upon a time' and is about a little girl called Cinderella and a dragon. However, Michelle's announcement of the story title describes the dragon first as 'live' and then as 'fierce', rather than friendly (perhaps to gain Josie's attention). Michelle and Josie recorded themselves in the 'quiet room', a screened off space next to the classroom which contained the computer, over-head projector and the class library. They told me that they wanted to make a tape for Josie's special needs teacher. This story is much shorter and I include the complete text:

Table 2.4

1	Michelle	Cinderella and the live dragon. Right. *(short pause)*. Right. Cinderella … *(whispers)* hoy, come on *(story voice again)* Cinderella and the fierce dragon by Michelle and Josie. Here it starts. Once upon a time the little princess went for a walk.
5		*(sound of skipping along)* Diddly, diddly, diddly
	Josie *(as princess)*	/diddly diddly
	Michelle	/Then she met this terrible, green dragon *(roars)*. And then she goes *(high voice)* 'Oh dear green dragon oh', on her knees she
10		goes 'Oh dear green dragon oh dear oh dear please don't harm me'
	Josie	*(high voice)* Oh dear green dragon oh dear oh dear please don't harm me
	Michelle	And then the poor dragon started crying *(sound of crying)*
15		'Why are you crying, little dragon?' Princess said
	Josie	Why are you crying, little dragon?
	Michelle *(as dragon)*	*(miserable high voice)* Because I've got no friends
	Josie	I'll be your friend
20	Michelle	Will you? I will not eat you up
	Josie	Come on, I'm – let's go cherry picking. That's where I was going
	Michelle	Come on. So they went cherry picking *(sound of 'la la' skipping)*. Cherry picking indeed! Then *(dramatic voice)* – they see the dragon's mother! 'Oh mummy, mummy, meet my
25		new friend, my new friend'. *(deeper voice)* 'What is her what is her name?' ⎡ Oh well
	Josie	⎣ Cinderella
	Michelle	Cinderella was really really frightened so she ran back home as fast
30	Josie	/Mummy!
	Michelle	/as she could screaming 'Mummy!'
	Josie	/Mummy!
	Michelle	/'Mummy mummy mummy mummy' and all that night and all that day the Cinderella was frightened. One night when
35		she was fast asleep Cinderella woke up in surprise.
	Josie	Oh!
	Michelle	and go 'Oh!'
	Josie	Oh!
	Michelle	in a very loud voice. Her mum and dad run in, all the servants
40		run in as well. And then they see the two dragons lying on her bedroom floor dead

Table 2.4 – *continued*

Josie	*(gasp)*	
Michelle	*(Dramatic voice)* In amaze she screamed	
Josie	*(screams)*	
45 Michelle	and the two dragons got buried that next morning and never was seen again. The end.	

The stories at home and school both start out with similar characters, but their stylistic features and the way they are developed in terms of plot and characterisation are very different. These differences are linked with the different contexts of their production. The bedroom story was close to 'playing house' role play and the easy flow of the characters' activities suggests that this was a familiar imaginative activity. The story reproduces what Bakhtin would call the primary genres of informal fragments of conversation around making cups of tea, doing the shopping and looking after small children. Cinderella is a little girl living in a home like Michelle's who 'plays out the front' and asks the dragon questions like 'Where do you live?' and 'Do you like living these?' Leisurely and rambling, the story unfolds through the children's reconstruction of everyday domestic activities, scaffolding Natalie's contributions to the older girls' play in a role which is not so different from her position in real life.

At school, in contrast, the girls said they wanted to record a story for Josie's teacher, and they knew that they only had fifteen minutes of break time to do it. The shorter, tauter structure of the second story, at least partly a product of the limited time slot available within the school curriculum, produces a more condensed narrative plot. It may also be closer to what the girls feel is a 'proper' story in school, where the domestic play genre would have seemed childish and inappropriate. In this second story, the voices on the tape are more heavily dramatised and stylistically distanced from their producers so that I was constantly aware of what Bakhtin terms the 'double-voicing'[3] of the character's utterances (the simultaneous presence of two different voices with their own separate intentions), and of Michelle and Josie's self-conscious production of the characters' words. Cinderella is now a princess with servants who goes 'cherry picking'. Rather than absorbing the genres of everyday speech, Michelle's narrator's voice in the school version indexes the secondary genres of written fairy stories: 'Cherry picking, indeed!', 'in amaze(ment) she screamed', 'and never was seen again'. The prosaic dialogue of the first story is replaced by

Cinderella's story book voice in the second: 'Oh dear, green dragon, oh dear oh dear, please don't harm me!'

The differences between the two stories also reflect the different participants and patterns of collaboration involved in their production. While in both stories Michelle skilfully orchestrates her own and other children's voices, the pattern at home was for her to take a strong lead, heavily cueing Natalie and to some extent scaffolding Sharon. In fact, the flavour of 'playing house' may be partly a result of Natalie's involvement in the story. In school, however, Michelle's friend Josie quickly takes on an independent role, introducing the idea of 'cherry picking' in line 21, which Michelle takes up and incorporates into the story. Michelle also follows Josie's cues in lines 28, 31 and 37. The first bedroom story also undoubtedly provides part of the context for the second story for Michelle (and myself). We can see traces of the cueing Michelle used at home continuing in the second story even after Josie initiates her own part, so that a pattern develops where Josie makes a contribution, Michelle retrospectively cues it, and Josie repeats it (lines 30–2 and 36–8). The story in school is much more of an equal collaborative production, as Michelle and Josie, almost instantaneously, pick up and follow each other's cues.

Creating these two texts offered the children different opportunities for expressing and exploring aspects of the self. In the bedroom, they take on the roles of nurturing mothers and recalcitrant children. Within the fairy story at school, interestingly, Michelle is free to fleetingly explore fears which are silenced within the genres of domesticity (as represented in the girls' play), or relegated to the forest outside. While the plot in Michelle and Josie's story is a kind of new permutation of the one played out only the day before (there is an attempt at making a relationship with the dragon, who is lonely and has no friends) the exploration of the dragon's vulnerability is only fleeting and he is not turned into an awkward child. Instead of domesticating the strange, the second story moves in the opposite direction. The fairy story world which was only hinted at in the bedroom story becomes the dominant framework of the story told in the school quiet room, where the dead dragons come in from the outside and end up in the very heart of the home, 'lying on her bedroom floor dead'.

Like the contrast between Julie's talk in the classroom and the girls' toilets, the two dragon stories above show how children's language use is sensitive to changes in social context, and how they draw on the generic potential of different settings to produce imaginative stories involving alternative ways of viewing, representing and evaluating experience with different possibilities for the expression of identity. The two stories' rather different generic qualities reflect their realisation within the social practices of the home and school, respectively, and the local social practices, in each case, are absorbed into the narrative production.[4] There is also, of course, a sense in which the talk in the examples above is itself an important element in constructing and holding the context. Even as it is used, it establishes a particular kind of generic frame, whether of imaginary role play, or telling fairy stories. Similarly, in Julie's earlier example, the dialogues themselves sustain the genres of doing mathematics, or gossiping and teasing. Talk holds a current context, and it can also contain references to other contexts. As we saw in the first bedroom story, Sharon refers to an alternative context (the black dark forest) within the story. The invoking of alternative contexts, and articulating the relationship between them, is an important resource for producing meaning in talk, as I shall begin to explore below and will return to in later chapters.

The intertextual construction of the present

Teacher-pupil dialogues, concerned as they are with inducting children into school institutional practices and procedures, frequently contain references to past and future contexts. The past is invoked to establish precedent and mark significant activity and knowledge, as in *Remember how we did this last week ... what did I tell you we called this ...* and the future invoked to set goals and direct attention: *We have to move on to another topic next week ... you're going to need to know this for the test.* In many ways what constitutes the present, and how it should be evaluated, is constructed through intertextual referencing to various points in the past and future. This pattern of referencing backwards and forwards in time is closely connected with the ways in which knowledge about curriculum content and about the ground rules for classroom procedures is constructed within the classroom.[5] Children are continually being referred to the past and to the future in the course of work on classroom activities, the staging of curriculum syllabi across weeks and terms, and their own career trajectories through the different age-structured stages of the educational system. This linear time referencing, and the kinds of commitments and accountability it entails, are reproduced at a micro level within specific interactions, as I illustrate in Table 2.5 below.

It is a few minutes before the end of the school day in Camdean and the large sunny classroom is littered with detritus from the afternoon's activities, when pupils have been recording and mounting the results of a scavenger hunt in the school grounds. In the evening, pupils' parents will be visiting the school to meet teachers and talk about their children's progress. A few children are doing some desultory tidying while the majority are sitting expectantly at their tables, waiting for the bell to signal the time to go home. Miss Potts is restlessly pacing, with increasing irritation, around the room:

Table 2.5

Miss P.	What are your parents going to think, coming into a mess like this? Well they're not coming into a mess like this. Tough. You sit there and I'll clear up. And when I've finished, you can go home. OK?
Some pupils	*(uncertain)* ⌈ yea ⌊ no
	(pause while T moves round room)
Miss P.	Or are you going to cooperate?
Pupils	*(a few girls' voices)* Cooperate
Miss P.	I think about ten people in this room are doing clearing up. I said at the beginning that I wanted all of this work first of all put over the back. I've had five people come to me *(mimics whining voice)* 'What do we do with our work?' Which proves what?
More ps	Not listening
Pupil	Not listening
Miss P.	You just don't bother to listen. There's buckets and things all over the place, mess around, floor's a disgrace. Now there is FIVE minutes and you're not going because you've got trays out. I suggest that you get cleaned up NOW. Anybody messing around will be in trouble.

The physical context here is especially important because an aspect of it (the mess) is the immediate subject of the talk. Miss Pott's use of indexical or deictic terms: personal pronouns ('you', 'your', 'I', 'they'), the demonstratives 'this' and 'there' clearly signals the subject of her harangue: the state of the classroom and her displeasure with the children. The separation and opposition between 'I' and 'you' here contrasts with Miss Pott's more inclusive use of 'we' on other occasions, for example when she is guiding students through a mathematics calculation on the board. Indexical terms like pronouns and demonstratives are one of the most obvious ways in which speakers map out the contexts they are talking about, and grammatically encode the relationships between people, objects and actions in talk. Terms like 'this' or 'him' may appear relatively neutral when taken out of context, but their use by speakers always conveys a particular viewpoint: who counts as 'us' or 'them', the implied boundaries for 'here', the authority of 'I' and the positioning of 'you' (Hanks, 1996). Contexts are navigated through the use of different tenses, personal pronouns, demonstratives and deictics of place (here or there) and time (yesterday, today, tomorrow, now, then) to create a moral landscape in accordance with a particular evaluative perspective.

In Table 2.5, while the focus is ostensibly on the here and now (the mess), Miss Potts invokes another context to back up and strengthen her own position when she refers to the impending parents' visit to the school that evening. What the children's parents are going to think, in the future context of their evening visit, is used as an authoritative perspective to organise and galvanise their activity now in the present. In her harangue Miss Potts also refers to another context in the past, using reported speech. She mimics a child's whining voice 'What do we do with our work?' to remind pupils of the exchange she had with them earlier in the afternoon, and of the confusion and disorder which has characterised the last twenty minutes. The reported speech holds up and illuminates a momentary previous context which is also used as a resource for getting her point across in the here and now. Again, in Miss Potts' question 'Which proves what?' she is also implicitly referring to similar conversations from other occasions in the past. In their rapid recognition of the answer she wants, her pupils are not just responding to Miss Pott's question now, but also to the memory of her voice and the response of 'not listening' which she has cued on previous occasions.

Most of Miss Potts' comments in Table 2.5 are in fact structured around temporal relationships between actions and their consequences (or lack of consequences). 'When I've finished, you can go home', 'I said at the beginning that I wanted ...' and 'Anybody messing around will be in trouble'. The references backwards and forwards across time within the lesson, the references to the future parental visit and an intermediate future when 'you can go home', together with the implicit references to previous behaviour and dialogue in the past are linked to what might be termed the linear production of knowledge in school. Knowledge and procedures are built up in a planned, staged structured process over weeks, terms and years, in relation to specific short and longer term educational goals. The teacher talk I recorded is full of these kind of linear cause and effect connections, as children were trained to organise their behaviour and activities in terms of particular chains of inputs and outputs.

When Miss Potts invokes the future to urge pupils to clear up the mess and the past to condemn their lack of attention, the meanings of particular words and phrases, and of her overall message, emerge within the context of institutional practices and speech genres in a school classroom. Here, teachers and pupils are expected to conform to particular kinds of hierarchical relationships and authoritative definitions of what counts as worthwhile knowledge and appropriate activity. Deictic references to the immediate context in the teacher's utterance, for example 'this work', and 'over the back', depend for their meaning not just on the shared physical context, but also on its construal within established social practices which mark what counts as work and what should be done with it. Similarly, the meaning of having trays out and indeed of 'clearing up' and 'messing around' are all clear to pupils in terms of established procedures and relationships within the classroom (though Miss Potts' final description of the mess suggests she feels the need to reiterate some of these more explicitly). At least some of the pupils know that 'Or are you going to cooperate?' is not actually a question, but a direction. The use of the term 'cooperate' is consistent with the school policy of encouraging pupil autonomy and self respect, but on this occasion is more or less synonymous with *do as I tell you*. At this point in the day, when the teacher wants the classroom tidied and the children want to go home, the pupils know that Miss Potts has a certain amount of institutional power to keep them there until what she wants has been done.

Miss Pott's classes often started and ended with a few public reprimands or a general 'dressing down'. One or two boys occasionally challenged her authority during these harangues and were punished by having privileges withdrawn, for example being excluded from physical education or, on one occasion, sent to the head teacher's office. This kind of recurring public harangue re-established and underlined the ground rules of classroom behaviour and activated sanctions against those who failed to conform. Children's remarks suggested that they expected and sometimes welcomed these reprimands in the classroom context, which demonstrated the strictness that was part of being a good teacher. This may explain why pupils, once they realise that this is one of Miss Potts' harangues, cooperate fairly readily in the dialogue she cues and produce the required responses 'cooperate' and 'not listening'.

More tightly structured speech genres like the dialogue in Table 2.5 tend to involve fairly fixed and sustained interpretative frames with clear positions for the participants, and institutionally defined relationships between them. A breaking of the frame may threaten a breakdown of the speech genre and the institutional discipline it encodes. However, these frames were occasionally transformed through unusual events such as when, on one occasion during a class telling-off in Lakeside, the head teacher entered the classroom for a few seconds, wearing a woman's wig. (There was a rational explanation for this, which I can no longer recall). The frame of 'teacher haranguing pupils' was momentarily transformed into a frame of 'head teacher playing a joke on the class', where teacher and pupils were repositioned and brought together as his (rather bemused) audience. The speech genre of classroom teaching, however, still sustained the overall context and when the head teacher disappeared, the children immediately turned back to their work. The frame transformation had been a brief momentary aberration.

Microcontexts: manipulating frames

In the teacher-pupil dialogues I recorded, the reference points for evaluation remained fairly constant, knitted into the school processes and procedures. This was not so much the case in talk among children themselves. The children were less orientated to the longer term processes of input and output which dominated teacher-pupil talk, and they frequently switched between frames at a micro level within conversation in order to rekey what was going on, reaccent the evaluative meaning of a previous utterance, and reposition themselves more favourably within an interaction. In contrast to the linear referencing across time within teacher talk, the informal talk among children was not so much orientated towards cause and effect relationships between the past, present and future, as towards what might be termed more horizontal connections between alternative interpretations of interactions or events within a single time frame.[6]

In the extract in Table 2.6 below, pupils in Julie's class are drawing pictures as part of follow-up work to a reading by their teacher from *The Silver Sword*. The conversation occurred shortly after Miss Potts announced that pupils would be getting their school reports to take home at the end of the week. This extract shows how children can invoke a number of different frames, in rapid succession, for a past event. Mr. Clayson is the head teacher at Camdean.

Table 2.6

Pupil 1	Since I started at this school I've only been to see Mr. Clayson once
Pupil 2	Neither have I
Julie	*(gasps)* I've been there about ten times, always going to Clayson every single day. Wack wack wack because she's been a good girl! I normally go there because I say I've been involved, when I'm not. I stick up for my other friends
Pupil 3	I know, you're trying to get your nose in and things
Julie	I'm not, I'm sticking up for my friends and I say that I was doing it as well.

At the opening of the conversation Pupil 1 and 2's initial interpretative frame is an assumed shared understanding about the significance of being sent 'to see Mr. Clayson': it is a fairly awesome punishment meted out for particularly naughty behaviour. Julie, however, reaccents the meaning of being sent to the head teacher. She jokes irreverently that she's sent to 'Clayson' every day, caricatures what happens to her there (corporal punishment was not used in the school), and inverts the normal relationship between behaviour and punishment. In this way Julie playfully subverts school institutional notions of right and wrong and rewards and punishments and invokes a new evaluative framework within which loyalty to one's friends takes precedence over honesty as defined in school terms ('I normally go there because I say I've been involved when I'm not. I stick up for my other friends'). Thus Julie claims that in her case punishment constitutes martyrdom to friendship rather than a just response to bad behaviour, and presents herself as a feisty individualist whose integrity in personal relationships is not to be undermined by school norms. This second frame, however is in its turn contested by a third pupil, who claims that Julie's actions should not be interpreted as loyalty, but as nosiness. The comment 'You're trying to get your nose in' retrospectively re-evaluates or 'reaccents' Julie's previous comment. The issue of Julie's motives is never completely resolved and participants are left with these rather different possible interpretations of her actions.

Meaning is also left unresolved in the next example in Table 2.7, where Julie and David are sitting together eating their sandwiches at lunchtime. Here, Julie sets up two possible different interpretative frames ('children playing together after school' and 'girl wooing boy') to produce the ambiguity which is an important part of her strategy in engaging David's attention:

Table 2.7

Julie	Do you know where I live? Right if you go along Redlea the only blue door, that's where I live. The only blue door in Redlea
David	Only?
Julie	Right, if you can't get through, go to my next door neighbour's, that side (...), go through her place, jump over the fence and go down my path
David	Which number do you bang on?
Julie	One three four. And if you can't get through, go to, go round to number one three two, go through the fence, over the wood ⌈ (...)
David	⌊ you got a bike?
Julie	Puncture (...) got lost. I got skates. I can hold onto the back of your bike and go oooooh! *(pause)* Do you really go out with thingy *(pause)* Ma –
David	Who?
Julie	Mellie
David	No
Julie	What, did she chuck you? Why? *(pause)* Do you think Warren will mind if I move onto your table?
David	No. It's my table, I was the first one on it, so I own it
Julie	You don't, the school does. What's the hottest part of the sun? What's the hottest part of the sun? *(pause)* Page three!

The conversation starts with the knocking on doors which invokes the 'children playing after school' frame. Julie's question about whether David is going out with Mellie (with the possibly disingenuous pause over Mellie's name), and her request, following David's answer, to move onto his table, retrospectively adds a different kind of meaning to her previous invitation and hints that what is going on here is not children planning play but 'girl wooing boy'. This frame casts a particular light on Julie's skilfully deflected request to sit with David ('Do you think Warren will mind') and her ambivalent response to David's stated ownership of the classroom table. On the one hand, she quickly contradicts his assumption of dominance about owning the table: 'you don't, the school does', but she follows this up immediately with a joke 'what's the hottest part of the sun?' which relies for its humour on a pun between the sun and the *Sun* newspaper, with its regular Page 3 photograph of a semi-naked female model representing a rather passive female position within a dominant male gaze.

In one sense Julie is using language as a resource, drawing on both childhood and teenage speech genres within these alternative interpretative frames, in order to negotiate her relationship with David.

But these genres are also themselves shaping the choices of meanings available. The words 'go out with', 'chuck' and 'hot' all have specific generic connotations and invoke particular kinds of gender relations, potentially positioning Julie in ways which may not fit with her current assertive management of interactions with David. The same resources which Julie draws on to present and realise herself through talk construct her in particular ways, through their generic associations.[7] However, the ambiguity and provisionality of Julie's approach allows her to try out and test these positions and values while retaining the facesaving[8] option, should David reject her advances, of the alternative conversational frame of children playing after school. While ambiguity and provisionality can on some occasions lead to confusion, they can also allow a speaker to take risks in trying out possible relationships and identities, without the loss of face which more committed language acts might entail. In a situation where Julie is tentatively sounding out David's reactions, this kind of ambiguity offers him an important role in establishing which meaning to take forwards, through his choice of interpretative frame in which to locate his response. In the event, David seems to stay firmly within the 'children playing' frame.

While this kind of frame manipulation was quite common in children's talk among themselves, and Julie was happy to reframe and reverse the meaning of school discipline, children were less used to ambivalent or transgressive framing within teacher talk, which as I've explained tended to be more linear and evaluatively fixed in its patterning of contextual references. Children's uncertainty when teachers deviated from this was illustrated particularly clearly at one of the school assemblies which were held weekly in Lakeside. These assemblies were led by a particular class who usually displayed work and sometimes performed music and drama for the rest of the school. On one particular morning, the assembly started with three 9 year-olds standing at the front of the hall, reading out poems they had written about animals. Although their voices were more or less completely inaudible, children from the rest of the school remained sitting silently in class rows on the hall floor facing the readers, with the teachers seated on chairs along each side of the hall. (I myself was at the end of one of these rows.) A boy from the presenting class then asked the teachers to come and sit facing him on two rows of chairs placed diagonally at the front of the hall. With exaggerated demonstrations of reluctance and loud exclamations of 'Oh no', around eight teachers went to the front of the hall.

Somewhat to my surprise, these teachers immediately started to act out the parts of naughty children, pretending to punch each other, pull each others' hair and tip chairs up. The 9 year-old boy 'teacher' initially looked rather embarrassed and unsure about how he should react, while some children among the classes seated in the audience laughed and make the occasional comment. The boy 'teacher' then pretended to try to restore order to his 'class', managing very skilfully as far as I could see to project his dramatic role of a teacher trying to control naughty pupils, while still communicating the restrained respect required by his 'real' role of pupil. He did this through clearly marking his actions as playacting with exaggerated body movements, but remaining ultimately fairly ineffective (he did not, for instance, try to physically stop the 'fight' which was developing between a couple of the teachers acting as 'pupils').

While the boy teacher was quite remarkable in his simultaneous management of two frames which gave him contradictory role positions, the children seated watching on the floor were not so adept. As the teacher 'pupils' at the front became more unruly, some of the seated children began to imitate them fairly freely, and several scuffles broke out as the noise level among the seated pupils rose. The teacher whose class was taking the assembly now quickly stepped out of the role of naughty pupil, straightening his body with a loud 'shh' and glowering at the pupil audience. Some seated children echoed this 'shh', and the hall quickly fell silent, the pupils apparently somewhat relieved that normal power relations had been resumed. The teacher 'pupils' at the front settled down and their boy 'teacher' read them versions of fairy stories which had been written by his class for younger children. There was still some intermittent whispering among the other classes watching and at one point the head teacher interrupted the reading of the story to order a child out of the assembly to go and wait by his office.

I got the impression that many children were not familiar with this kind of role reversal sketch, and were in fact quite confused by the simultaneous holding of two different frames which it required. As they went up to class after assembly, Darren and Martie playfully re-enacted the teachers' carnivalesque behaviour, jostling each other on the stairs. When the children were milling around rather noisily later as they got ready for lunch, Mrs. Kilbride remarked 'And you wonder where we got our ideas from in this morning's assembly. Think about it.' The children looked puzzled, and there was no evidence in my recordings to suggest that these children (who were the oldest in the school) saw the teachers' behaviour in the sketch as any kind of comment on their own. One of the metamessages of the teachers' performance (*this is how your behaviour seems to us*) may well have been lost on the majority of pupils.

Conclusion

In this chapter I have begun to build up my analytic framework for examining the contextualisation processes in children's talk, through exploring the ways in which children draw on the generic resources of different settings and use these for meaning-making. The speech genres of teacher-pupil classroom dialogue, pupils' talk with each other about classroom work, gossip in the toilets, imaginative play at home and story performance in school all involve different uses of language, different kinds of content themes and different reference points for evaluation. These genres offer pupils alternative opportunities for relationship and for expressing and presenting, or silencing, aspects of themselves. Compare, for instance, Julie's use of language in Miss P's dressing down of the class, with her conversation with Carol and Nicola in the toilets. Children's imaginative texts, I have suggested, encode the generic practices which were involved in their production. I have also looked briefly at how, within a context or invoked context, evaluative perspectives and relationships between people and objects are mapped out through the use of grammatical indexical forms: tenses, pronouns, demonstratives and deictics.

While there are general patterns of theme, relationship and evaluation across the different speech genres which emerge in the data, I use Goffman's notion of interpretative frames to examine the more subtle, moment by moment, negotiations of evaluation, positionings and alignments at particular points within a genre. In teacher-pupil dialogue these frames tend to be fairly consistent and sustained over time, knitted into institutional practices with a strong institutionally derived evaluative framework for judging individuals and their actions (the good teacher, the diligent or badly behaved pupil). Pupils and teachers expect this consistency of framing: when teachers break the frame, for instance when the head teacher came into the classroom wearing a wig and when the teachers pretended they were disruptive pupils in assembly, the fracture is strongly marked and often carnivalesque, a moment of release for teachers after which normal practices are quickly resumed. Normal contextualisation patterns within teacher-dominated talk are made within a consistent frame, almost synonymous with the speech genre, and involve the referencing across time which ties in with linear conceptions of pupil progress and the staged structuring of knowledge formation within school.

In pupils' informal talk, in contrast, the children frequently invoke alternative frames which reaccent previous contributions and reposition themselves more favourably. A change in framing always involves some kind of change in evaluation, as when going to see the head teacher is given three different meanings in rapid succession and when meeting after school can be seen either as children's play or as part of becoming boyfriend and girlfriend. In each case, certain words and gestures could be evaluated differently, depending on the interpretative frame. Julie also uses what might be termed 'frame ambiguity' to protect her face in a delicate interaction with David, holding the alternative interpretative frameworks as potential resources of meaning for both of them within the interaction. In contrast to the fixed, formalised knowledge involved in schooling, this kind of frame switching is connected with children's more fluid, multi-perspectival, fragmentary construction of knowledge about their social world, and about the people and social practices within it. Thus the patterning of contextualisation through framing within a genre is related to the nature of knowledge being produced, whether the relatively fixed, systematically organised school curriculum knowledge, or the knowledge about social practices which are themselves inherently dynamic and multi-voiced.

As I argued in Chapter 1, the taking up of evaluative positions is an important part of children's ongoing developing sense of self. Children's inclinations to evaluate and act on the world in particular ways are expressed in part through their contextualisation strategies, which foreground particular view points, relationships, and social practice. These contextual connotations, however, also play a central, dynamic and sometimes unpredictable part in the negotiation of meaning. In addition to using language for their own communicative goals, speakers themselves are in some ways produced, as people, through the generic associations of the contexts they invoke and the ways in which these references are dialogised within talk. Contextualisation is in this sense doubly implicated, both as a resource for individual speakers and as a socialising force, in the meaning of children's dialogue and their negotiation of identity.

3
Dialogue and Collaboration: Girls and Boys

> Utterances ... echo each other in a 'tenacious array of cohesive grammatical forms and semantic values' and intertwine in a 'network of multifarious compelling affinities'. One cannot therefore understand the true meaning of any conversational utterance without considering its relation to other utterances.
> (Tannen, 1989, p. 97, with quotations from Jakobson, 1960).

Janet   What happens if you want to stop being somebody's boyfriend?
Kieran Chuck 'em
Kevin   Dump 'em

In this chapter I take up the ideas about dialogue and dialogicality I introduced in Chapter 1, in order to look at how children accomplish collaboration within talk. Talk is always part of social practice, underpinned by common understandings and histories and tied to shared contextual meanings through generic patterning and interpretative frames. All talk therefore assumes a certain amount of shared knowledge and goals at a basic level and is, in essence, collaborative (although this does not, of course, preclude misunderstanding). In addition to the shared understandings on which talk is predicated, all utterances are also, as I discussed in Chapter 1, both responsive and addressive. Speakers and writers orientate their utterances, explicitly and implicitly, to other speakers in the past and in the future.[1] This dialogical tendency is not just expressed through turn taking in talk, but permeates across turns. Rather than listening to someone else and then responding, the children's talk was much more overlapping, fragmented and recursive.

They often completed each other's utterances, repeated and took over each other's voices and quoted voices from elsewhere. These dialogical interdependencies cross-cutting children's talk which we saw for instance in Julie's story about swearing at her mum (Table 1.1), and in the retrospective challenging of meaning in the conversation about being sent to the head teacher (Table 2.6), make it difficult to pinpoint the author of particular ideas, or even, on occasions, to identify who counts as the speaker and who the listener.

Goffman (1981) provides a first step towards deconstructing the speaker-listener roles, suggesting that there can be six basic positions in relation to what is being said within a conversational frame. Speakers may assume any combination of three roles: the *animator* who produces the utterance, the *author* who is responsible for its wording or the *principal* who is ultimately responsible for the views expressed. Thus, for instance, in quoting someone else's words we may, like Natalie repeating Michelle in the story in Table 2.2, be simply the animator, rather than the author or principal of what is said. And, for Goffman, listeners may be either an *addressed recipient*, the rest of an *official audience* or *unofficial bystanders* including over-hearers and eavesdroppers. I myself took up various combinations of one or more of these listening roles, in talking with children and making the recordings.

However, while this framework starts to unravel the different kinds of voices, commitment and interactions which may be part of a particular conversational exchange, it still doesn't address the ongoing dialogic links *between* utterances which I found were a central part of meaning-making in the children's talk. In the quotation at the beginning of the chapter, for instance, Kevin appears to be the animator, author and principal of 'Dump 'em', but in choosing this wording he is echoing Kieran's 'Chuck 'em', with its similar slang term and parallel structure. Kevin frequently takes his cue from Kieran and the dialogic link he makes here is an important part of the interpersonal meaning of his utterance, in its expression of a social and evaluative alignment with his friend. Again, when children report someone else's voice, they do not usually, like Natalie, simply relay the views of the principal of the original utterance, but almost always reword and reframe reported utterances in line with their own intentions. There is, Bakhtin suggests, a dialogical relationship between the speaker and the voice they are reporting, which is expressed through the way in which the voice is reported (as in Miss Potts' parodic representation of children asking what they should do with their work Table 2.5). The animator of the reported speech adds their own meaning, becoming in effect its author and co-principal. In this chapter, I shall start deconstructing the speaker-listener model through examining the dialogic links between different children's utterances as they talk together, looking at how these are involved in constructing evaluative, referential meanings and how the dialogic links speakers make also construct and express interpersonal relationship and aspects of personal identity. I take up questions about the dialogic links invoked by reported voices, in subsequent chapters.

Ideas about talk and collaboration within education have often been associated with liberal education policies advocating children's support and extension of each others' learning through group work and other cooperative activity.[2] I shall, however, be focussing here on children's talk about non-curriculum topics and tracing interactive patterns associated with the production of less formalised kinds of knowledge. The kind of collaborative talk valued by many educationalists, where the exchange of views is mutually supportive, has also been traditionally seen as feminine.[3] Some linguists' findings have suggested that men are more hierarchical and competitive and women more egalitarian and connection seeking, and that particular themes, language choices and interactive strategies are associated with a particular gender.[4] Such findings have sometimes been interpreted in terms of a rather fixed relationship between language style and gender identity, for example, a child is seen as verbally competitive because he is a boy. More recently, researchers influenced by poststructuralist ideas have become more interested in the various contextualised ways in which gender is performed and produced through language, and how a child presents themselves as a boy, through their choice and use of language.[5]

I shall start by looking at the dialogic patterns in the talk between pairs of friends, in their interviews with me. The interviewees' presentation of their friendship through close collaboration was part of the generic patterning of language use, themes and evaluative stances which emerged within this context. I then look at the interactive patterns in talk about non-curriculum topics among groups of children on their own. Finally, I consider the relationship between gender and communicative style which emerges from different contexts within the data, and suggest how the differences I found can be interpreted within the more emergent, processual view of identity that I outlined in Chapter 1.

The duet of friendship

In my interviews with the children in friendship pairs, they often expressed dimensions of their friendship to me through the ways in which they interacted and orientated towards each other's utterances, as well as through their stories of shared experiences and displays of knowledge about each other's lives. Identifying oneself as someone else's friend involves a combination of language use, interaction, choice of topic and evaluative stance, and there was often a subtle negotiation around these, within the interview context. A particularly common collaborative pattern in my interview data is a series of linked utterances, sometimes overlapping or repeating each other, which expand on a particular theme. Here, for instance, are a number of examples from my interview with Kevin and Kieran, who frequently extended and elaborated each other's comments. They are talking in the first example in Table 3.1 about being in a gang, in the second about the cartoon stories Kevin designs at home, and in the third about having girlfriends.

Table 3.1

a.

Janet	And then what did the gang do?
Kieran	Just went round
Kevin	Play football
Kieran	Telling jokes and
Kevin	Tell jokes

b.

Janet	What kind of stories?
Kevin	Make up funny stories about characters
Kieran	There's one of the boys has spiked hair
Kevin	Has spiked hair, wears a T shirt

c.

Janet	Have you had girlfriends before?
Kevin	Yea, Lisa Smith, I've been out with her before, I went out with her for about a year when I was in year, when I was in second year
Kieran	Yea, till third, weren't it?
Janet	Why did you break up?
Kevin	I don't know. Just got bored with each other
Kieran	Go out with them too long you get bored
Kevin	Yea
Kieran	It's the same thing really, ain't it, you try to get someone different.

I was particularly struck in the interviews by the extent and detail of children's knowledge about each other's lives, which enabled them to collaborate in reporting their friend's individual experience, as well as events which they had both shared. We can see a recurring pattern in the first two examples (and in the example at the head of the chapter), where Kieran answers me, and Kevin provides an additional supportive comment. In example (c) however, where the focus is on Kevin's experience with girlfriends, Kieran provides a supportive question 'Yea, till third, weren't it?', and two further turns where he agrees with his friend about getting bored with girls. On the tape Kieran's further explanation about 'wanting to get someone different' sounds defensive of his friend and this kind of warranting and supporting of a friend's experience occurred frequently in the interviews. Within this interactive pattern, there was also a considerable amount of repetition of words and phrases. In the first two examples Kevin echoes Kieran's final phrases 'Telling jokes' and 'has spiked hair', and in the third example Kieran echoes Kevin's phrase 'get bored'. This repetition, which seems to operate at an unconscious level, expresses the boys' orientation to each other and also confirms and warrants their experiences.[6]

The term 'duetting', used by Falk (1980) to describe the way in which couples sometimes talk to a third party, seems an apt description of the boys' talk here. Falk suggests that where the partners have mutual knowledge of a topic, a sense of camaraderie and a common communicative goal, linguistic patterns will include speakers repeating or paraphrasing each other, talking simultaneously but not in competition for the floor and overlapping and continuing each other's turns. In all three of the examples above, Kevin and Kieran paraphrase and continue each other's turns. Other friendship pairs of girls and boys in the interview also frequently duetted (all children chose to be interviewed with a friend of the same gender as themselves). In the first example in Table 3.2 below, Geoffrey completes Lee's utterance, rapidly orientating to the content of his turn, and in the second example Laura completes what Melissa is saying. In the third example, Melissa breaks in twice to complete an explanation and Laura adds an additional meaning ('or don't play with them ...').

It is sometimes difficult to decide whether two children are sharing an utterance, or whether it is actually the second child who adds an additional point, encoding it as if completing the previous utterance. In example (a) for instance, Lee's use of the term 'where' in 'where he busted his arm' retrospectively makes Geoffrey's 'up to the very top' (which itself had extended Lee's previous comment), incomplete. Utterances are not only multifunctional in simultaneously expressing referential, interpersonal and emotive meanings, but their functions can also be retrospectively extended, or reframed, through the backwards links made by a subsequent speaker. Lee's 'Where he busted his arm'

Table 3.2

---

a. Breaking an arm
Lee	Yea we went down there as well
Geoffrey	Up to the very top
Lee	/Where he busted his arm

b. Explaining what happens in club meetings
Janet	What do you have meetings about?
Melissa	Just talk. What work you've been doing, and
Laura	Boys *(laughter)*

c. Explaining a club rule
Janet	What does 'No using' mean?
Laura	It means
Melissa	No going off
Laura	Like, when you're playing with someone, ⌈ you don't go
Melissa	⌊ you don't go off and play
	with someone else and never speak to them or anything like that
Laura	Or don't play with them or talk about them behind their back and things like that.

---

adds new significance as well as a linked clause to Geoffrey's 'Up to the very top', as the friends build collaborative grammatical structures on the hoof, within ongoing dialogue. And Laura's echoing of her friend's phrase 'anything like that' in 'things like that' (Table 3.2 (c)) is another example of the repetition and parallel phrasing which is typical of duetting between friends.

In conveying shared knowledge about events and practices and expressing friendship, children's utterances may be so closely dialogically aligned that they may speak, as it were, with one voice. There can, however, be quite subtle negotiations involved, for instance when Karen and Helen were telling me about Karen's brother's accident.

Table 3.3

Janet	How long ago was that, then?
Karen	That was
Helen	/About three months
Karen	About three months ago
Helen	He was going boxing, he can't do that till next season, now
Karen	He's just been getting on everybody's nerves
Helen	He was going to get in a team or something, weren't he?
Karen	Yea, just for the England boxing club, for the juniors but he can't do that now.

Although it is Karen's brother who is the subject of the conversation, Helen cuts in here to complete Karen's utterance 'That was' with 'About three months', and initially provides more detailed information than her friend 'He was going boxing, he can't do that till next season, now'. In Karen's comment which follows, 'He's just been getting on everybody's nerves', she exercises the right as a family member to make a derogatory comment about her brother and may also be claiming the right to lead on the story at this point. (Although children often made disparaging remarks about their own family members, they avoided doing this about other children's relatives to their face and it would have been very unusual for Helen to have the right to make this kind of comment here.) Helen seems to acknowledge Karen's right to lead in her responding deferral 'He was going to get in a team or something, weren't he?' which in effect hands the story over to her friend (while still also displaying further detailed knowledge of Karen's brother). In conveying this kind of information, Helen is expressing her closeness with Karen to her and to me and the delicate balance between supporting Karen and displaying intimate knowledge to a third person whom she wants to impress is skilfully negotiated. The business of who has the right to tell what to whom is at the very heart of friendship[7] and in the interviews, where children revealed quite intimate details about their personal lives, friends would often provide leading supportive questions or comments which demonstrated their familiarity with the content of what was being said (thus warranting its 'truth'), while being careful not to usurp their friend's right to lead in an account over which they had greater personal rights.

Where children are relating a shared experience, the pattern of the interaction not only serves to elaborate and extend the account. It also sometimes seemed to express, through the way an event was represented by friends in the interview, something about the texture of the relationships and interactions within the original event being reported. In other words, the particular interactive style of the joint account relayed something important about the topic. Sam and Simon, for instance, often played together out of school, and talked to me at length about the places between the railway line and the farmer's field where they built their camps and about the transformation of Simon's garden shed into a museum for their collection of animal bones. The easy give-and-take of their relationship and shared activities is reflected in the collaborative style of their explanation about finding a man's rucksack along the canal.

Table 3.4

1	Simon	The other day about a month ago
	Sam	/Cause not a lot of people go over there
	Simon	/About a month ago, we found a rucksack and it was this man's,
		three pairs of trainers, a blanket, a toothbrush, a pair of pants and
5		you know them things you relight, you refill your lighter with,
		and one of ⌈ them
	Sam	⌊ Gas (....) so we sold it for 55p, it was full
	Simon	Yea and he kept the rucksack, he's still got it now
	Sam	He took the blankets for his shed
10	Simon	Yea but I had to throw them away because they smelt a bit iffy
		and there was clothes
	Sam	I think I've still got the rucksack
	Simon	You have.

While Simon starts the account, Sam quickly adds an important piece of information ('Cause not a lot of people go over there') and helps Simon out when he struggles to describe the lighter refill. Simon responds to Sam breaking in with the additional information about the gas lighter not by competing to reclaim the floor, but by orientating his next remark to Sam's experience 'Yea and he kept the rucksack, he's still got it now', whereupon Sam responds with a similar reference to Simon, 'He took the blankets for his shed'. The referential and interpersonal meanings of the talk here are closely tied in to the turn-taking structure. Thus Simon's 'Yea and he kept the rucksack, he's still got it now' (line 8) not only extends the account, but refers to Sam's experience in a way which acknowledges and accepts his friend's interruption as a bid to share in telling the account. Rather than taking over the account at this point, Sam as it were returns the compliment 'He took the blankets for his shed' (line 9). Like the re-adjustment which occurs in Karen and Helen's sharing out of the collaborative account earlier, Sam and Simon manage a subtle re-orientation towards each other's speaking rights (which have important consequences for their friendship) and shift from Simon leading the story to a more evenly balanced collaborative telling. In the next two turns Simon expands on Sam's comment about the blankets (line 10) and then Sam expands on Simon's comment about the rucksack (line 12), also orientating to his previous turn about throwing things away. In the final turn, finessing this ritual dance of friendship, Simon's comment 'You have' clinches the boys' display of close shared knowledge and mutual alignment.

In contrast to the amicable give-and-take of Sam and Simon's communicative style, the joint story by Karlie and her friend Nicole in Table 3.5 below reflected the rather different tone of the experience being recounted. Nicole was talking about what she did with her boyfriend.

Table 3.5

Nicole	I kissed him once, that was in school, they all pushed me to him. It was funny, weren't it?
Karlie	Yea, ⌈ he wanted to kiss her
Nicole	⌊ I didn't want to kiss him
Karlie	/So we was trying to push her to him
Nicole	/I didn't want to kiss
Karlie	/And then he didn't want to so we just grabbed both of their heads and then just pushed them together.

Nicole's first turn is initially a complete minimal narrative: 'I kissed him once, that was in school, they all pushed me to him' with a concluding evaluative comment: 'It was funny, weren't it?' This final question invites a turn from Karlie and as the story is taken up and expanded by the two girls, 'I kissed him once' retrospectively takes on the function of the kind of abstract which speakers often use to introduce a story in conversation and 'that was in school, they all pushed me to him' as the scene setting. We then hear, in this slightly longer story, how 'he wanted to kiss her', 'I didn't want to kiss him', 'So we was trying to push her to him', 'I didn't want to kiss', 'and then he didn't want to so we just grabbed both of their heads and then just pushed them together'. Thus, the fuller, collaboratively produced narrative 'refunctions' Nicole's initial utterance, turning it from a complete, self-contained mini-narrative into what William Labov[8] calls the abstract and orientation sections of the slightly longer story. Just as Geoffrey and Lee expanded on each other's comments, retrospectively changing both the grammatical status and the semantic significance of previous utterances, we can see in Nicole and Karlie's account here how this retrospective re-functioning can also happen at the level of narrative structure. The style of the telling is an iconic representation of the original incident, the girls' contradictory voices replaying the half joking struggle when Nicole's friends tried to push her and the boy together. While Sam and Simon's sensitively tuned turn taking reflects their comfortable relationship in the adventure of finding the rucksack and sharing out its contents, Karlie and Nicole's choppy interaction reflects, both in the structure of the talk and its meaning, the interpersonal pattern in the kissing incident.

Producing unformalised knowledge in group talk

The kinds of overlapping and merging of talk in the interviews which I described above also occurred in conversations among children in the classroom. For instance, in the example below Julie, Alice and Susie (from two linked classes of ten to eleven year-olds) are working on mathematical calculations based on fictional cafe bills. The morning session in Camdean has nearly ended, and the girls are discussing how classes get allocated to different lunch sittings.

Table 3.6

Julie	This makes me think about school lunch
Alice	We've never been second or first, ⌈ have we?
Susie	⌊ Our class, our class is always one
	of the last to go, aren't we?
Alice	Yes, because we ⌈ have
Susie	⌊ Just because ⌈ Mr. Gorman
Alice	⌊ Mr. Gorman
Susie	Oh yea, Mr. Gorman volunteers us to go last
Julie	We've never been first
Alice	Mr. Gorman always, he volunteers for mine and your class, he volunteers for our class to go last!

Alice and Susie repeat each others' words, and overlap and complete each other's turns. Utterances like 'Yes because we have' and 'Just because Mr. Gorman' do not make much sense on their own, but meaning is produced cumulatively across the different contributions. The girls' voices blend together, sharing what Goffman would see as the authorship and principalship of the words. Alice's summative comment draws Julie's, Susie's and her own previous comments together in terms of their content and evaluative stance, simultaneously expressing the social and evaluative alignment between the three girls.

This kind of overlapping, almost simultaneous yet relatively harmonious talk has been associated with conversation among women friends.[9] However, collaborative negotiation in girls' informal talk is not always as harmonious as in the extract above.[10] In the next example, where Jenny and Angie in Camdean are sitting together finishing off some work from earlier in the day, there is a similar close negotiation of meaning, but the speakers have opposing perspectives, and there is none of the overlap, repetition, or completion of each other's utterances which is typical of 'duetting'. When Jenny cuts in 'No, I was the one', this is an interruption registering disagreement, not a kind of shared voice.

Table 3.7

Jenny	I'm going to tell Kerry
Angie	What?
Jenny	That we said we were going to ignore her
Angie	I never said that, you did
Jenny	Yea you did, you did as well
Angie	I said just to pretend that she's not there
Jenny	Yea, that's still saying to ignore
Angie	I was the one who thought of ⌈ it
Jenny	⌊ No, I was the one who thought of it
Angie	And you went along. *(To Kerry, who has just returned to the table)* Right, we were going to pretend that we couldn't see you, right. And just now when I says that she never thought of it, but I thought of it, right, and then she went along with it. *(Pause)* I'm sorry, Kerry
Kerry	It's alright. I like a good joke, anyway.

This exchange, like the example in Table 3.6, is about evaluating people's actions. But whereas Julie, Alice and Susie were fairly unanimous in their complaint about Mr. Gorman, Jenny and Angie are directly opposed. The expression 'I'm telling' usually means informing a teacher or parent about someone's misbehaviour, and there are possible shades of this in Jenny's first remark. Although they seem to establish a functional equivalence between ignoring Kerry, pretending she is not there and pretending not to see her, Jenny and Angie do not reach agreement over who said what, and whose idea it was in the first place to ostracise Kerry. Although it is Jenny who says she is going to tell Kerry, it is Angie who does the actual telling, usurping Jenny and at the same time making a positive friendship move towards Kerry in her apology. While Kerry acknowledges the apology ('It's alright'), her final comment reframes the whole event as a joke, so that Jenny and Angie's plans are re-evaluated as benign rather than malicious. Peace is restored between the three girls, but in terms of meaning we are left with a range of possibilities: that it was Jenny who hatched the plot to ignore Kerry or that it was Angie, that Jenny and Angie meant to be nasty to Kerry or it was all a light-hearted joke, and that Kerry hides her hurt or is genuinely not bothered. In spite of Kerry's final comment, these alternative interpretations are not necessarily resolved, but could be drawn on selectively by any of the three participants in future dialogues.

The examples of collaborative talk in Table 3.6 and Table 3.7 both came from relatively intimate conversations between a small numbers of children who were sitting together doing their work. The talk I recorded among larger groups of children also involved moments of duetting, and, in addition, a considerable amount of sparring, particularly among a number of the more dominant boys. The next two examples, first of boys' talk and then of a group of boys and girls together, include what looks like the kind of competitive, conflictual talk that has been associated, in some discussions of language and gender, with men and boys. Children in these choppy, competitive discussions throw in fragments of personal experience, vying to demonstrate some kind of personal expertise and struggling to gain the conversational floor for a longer turn. However, I shall suggest that this kind of talk is also collaborative: a shared topic is developed across children's individual turns and a considerable amount of cumulative information is shared. What makes the talk seem competitive or conflictual is, in each case, the challenging between just two boys. Meanwhile, other boys use the same kind of supportive strategies that are found in the interviews. The first example in Table 3.8, from the recording of a group of around eight boys in the swimming pool changing room, is typical of the boys' talk in larger group interaction. The boys had placed a small cassette recorder on a bench.

Table 3.8

1	Darren	What about on telly, those, those, that em diving Olympics thing, they have em real high diving board, they stand backwards and there's like flip theirselves right way round and just ⌈ hit the water
5	Geoff	⌊ Yea I bet that hurts
	Martie	Sh, no it doesn't, the higher it is
	Darren	/Oi, where's your er (....) comb
	Martie	A brush, there, it's in my bag. The higher it is, it isn't harder to dive off, it's harder to go down cause the pressure is pushing you
10		up, the gravity
	Darren	/About pressure and all that *(laugh)*
	Martie	The gravity is bringing ⌈ you towards the ground
	Darren	⌊ Who's ever been in a racing car?
	Boys	Me, me
15	Darren	A formula one?
	Boys	Yea, yea
	Darren	While it's going, yea?

Table 3.8 – *continued*

	Boys	Yea, me
	Darren	A formula three thousand (….) ?
20	Martie	A formula three thousand isn't as power, powerful as a formula one
	Darren	I never said it was, so?
	Martie	I've been in a formula one
	Boy	I've been ⌈ (….)
	Darren	⌊ What about G-force, your head's like that. You're
25		going round the corner and you're going *(motor noises)*, no, but with G-force, your head, right, cause, cause you're going one way and the wind's blowing the other, your head's going *(car noise + laughter)*
	Geoff	Yea, I'd laugh if a racing car driver, if his head came off *(general*
30		*loud laughter)*
	Darren	And his car just went off the edge and went right through the finishing line.

My first impression in listening to this talk was a sense of competitive jostling for the conversational floor, and for opportunities to display technical knowledge.[11] In fact, apart from competition between Martie and Darren, the exchange is essentially collaborative rather than conflictual. Darren maintains his dominance not through continually holding the floor himself, but through the ways in which he orientates to others, eliciting their responses and orchestrating the conversation. In lines 1, 13 and 24, each time he introduces a new topic, Darren does so in terms of a question inviting a sharing of experience: 'What about …?' 'Who's ever been …?' 'What about …?' and in lines 13–19 he uses a series of questions to hold the floor (a feat not many children could have accomplished). In line 11 he picks up on Martie's mention of gravity ('About pressure and all that') and in his final turn he extends Geoffrey's suggestion about the racing car driver's head coming off in the same kind of duetting structure as I found between friends in the interviews. Apart from Martie, the other boys seem to help to sustain Darren's dominant position. For instance, both of Geoffrey's comments in lines 5 and 29 start with 'yea' or 'yes' and then expand on the topic in Darren's previous turn, thus supporting his claims to knowledge and to lead within the conversation.

At the level of topic content, in Darren's comments on G-force and racing drivers he addresses questions concerning conflict between forces of movement and gravity that were first introduced by Martie in relation to Olympic divers. These questions are not discussed any further, and members of the group may be left with a number of fairly hazy ideas about the physics involved. Martie said later in his interview with me that he was thinking of the water pressure pushing against divers when they enter the water (which doesn't necessarily support his argument about high dives and pain). In spite of the asymmetric power relationship and the struggle between Darren and Martie, however, all of the boys present will have heard or taken part in ways of talking about pressure, gravity and G-force, which they can draw on in future occasions. This gathering together of bits and pieces of references and explanations, with analogies being made across different segments of experience, was typical of the way in which children built up general, unformalised knowledge, in contrast to the concise explanations given by teachers or in books, and the linear structuring of references and knowledge in teacher-dominated talk.

Example 3.9(a), from talk among a group of both boys and girls, shows this same kind of process happening, and developing into a

Table 3.9(a)

1	Darren	Oi – you got a comb? Did you get up late?
	Tina	No, no, I was just messing around – went barmy with it this morning
	Sherri	Permed it, and it went ⌈ (....)
5	Darren	*(to Tina)* ⌊ Do you curl your hair?
	Tina	No. Perm
	Darren	Soft perm *(laughs)*
	Philip	Is that a soft perm?
	Sherri	No, it's a cold perm
10	Darren	*(to Sherri)* Have you ever smoked? *(pause)* Have you?
	Geoff	He has
	Darren	I have. You don't know how to. You go *(laughter)*
	Geoff	Probably go – she, she'll go *(sound of sharp intake of breath and laughter)*
15	Philip	No, she'd probably go like this
	Sherri	No I put it, I put it round like this
	Darren	I do it like, I go, I go
	Sherri	I go like that
	Geoff	I go like that
20	Sherri	What are you doing? *(laughter)*
	Geoff	I'm doing that on ⌈ (.....)
	Darren	⌊ I had a cigarette like that little, yea, I went into Stars and I used to go *(miming)* arrrrh, blinking (.....)
	Geoff	Guess what I done, right what I done, I had one of my dad's
25	Philip	/Oh, look I done it, I had this fag like that, right, ⌈ you put
	Darren	⌊ no, no, that's a
		⌈ cigar I went
		(makes sound of choking)
	Philip	⌊ No, no,
30		you get fags like that, right, you put the end in your mouth, don't bite make sure your lips aren't wet, breathe back, and smoke comes from your thing.

longer and more detailed discussion. Tina and Sherri combined being 'good pupils' with also being the objects of sexual interest for the more dominant boys like Darren, who was 'going out' with Sherri. Geoffrey and Alan often hung around at the edges of groups of more dominant boys, asking questions and trying to get in on a piece of the action. The topic of smoking arises as the children are chatting over their mathematics work. 'Stars' is the local newsagent.

Having lost face in terms of his knowledge about hair styling (through mistaking a cold perm for a soft perm), Darren challenges Sherri about smoking (line 10), a topic where he can demonstrate more secure personal knowledge. Supported by Geoffrey (line 11), he proceeds to tease Sherri about her lack of experience, aided by Geoffrey and Philip in lines 13 and 15. Listening to the tape, I was struck by Sherri's good humoured countering of Darren's teasing. In this and other conversations she presented herself as knowledgeable about topics like smoking or sex, but her personal style tended to be both self-assured and relatively unassertive. Sherri, Darren, Philip and Geoffrey then give overlapping accounts of experiences of smoking cigarettes and cigars (lines 16–32), with Philip and Darren beginning to challenge each other (lines 25–9) and Philip gaining centre stage momentarily with his concise explanation of how smoking is done, in the final turn. The conversation then moves on (see Table 3.9 (b) below), via roll-ups (a hand-rolled cigarette) to dope (cannabis), with a short intermission where the school secretary arrives in the classroom to ask for the children to return their dental forms.

The topic development here, from hair styles to smoking cigarettes to smoking roll-ups and dope proceeds through the jostling for turns, taunting and teasing among children, with individuals now and then gaining the floor long enough to give a brief explanation or anecdote. Darren's claims of expertise are persistently challenged by Philip (lines 64, 76 and 78), and there is a continual struggle for dominance between the two boys from line 39 onwards. The topic development is in fact prompted by Philip's 'You can't get a fag that big anyway!' which Darren counters with 'Yea, a roll-up' (line 37) and he then tries unsuccessfully to start an anecdote in lines 38 and 40, but is cut short by Geoffrey's question about dope. After the school secretary's interruption, Geoffrey returns to the question of dope again, and after struggling with Philip to respond to Geoffrey (lines 62–5), Darren manages this time to tell an anecdote (lines 70–5), and is challenged again by Philip.

While this discussion is strongly driven by social agendas (the rivalry between Darren and Philip, the boys' desire to display themselves as

Table 3.9 (b)

Tina	My Dad can do that (.....) I only had two drags, that's all I had,
Philip	You can't get a fag that big anyway!
35 Tina	He goes, he goes 'I'll see you later, then', I go *(laughter)*
Geoff	I still have a stomach ache, I got well (....)
Darren	*(answering Philip)* Yea, a roll-up *(laughter)*
	I found this roll-up
Philip	That's the only one
40 Darren	Once, I found this roll-up, right
Geoff	Have you ever smoked dope before?
Darren	I've smelt the stuff
Philip	It smells disgusting
Darren	It stinks
45 Philip	Roll-ups are disgusting!
	(70 secs)
school sec	*(next to them)* And could you bring it back to me tomorrow?
Mrs K.	Er can we have some shut up in here. May I remind all of you
	that there is a dental inspection tomorrow. And please can we
50	have our dental forms back
school sec	Okay, so could you get it signed, I meant to give it to you on
	Friday but I forgot, so if I can have it tomorrow? *(sounds as if*
	she's next to them, then leaves classroom)
Geoff	Medical, got a medical thing
55 Darren	Let's have a read at the bottom? What's it say? 'Please return
	the – whatever' *(laughter)*
Geoff	/'form'
Darren	/Back to the school by Tuesday,' – got to bring it back tomorrow,
	man 'Thank you'
60	*(90secs)*
Geoff	Have you ever smoked dope? Is that that black stuff which melts
Philip	No, it don't melt, it's black, it's black, yea
Darren	Yea you got, and it's hard and you have to melt all the (.....)
Philip	You have to get it so it goes you have to burn it so it goes
65 Darren	/Yea
Pupil	yea, like that, well that is (....)
Philip	Lovely, innit
Darren	Sick
Tina	*(protesting voice)* It's lovely
70 Darren	My mum used to smoke it and like you could smell it, and she
	goes, she ⌈ goes out
Pupil	⌊ (.....)
Darren	she goes out to make a cigarette and I go *(sound of rapid inhaling)*
	and she comes back in *(sound of coughing)* 'What's wrong with
75	you?'
Philip	You don't do it like that, you smoke it in the fag
Darren	I know, right
Philip	But you didn't, you done it completely wrong.

experts to each other and to the girls), it also involves the collaborative accumulation of a shared pool of knowledge.[12] The children involved hear and see a collection of demonstrations about how to smoke a cigarette and Geoffrey, Darren and Philip all contribute information about what cannabis looks like and also their personal evaluation of it. Philip explains you have to put it inside a cigarette. Darren and Philip say 'I've smelt the stuff', 'It smells disgusting', 'It stinks', 'Roll-ups are disgusting!' (lines 42–5), while Tina counters 'It's lovely' (line 69). Between them, the children share and exchange a fair amount of technical vocabulary: cigarette, fag, cigar, to have a drag, roll-up, dope, together with information about what these look and smell like, how to use them and what they think of them. Children involved in this conversation could now try smoking a cigarette (if they have not done so already), and could probably also recognise dope smoking, and, perhaps most importantly of all, know how to talk about various kinds of smoking, using the appropriate vocabulary.

Gender, communicative style and identity

When I looked at the children's different uses and experiences of talk right across the school day, there initially did seem to be some communicative strategies and language uses which were particularly connected with gender, for example the girls' interactional style when they were talking about going to lunch in Table 3.6 seemed similar to Coates' (1996) description of floor-sharing in talk among women friends and the more challenging style of some of the boys in Tables 3.8 and 3.9 seemed consistent with accounts of men's talk as more hierarchical and competitive (Tannen, 1990). On the other hand, in the interviews where I had a good rapport with the interviewees (which was in most cases), both boys and girls used a much more mutually aligned speaking style, repeating, paraphrasing, overlapping and continuing each other's turns and sometimes addressing quite personal topics. Talk among girls could also include competition and conflict, as when Jenny and Angie argue about ignoring Kerry. And in the large group talk about forces in Table 3.8 and smoking in Table 3.9, boys also build on each others' comments, share experience and co-construct knowledge (albeit fragmentary and unformalised). There were thus cross-cutting patterns of collaboration, competition and conflict within many stretches of conversation among both boys and girls.

It is not the case, then, that particular interactive styles are exclusively associated with either boys or girls. One pattern which did seem to prevail was connected with context. While both boys and girls were mutually supportive in the more intimate context of the interviews, in more public contexts some of the more dominant boys often seized the opportunity for displays of a more macho kind of masculinity. Indeed, it was often the interactive style of these dominant boys and their propensity for competition and display which created a more public arena in the first place, as their voices rose and other children stopped to listen. While the talk about smoking begins with Sherri and Tina taking an active part, they drop back and only contribute occasionally once the discussion between Darren, Philip and Geoffrey gets going. Thus social activity within different contexts seemed to offer different kinds of opportunities to perform various ways of being a boy, or a girl, through talk. This was only the case, however, in terms of tendencies among particular dominant children, and the children as a whole displayed a wide range of interactive styles.

In fact, assertiveness in speech style and the speaking rights of individual children in different contexts seemed to depend on a complex mix of social background, gender, age and other individual characteristics. There was a considerable range in terms of maturity within the mixed year class of 10–12 year-olds in my main research site, which included those who still looked very much like children at one end of the spectrum and much more physically mature girls and boys at the other. Within this very mixed group of children, different individuals exercised power through talk and expressed aspects of gender in different ways in various settings across the school day. Connell *et al.* (1982, 1995) suggest that there are multiple forms of masculinity and femininity, with a symbolically powerful hegemonic masculinity in contemporary Anglo-European society which is signified through assertive heterosexuality, toughness, canniness, and social dominance. In the talk in larger groups, there was an orientation towards this kind of hegemonic masculinity, by the more physically mature and dominant boys.

There were also some differences in what boys and girls talked about. I could not easily have imagined the boys involved in Jenny, Angie and Kerry's emotionally complex, highly-charged negotiations (Table 3.7), or the girls having the conversation about G-force and racing cars (Table 3.8). And when children talked about boyfriends and girlfriends, for instance Kevin and Kieran's talk about getting bored (Table 3.1 (c)) and Nicole and Karlie's about Nicole kissing her boyfriend (Table 3.5), they took up strong gender alignments expressed through their orientation to heterosexual activity.[13] I suggested in Chapter 2 that Julie's talk in the girls' toilets (Table 2.1) invoked a speech genre connected with teenage romance and desire. Julie's combination of language forms and particular themes indexes social stances and activities which in their turn help to index a particular kind of gendered identity (Ochs, 1992; Duranti, 2001). Children's orientation towards this particular sphere of heterosexual social activity in their talk about chucking and dumping boyfriends or girlfriends, aspects of personal appearance, references to 'hot' images (Table 2.7) and teasing flirtation (Table 3.5) all represent the gradual accumulation of acts, choices and alignments which will, over time, produce their particular individual gendered identity.

Eckert and McConnell-Ginet (2003) suggest that children become adolescent through gradually accumulating adolescent acts, and take on a gender identity through an accumulation of various choices of linguistic and communicative resources which combine with other aspects of personal style like clothing, hairstyle and ways of walking. Thus Julie combined a rather childly appearance (pageboy blonde hair, pastel coloured T-shirts and skirts and neat white ankle socks), with a more assertive, feisty, persona and a growing interest in heterosexual activity expressed in her talk. Darren was already going out with Sherri, and his expensive trainers, gelled hair and confident walk were important symbols of his adolescent identity and powerful social position within the class. He performed being male and socially dominant through frequently holding the conversational floor in large groups, and representing himself in talk as tough, canny and heterosexual.

This self-styling by children was done in the context of the institutional marking of gender difference within school. Although gender was not often used explicitly as an organising principle in the classroom organisation or teaching which I observed, it emerged clearly in spatial divisions in cloakrooms and changing rooms and in children's choices of friends and work-partners in the classroom, which was strongly policed by the teasing which greeted any attempt at close cross-gender relationship. Even the children who were 'going out' with each other tended to sit and work with same gender friends in the classroom. Children could make creative choices about personal style, but these needed to be comprehensible and acceptable to others in order to be interpreted. Children's references to the genre of heterosexual romantic relationship show how they themselves are inserted into these genres and produced as particular kinds of heterosexual beings, in the course of ongoing informal conversation and social practice.

Conclusion

In this chapter I have described the different patterns of collaboration which I found in the children's talk, both in my interviews with friendship pairs and in children's group talk among themselves. I have looked at how children's utterances always face both backwards and forwards, as Volosinov suggests and how responsivity and address-ivity are expressed, for instance, within repetitions, jointly-produced comments, floor sharing and the retrospective 're-functioning' of utter-ances by subsequent speakers. I have considered the implications of this dialogicality for the referential and evaluative content of children's talk and for the expression and creation of particular relationships between speakers and particular gender identities.

In the interviews, I found that both girls and boys produced 'duetting' with friends of the same gender, repeating, paraphrasing and expanding on each others' utterances. The children orientated towards each other through their management of turn-taking and their collaborative construction of grammatical structures, and in the development of themes across their interaction. While utterances had simultaneous referential and interpersonal functions within a particu-lar moment, they could also later be retrospectively refunctioned in the course of the recursive, accumulative production of meaning. This talk expressed the children's friendship through their shared evalua-tive alignments and through the display of close knowledge about each others lives, delicately balanced with the negotiation of individ-ual speaking rights. Their collaborative accounts sometimes iconically represented the interactional tone of the event being related, but even where Karlie and Nicole replay a half joking struggle, they are agreed about its 'funniness'.

In children's group talk, I found supportive duetting and also conflictual talk within groups of both girls and boys. Although some girls' group talk seems to illustrate the egalitarian, connection-seeking, floor-sharing style which has been connected with women in some sociolinguistic research, I have shown that this kind of talk also happened between boys in the interviews and occurs too in their larger group talk. And while Tables 3.8 and 3.9 include the kind of competi-tive jostling for the floor which has been identified as a style connected with men, I have shown that this talk also includes collaborative features, and that the overall effect of such interactions can be the pooling and exchanging of experiences from different members of the group, in relation to a common theme. Competition in the large group conversations was mainly between just two boys (Darren and Martie in the changing room and Darren and Philip in the talk about smoking) and girls also, like Jenny and Angie in Table 3.7, produced conflictual talk.

Rather than being a question of simple correlation between gender and linguistic forms and functions, there are more complex interactions between gender and other linguistic and social phenomena. Children make choices in how they use language, what they talk about, the evaluative stances they take and how they present themselves as similar to and different from others. The expression of gender identity emerges, in this sense, through the history of a child's particular choices in relation to language and other aspects of style. But children make these choices in the context of ongoing conversations and interactions with peers and adults, in the course of social practices which encode their own history of gender differentiation, all of which shape children's individual feelings and desires. Particular uses of language index stances and activities which in their turn index a particular gender, and this is both a resource for children to draw on, and a limitation to their creativity.

Finally, I have pointed out that although meaning-making in talk is essentially collaborative, this should not be taken to imply that a shared history of communication between people is one of agreed and mutually accepted knowledge. On the contrary, there is frequently ambiguity, inconsistency and conflict as speakers present and negotiate alternative perspectives and interpretations which they may then revisit in the future.

4
Reported Voices and Evaluation

> In real life we hear speech about speakers and their discourse at every step ... people talk most of all about what others talk about – they transmit, recall, weigh and pass judgement on other people's words, opinions, assertions, information.
>
> (Bakhtin, 1981, p. 338)

Michelle The boy, he's ugly, but he's got a nice personality. He's seven and he's nice to me, he goes 'Do you want to watch telly? Watch whatever you want!' He's so nice.

One of the things that first struck me when I listened to the tapes I collected was how frequently children quoted and reported other people's voices. In the course of relating an experience, arguing a point or giving an explanation they frequently reproduced the words of parents, teachers, friends and other people in their lives. Why is this kind of recreated dialogue, like Michelle's quoting of the boy's voice in the example above, such a ubiquitous feature in the children's talk? What does reproducing a voice accomplish that a straight account would not? In this chapter I begin to answer these questions by focussing on examples in children's talk where the reported voice is fairly clearly marked as separate from the speaker's own.[1] In Chapters 5 and 6, I look at the animation and orchestration of reproduced voices by children within their anecdotes and stories and, in Chapter 7, I move on to examine examples from their talk where the boundaries between the speaker and the voices they are reproducing are less clear-cut and other voices appear to merge with the children's own. These four chapters provide the heart of my argument about the crucial role of reported and appropriated voices in the evaluative processes in children's talk.

Reproducing a voice does not just invoke another speaker; ways of speaking and specific linguistic features may also index stances, activities and relationships, speech genres and scenarios. For instance when Kim says 'She always goes *(cross voice)* "Get on with your work, Kim!"' she invokes her teacher's stance and an aspect of their relationship, and through these an associated classroom context. Kim also conveys some of her own negative feelings about the teacher. As Volosinov explains, 'reporting' always involves transformation; voices are not reproduced 'straight' in the reporting context, but are reworked and reaccented in particular ways by the speaker doing the reporting, in line with their own purposes. Whether in a conversational anecdote, a work of fiction, a polemical article or a defence attorney's summation, reported speech always includes an element of evaluation. Words are selected, changed or edited, or a whole quotation is slanted in a particular way.

Researchers of adult talk have found that reported speech seems to be an enormously evocative way of representing and commenting on experience and drawing listeners in.[2] The children I studied created voices to invoke and comment on people, their behaviour, relationships, emotions and values, within the context of recreated events and scenarios. The immediacy and specificity of their reported voices catches the listener's attention, for instance by showing *how* a boy's nice personality is expressed through reporting his comment 'Watch whatever you want!', rather than just stating blandly that *he's nice*. Reported speech is perhaps particularly powerful for children because so much of their own experience is mediated and controlled through dialogue with adults, both at home and in school. As Steedman (1982) puts it 'in most children's lives, the words of adults are what move events forwards, forbid and prevent action ... people talking to each other, and the effects that this talking had was the most important and powerful event that children ever witnessed' (p. 90).

Michelle's comment about the boy's 'nice personality' occurred in an interview conversation where she and Kim tell me how their teacher is sometimes nasty to them, and where they struggle to understand Michelle's father's violence towards her mother (see Chapter 6). The boy's niceness provides an important reference point in the girls' exploration of the rights and wrongs of the behaviour of the adults who dominate their lives. Children's evaluation of the perspectives represented in the voices they report (like Michelle's approval of the boy's niceness) is shaped by, and instantiates, social values and beliefs from their social world but it can also express their individual personal experience and reflections. Through their representation and evaluation of other voices, children can express their own position and perspective in powerful ways.[3] Thus, while the talk of people of all ages is full of other voices, the ways in which children represent the voices of significant others are a particularly important part of their ongoing active engagement in their own socialisation, and in the dialogical construction of their sense of self.

In addition to individual speakers setting up a reported voice in this kind of way, the reported voice is also, however, introduced into a particular conversational context and its meaning is shaped through various dialogical links within that context. In this chapter I build on previous discussion about contextualisation and dialogicality as I begin to unpick the dynamic relationships between a child's voice and the voice they are reporting, and between the reported voice and the reporting conversational context. I shall look at how these two related sets of dialogic relationships contribute to the children's ongoing construction of meaning.

Representing voices: grammatical and other cues

In an influential study of the presentation of speech and thought in literature, Leech and Short (1981) use a cline to represent grammatical forms ranging from those where the author's voice is most dominant to those where the character's voice and perspective are more prominent in the meaning being conveyed. The more indirect the speech presentation, the more the perspective of the author dominates; the more direct the reporting, the more the perspective of the character comes to the fore. Thus forms range from the author-dominated 'narrator's representation of a speech act' (e.g. *he shouted*) through 'indirect speech' (*he shouted that he couldn't come just then*), 'direct speech' (*he shouted 'I can't come now!'*) to free, direct speech, where the characters apparently speak directly to the reader without a reporting clause, or sometimes without inverted commas (*I really can't come now!*).

Leech and Short point out that the foregrounded perspective is signalled by deictic cues.[4] In direct speech, where the character's perspective is foregrounded, deictics of time and space emanate from the character (in the example *he shouted 'I can't come now!'* the present tense *I can't come* and the adverb *now*). In indirect speech, where the author's perspective is foregrounded, deictics emanate from the author (in the example *he shouted that he couldn't come just then*, the past tense and the adverbial clause *just then*). Leech and Short also identified a hybrid form 'free indirect speech', which falls between direct and indirect speech on the cline and which they suggest is a mingling of the reporting and the reported voice (e.g. *he really couldn't come now*), often with the grammatical structure of indirect speech but the deixis and emotional force of direct speech. Free indirect speech is used in narrative where the voices of the author and a character are in some way mingled.[5]

Table 4.1   Speech presentation cline (adapted from Leech and Short, 1981)

narrator's repres.	indirect	free indirect	direct	free direct
Author's perspective	◄─────────────────────────►			Character's perspective

The children's use of reported voices in their talk closely matched Leech and Short's literary taxonomy. Children tended to use direct reported speech where they wanted the evaluative perspective of the voice to come through clearly. For instance, in 'Do you want to watch telly? Watch whatever you want!' Michelle represents the boy using the present tense and referring to herself as 'you'. So this is his time frame and his perspective, and she wants what he says fully brought to life because it clearly supports her claim 'he's nice to me'. In contrast, as we shall see later, when children want to distance themselves from the voice they are representing, they use more indirect forms. However, children are not like the authors of novels who have ultimate control over their fictional characters. The 10–12 year-olds in my study often reproduced the voices of adults who wielded considerable power over their lives and there is thus much more of a sense of struggle in the ways that children attempt to problematise or criticise the evaluative perspectives reflected in the more authoritative voices they reproduce.

In addition to this grammatical cline, recent research on spoken language shows how, in oral language, speakers use prosodic cues such as variations in pitch, volume, pace and rhythm, together with non-verbal cues like laughter, to convey a particular kind of voice and its evaluation.[6] Thus, for example, Miss Potts produced a higher-pitched, whining voice in her parody of children asking 'Where do we put our work?' (Chapter 2). In spoken language, prosodic cues are as important as grammar in communicating a speaker's evaluative stance towards the voice they are reproducing. In addition, as I discussed in Chapter 3, meaning in ongoing conversation is produced collaboratively and dynamically and the evaluative force of a reported voice also emerges, as I shall illustrate, through its dialogic relationship to other utterances within the conversation. In addition to these dialogical processes, the significance of reported voices, like other aspects of meaning-making in talk emerges also through various kinds of contextualisation.

In order to interpret the evaluative significance of a represented voice, in addition to grammatical and prosodic cues, I needed an ethnographic understanding of the current conversational context and I also needed an ethnographic understanding of the events and scenarios which were being depicted. Thus, for instance, I hear the boy in Michelle's account telling her to watch whatever she wants in the context of the children's reports about arguments with siblings and parents over different television channels. While a few children had televisions in their bedrooms, many were still involved in ongoing family struggles over programme preferences and which channel the set should be switched to. So, in this context, 'Watch whatever you want!' is particularly striking evidence of the boy's 'nice personality'. In order to interpret the evaluative force of Michelle's represented speech in relation to the point she is making, I draw on the associations it invokes for me from my experience of listening to the children and, to some degree, entering into their worlds.

In the analysis below I shall look at how the evaluative meaning of reported speech is conveyed through combinations of:

– grammatical form
– prosodic and non-verbal cues
– the dynamics of ongoing dialogue
– contextual links to other conversations and contexts

Invoking and evaluating people

When children wanted to talk about someone's character, they often did this through invoking what that person had said, as Michelle did in the example above. In the two examples in Table 4.2 below, two girls collaboratively produce an evaluative comment about a teacher in the course of chatting over their work. Like Michelle, they use an example of direct reported speech to illustrate the characteristic they are talking about. In the first example, Julie and Kirsty are discussing their class teacher Miss Potts and in the second, Jenny and Tracy are commenting on their deputy head teacher, Mr. Sinclair, who is covering the class while their class teacher, Mrs. Kilbride, is absent.

Table 4.2

---

a. Miss Potts

Julie	D'you remember that time when we had to make words out of thingy and I said 'cod' and she said (*measured tone*) 'You cod be right'
Kirsty	(*laugh*) Yes
Julie	She, she might be a bit strict but
Kirsty	/She is funny
Julie	Yes I know, she goes (*posh voice*) 'Oh I'm beautiful!'

b. Mr. Sinclair

Jenny	That Mr. Sinclair seems as though he's really, you know, nasty and strict, but he ain't. He's soft
Tracy	/Cause Miss would tell us off if we was doing our hair, wouldn't she?
Jenny	You see the way he's standing there? He never shouted at those boys like he does in assembly (*gruffly*) 'If you can't pray quietly then don't pray at all!'
Tracy	Yea.

In both exchanges the direct reported speech demonstrates a teacher attribute: the parodic 'Oh I'm beautiful!' provides an example of how 'she is funny' and 'If you can't pray quietly then don't pray at all!' is an example of Mr. Sinclair's apparent strictness. In each case children put on a clearly stylised voice: the higher-pitched drawn out vowels of the 'posh' rendition of Miss Pott's own self-parody in the first case and the lower-pitched gruff representation of Mr. Sinclair's comment in assembly in the second. As Leech and Short point out, this directly reported speech clearly conveys the teachers' perspectives.

While we get a reasonably good sense of Miss Potts' and Mr. Sinclair's viewpoints, however, these are given a particular evaluative significance within the girls' conversation. Miss Potts' funniness exemplified by her comments 'You cod be right' and 'Oh I'm beautiful' are set alongside her strictness, to produce an overall positive evaluation and a sense of Julie and Kirsty's fond respect. In contrast, Mr. Sinclair's strictness in assembly, 'If you can't pray quietly then don't pray at all!' is juxtaposed with what Jenny and Tracy view as his inappropriate softness in their classroom to produce an overall negative evaluation. In other words, the evaluative function of the reported speech is conveyed not only through prosodic cues and grammatical framing, but also, collaboratively through the way in which it is contextualised within the reporting context. The relationship between the reported voice and the reporting context is, as Volosinov suggests, key to understanding its meaning and significance: 'Reported speech is speech within speech, utterance within utterance, and at the same time *speech about speech, utterance about utterance'*. (Volosinov, 1986, p. 115, emphasis in the original).

My interpretation of the evaluation here also relies on my ethnographic work in the school. Strictness, softness and nastiness were seen by the children as significant teacher attributes. Softness in teachers was despised and strictness respected, but teachers who often got cross with pupils, or humiliated individuals, were 'nasty'. The ideal teacher in the children's eyes was one who had good control of the class, but who was also fair, pleasant and kind to individuals and could 'have a laugh'. In the first exchange, Miss Potts is positively evaluated for her combination of strictness with a readiness to laugh at herself. By contrast, in the second exchange Mr. Sinclair is doubly negatively evaluated: he picks out and humiliates boys in assembly, and is too soft in the classroom.

While the comments about Miss Potts and Mr. Sinclair provide fairly straightforward examples of how a personal quality is conveyed through reported speech, more complex discursive work is sometimes needed in order to report a voice that appears initially to reflect negatively on the reporter. When Josie was talking in her interview with me about the difference between what her mother thinks of her and her own sense of herself, for instance, she said 'I've got a Barbie (*doll*) and if I've got problems, I talk to her. My mum says I'm a baby, but it's just the way I am'. Through the clear separation of her mother's voice from her own and its more distant reproduction as indirect reported speech, Josie exposes and evaluates a difference between an external judgement by an adult (of being 'babyish') and her own emerging sense of the kind of person she is. This kind of distancing through indirect reporting also occurred when Kim reported Mrs. Kilbride's criticisms of her. Kim had been telling me in her interview about her father's advice to her for dealing with their class teacher, Mrs. Kilbride. She said her father told her that 'if she touches me I have to slap her back or have a go at her that I'll tell my Dad and my Dad will have a good slap for me'. I asked her if she thought Mrs. Kilbride was likely to slap her and the conversation continued as follows.

Table 4.3

Kim	She can be really, she's nasty to me, she don't like me at all
	⌈ She thinks
Michelle	⌊ She can be really nasty
Kim	She says that I always go me own way and I never go by the rules like I always go that door over there, it's only for visitors
Michelle	*(laugh)* You do as well don't you only you don't get done for it
Kim	When she can be nasty we go the wrong way, don't we, to get her back.

Here, Kim indicates the distance between Mrs. Kilbride's and her own evaluative viewpoints through using indirect rather than direct speech ('She says that ...'). Reporting Mrs. Kilbride's voice directly (e.g. *You always go your own way and you never go by the rules*) would have foregrounded Mrs. Kilbride's negative evaluation of Kim's behaviour, thus involving considerably more discursive work in order for Kim to express her opposition. Using indirect reporting is more economical, and, as Leech and Short suggest, allows the author more control over the reported speech. At first it wasn't clear to me whether 'like I always go that door over there, it's only for visitors' was intended as a continuation of Mrs. Kilbride's indirect reported speech or a shift into Kim's own voice. It seems close to indirect speech, possibly another example of what 'she says'. But it has the deictic reference points of direct speech: 'that door over there' is a reference within our current context and 'it's only for visitors' an explanation for myself, her current audience. Kim's mingling of her own voice with Mrs. Kilbride's in this free indirect speech conveys an evaluative ambivalence: she is giving an example of Mrs. Kilbride's 'nastiness' but this also concerns her own rule-breaking and she might assume that I, as an adult, would disapprove.

Children often referred to rules and procedures to guide their own and other's behaviour, especially if it was within their interests to do so. But rule-breaking could also be seen as daring and admirable, especially if you could get away with it. Michelle's response: 'You do as well don't you only you don't get done for it', re-accents Kim's rule-breaking as much more positive in terms of peer group values (as well as signalling support and admiration for her friend), and Kim adds a further justification, using the evaluatively aligning indexical 'we': 'When she can be nasty we go the wrong way, don't we, to get her back'. It is significant that Michelle initiates this re-evaluation, creating an opening for Kim to then give her own contribution. In the interviews, when children introduced a sensitive topic which might reflect negatively on themselves, they often presented their own evaluative position rather tentatively and ambiguously, allowing (perhaps implicitly inviting) their friend to produce a more positive evaluation, which they could then confirm. In this sense the evaluative work is accomplished collaboratively (signalled in the interactive 'don't you', 'don't we'), with friends corroborating and warranting (i.e. authenticating) each other's perspective on their experience.

There is a more complex dialogue here between the reported voice and the conversational context than in the two earlier examples

where Miss Potts' and Mr. Sinclair's voices were fairly unproblematically quoted to illustrate children's perceptions of them as teachers.
What Kim and Michelle are saying about the problematic relationship between Mrs. Kilbride and Kim is conveyed not just through
Kim's reporting, but also through the dialogue set up between
Mrs. Kilbride's negative perspective and the more positive perspectives produced by Kim and Michelle. In this way, Mrs. Kilbride's
utterance is re-evaluated within the reporting frame dynamically
co-constructed by Kim and Michelle as 'nastiness' rather than
accepted institutional authority. The reported voice is dialogised, as
Bakhtin terms it, first through the way in which Kim does the reporting and, second, through the ongoing dialogue between the current
speakers. In the interview context these included myself, and there is
an interplay between Kim's, Mrs. Kilbride's, Michelle's and my own
points of view (or assumed points of view), which is part of the
dynamic meaning-making. It is also part of the dialogic process of
identification for participants, for example through Kim's impressions of how Mrs. Kilbride, Michelle and I might view her actions differently, as independence, disobedience or successful daring. As ever,
negotiations and evaluations of identity and unformalised knowledge
are closely integrated. How you are meant to behave in school, when
it is justifiable to break school rules, what that says about you as a
person, and how it is possible to be a different person from the ways
in which teachers see you, are all interconnected.

This strong connection between knowledge, social relationship and
identity also emerges clearly in the next example, in Table 4.4, where
Darren is talking with Martie and other friends in the school coach on
the way to their swimming lesson. Martie's remark about a hill they
can see through the coach window leads to an exchange about what
'exaggerating' involves.

Table 4.4

Martie	That drop? See that little hill? It's like that! *(holds hand to show steepness)*
Darren	It's not like that, it's like that *(holds hand at less acute angle)*
Martie	Oh yes, I'm *(slight emphasis)* exaggerating
Darren	My mum always does that. She pretends, she hits her head or something, and then she goes to somebody 'I whacked my head and all blood was coming out!'*(laughter)*, sitting there going 'Oh, oh!' and I, if I say something like 'Oh a thousand pounds', she goes 'Don't exaggerate, Darren!' I go 'What? I'm not'.

Here, Martie's slight stylisation of the word 'exaggerating', which evaluates his own previous comment, is picked up by Darren who says that his mother 'always does that' and reports her embroidered description of a trifling bump: 'I whacked my head and all blood was coming out!' As in the earlier example when Julie recreated Miss Potts' humour, Darren represents an attribute of his mother (proneness to exaggeration) using reported speech. He then goes on to report dialogue between his mother and himself to illustrate another feature of her behaviour: how, although she habitually exaggerates herself, she also scolds Darren for doing the same thing. Her reported comment 'Don't exaggerate, Darren!' is evaluatively accented within the discursive reporting context, through coming directly after an example of her own exaggeration. This pointing up of adult inconsistency is a theme which invokes numerous intertextual links with children's other accounts about adult injustices and double standards (for example Jenny and Tracy's negative comments in Table 4.2 earlier above about Mr. Sinclair). The dialogical link with other accounts of the kind *Here's another example of adult inconsistency!* strengthens the evaluative point Darren is making.

In demonstrating both his mother's and his own propensity for exaggeration next to each other ('all blood was coming out' and 'Oh, a thousand pounds'), Darren is simultaneously presenting her inconsistency and the similarity between them as habitual exaggerators. His response 'My mum always does that' also picks up and expands Martie's previous point and Darren is by implication aligning both himself and his mother with Martie, who also exaggerates. The identity and relational work going on here revolves around the three different uses of the idea of 'exaggerating' expressed through reported speech. First, there is Martie's narrator's representation of a speech act 'Oh yes, I'm exaggerating' suggesting an external critical voice (rather like Julie's 'I'm cheeky to my Mum'), then Darren produces his mother's voice exaggerating about whacking her head and finally he reports his own voice exaggerating about the thousand pounds. Darren's reported voices are also playful: his anecdotes are themselves frequently full of exaggeration, and Martie will hear Darren's comments about his mother in the context both of other children's stories about adult inconsistency, and in the knowledge that Darren is probably exaggerating about his mother's propensity to exaggerate.

Recreating events

As other researchers have also pointed out, the evocative power of reported dialogue is such that it can be used both to refer to specific events and also to invoke a more general category of event or social practice (Tannen, 1989; Myers, 2004). In the children's talk, this invoked category is then often used to contextualise a specific incident. It is as if the speaker starts by saying *This is the kind of thing I'm going to tell you about*; and then proceeds with their specific example. They may assume that their audience will only need quite minimal cues to recognise the genre of the dialogue. For instance, Terry described to me in his interview how a neighbourhood fight had started outside his house the previous night. He explained 'They come round and started effing and blinding and all that lot'. 'All that lot' refers to an exchange of insults and profanities which Terry expects he can leave to my imagination, and would probably feel uncomfortable repeating more explicitly in my presence. This brief indication of a particular kind of exchange is enough to enable me to imagine the sort of hostile, aggressive, provocative verbal behaviour Terry witnessed, which quickly escalated into physical violence. It also conveys Terry's evaluative perspective; he did not, for instance, say '*They came round and complained that my sister had stolen their walkman*', which could have been an alternative way of representing what happened (see his longer account in Chapter 6).

In describing a rather different kind of social interaction, Julie explained to me how she learned to swap pens, small toys and make-up with other children when she first came to Camdean. Julie uses fragments of dialogue to invoke the essential characteristics of a swapping transaction.

Table 4.5

Julie	'You swap that for what' an and they go 'nayee' or whatever. They go 'great' and get it out, and go 'Oh dear – forgot this' and I say 'I'll give it to you tomorrow, and I'll give you this stuff now and you give me that and I'll give you whatever tomorrow'. So they go 'uh'.

The use of dialogue by Terry and Julie in these two examples may be elliptical and perfunctory, but it is perfectly appropriate for the particular point in the conversation at which it occurs. In each case, fragments of reported speech are used to index speech genres, which in their turn index a neighbourhood fight and swapping practices. Terry clearly conveys to me as much as I need to know about the beginning of the fight, which he then goes on to describe at some length in later parts of the interview. I know from Julie's initial description that swapping involves agreement by both parties to exchange items, and that one transaction may be split over a number of days. Although her account seems fairly detached, she followed it by explaining about her own initial naivety when she first came to the school and her subsequent recognition of different kinds of value, for instance cost, newness, oldness and sentimental value (in relation to a pen her grandmother had given her). Her account above of how transactions are done is therefore given as evidence of the knowledge and experience she now has as a practised swapper.

As well as invoking a speech genre connected with a particular sphere of social practice, reported dialogue can also be used as evidence that this social practice actually took place. Although swapping had been banned in Julie's school, it was still a highly popular clandestine activity. The extract below records an argument between Julie and Ellie which occurred in the playground during the morning break. Julie won't agree to swap with Ellie now because, she claims, Ellie reneged on their swapping transaction the previous day.

Table 4.6

Ellie	Why won't you swap?
Julie	Well I swapped yesterday with you, but ⌈ you come and
Ellie	⌊ I didn't want to
Julie	/Right cause I swapped with you yesterday ⌈ (.......)
Ellie	⌊ I didn't want to
Julie	/Yes you goes 'Let's have the dog, then' and you gave me out your hand lotion and you went 'Black Jack, can't swap back'[7] and all the rest of it, and then as soon as you got to calling 'Are you coming?' hunted for me and you said that you wanted the lotion back. So I took the dog back, you took the hand lotion back.

To counteract Ellie's claim that she hadn't actually wanted to swap the previous day, Julie re-creates their dialogue, including the fact that 'you went "Black Jack, can't swap back" and all the rest of it', the rhyme children used to clinch a swap. Then, she suggests, Ellie had insisted on revoking the swap ('you said that you wanted the lotion back. So I took the dog back, you took the hand lotion back'). The dialogue here is a particularly significant part of the overall evaluative point of Julie's account because it is what she claims Ellie said which proves that a swap did in fact take place. If, as Ellie now claims, she had not wanted to swap, then she should not have said 'Black Jack can't swap back'.

Reconstructing the precise words of the ritual formula here is important because of its performative force, which is taken to accomplish an act (like 'I do' in a wedding ceremony). In most other cases, however, as I explained earlier, speakers do not usually report words exactly, but select, rephrase, edit and recontextualise. Usually, when children recreate a scene using reported speech, it is not possible to tell how they may have selected from and changed what was actually spoken on the original occasion. I do, however, have direct evidence of how Julie reworks one of the conversational exchanges she had with David. This is because she reconstructs the dialogue for friends even as it is happening, rather in the style of a simultaneous translation. In fact I got the impression that Julie's reconstruction (and transformation) of what was happening was rather more significant than the actual event itself.

During the dinner-break, Julie had been playing a pickpocketing game with some friends. The children were now milling about in the classroom before settling down for afternoon registration. The transcript example below starts with Julie 'muddling' and then 'pickpocketing' David (lines 1–6). In line 7 she then claims the attention of friends standing nearby and explains what she has been doing 'Right, I says to David.....' (lines 7–8). With these friends now watching, she turns back to David (line 9). After asking him if he is 'going out' with Mellie, she gets him to re-enact the pickpocketing for the benefit of her friends. Finally, in lines 16–18 she produces a new and slightly embellished account of the first pickpocketing 'last time' (i.e. in lines 1–6).

Table 4.7

1	Julie	David, can I pickpocket you? *(giggles)* Right, I'm going to muddle you a minute. Go like that *(turns him round)*. Right, now you do that *(puts his arms out, giggles)* Right and then I go to your side like that, and I stand there for about a minute or two
5	David	How is this muddling me?
	Julie	No, I'll just pickpocket you *(laughs)* Leave it, leave it, leave it *(turns to friends)*. Right, I says to David, I says 'Stand there, I'm going to muddle you' and I says 'You put your arms out like that' *(turns back to David)* David
10	David	Yea
	Julie	Are you going out with Mellie?
	David	No
	Julie	Alright, do that a minute, I want to try something. Right, do that. Put your arms up. Right you look straight to the side. Then I come to your side and then I stay there for a little minute or – two I pickpocketed you! *(turns to friends)* He said, he said last time, he said 'I'll murder you!' and I put his arms out like that and I said 'I've just pickpocketed you!' and he goes 'What?'
15		

After the second public 'pickpocketing', with David's silent and some-what bemused cooperation, Julie reconstructs the first pickpocketing (*last time*). As we can see from the transcript, David's only actual verbal contribution to this original pickpocketing was 'How is this muddling me?' However, in Julie's reporting of the event, she has him say 'I'll murder you!' and an incredulous 'What?' after she has success-fully pickpocketed him. David thus becomes a much more active and engaged participant within her reconstruction of their interaction. This reconstructed David is much more in line with Julie's evaluative purposes than the original rather more confused and monosyllabic real-life version. As in the exchange about playing together after school (Table 2.7), Julie seems to be managing her interaction with David so that it can be interpreted either as a child's game or as a flirtation. The physical contact involved in preparing David for the game the first time is accompanied by nervous giggling, and Julie's throwing in of the question 'Are you going out with Mellie?' poten-tially rekeys the interaction as an expression of romantic interest. Julie's use of reported dialogue to give a sort of running commentary on the pickpocketing is an important part of this alternative framing, because of the way she models a closer involvement in the (possibly flirtatious) game.

Significantly, Julie asks the question about going out with Mellie in front of her friends, who in Goffman's terms fall somewhat ambiva-lently between official audience and unofficial bystanders. Asking such a question in a private dialogue with David might seem too heavily loaded with personal interest, but in a more public context, where boys and girls often joked with each other, it can be more easily framed as 'just teasing'. Julie protects her own face by reporting the interaction which seems to be part of her ongoing project to engage David's atten-tion (and possibly to publicly indicate her interest in him), in a way which could also be seen as a child showing off her prowess in the pickpocketing game. Thus, in creating his fictional responses, Julie not only changes David's words to produce him as more engaged in their interaction, but also recreates a much more skilled and slick pickpock-eting operation than the one which had happened only a few seconds before.

So far, in this section, I have discussed the use of reported speech to invoke a type of interaction (angry swearing, swapping), and to recall and recreate a specific event (Julie's swap with Ellie and her pickpocket-ing of David). Reported dialogue from a previous context (even if only by a few seconds) is used to make an evaluative point in a current conversation: to convey to me the violence of Terry's fight and Julie's prowess in swapping, to prove to Ellie that a swap had taken place and to represent David as more actively involved in Julie's pickpocketing. In each case, there is a link between the present and one other context. In the next example, however, children use a comparison between two invoked past contexts to make an evaluative point in the present. Nicole and Melissa are teasing Kieran as they finish off their mathematics work. Melissa reminds Kieran that he cried on his first day at school and Nicole uses reported speech to invoke a shared experience with Melissa, which excludes Kieran, and which she uses to taunt him. The Warehouse is a youth club in the children's estate.

Table 4.8

Kieran	(*Melissa is flicking Kieran's hair with her pencil*) Stop that, or I'll punch you	
Melissa	Oh yea then, come on then, come on then	
Kieran	No I'm not going to waste my time	
Melissa	Do you remember the first day you come to school and you was crying because your mum was going to leave you? Yea?	1st past context
Nicole	Yea and do you remember I was frightened down the Warehouse?	2nd past context
Melissa	No	
Nicole	The first day you brought me over and I, you goes (*aggressive tone*) 'Yea I could beat you up and all these kids as well'. But I never cried	2nd past context
Kieran	I never cried	1st past context
Melissa	Yes you do, you were hiding behind the table	1st
Kieran	That's a lie	1st
Melissa	That was you	1st
Kieran	Was it hell	1st
Nicole	(*imitating a teacher's authoritative voice*) Kieran, will you sit down and get down to your work! Where are we now? Miss, can you help me?	Reframing of current exchange

Melissa invokes the first past context to the current exchange, Kieran's first day at school, through a narrator's representation of a speech act 'you was crying'.[8] Nicole invokes the second past context, her first day at the youth club, through recalling an exchange with Melissa where she is, by implication, much more courageous than Kieran: 'You goes (*aggressive tone*) "Yea I could beat you up and all these kids as well!"'. Although this second past context is not referred to again after the brief exchange between Melissa and Nicola, it has created a powerful intertext for the continuing conversation between Melissa and Kieran and the evaluation of Kieran's purported behaviour. Like Kieran's first day at school, this is another 'first day' for Nicole, but a more frightening one (she suggests) because it is at the local youth club full of tough kids and Melissa, the very person to whom Nicole might have turned for protection, threatens her. Nicole is, in effect, telling Kieran *I had a much more frightening 'first day' but, unlike you, I didn't cry.* It is the evaluative relationship between the two 'first day' scenarios invoked in the two parallel conversations (between Melissa and Kieran and Nicole and Melissa) which provide a continuing theme within the interaction.

The conflict between Kieran and Melissa escalates until Nicole defuses the situation by taking on an imaginary teacher's voice 'Kieran, will you sit down and get down to your work', following this immediately by calling Mrs. Kilbride over to help her. Nicole's use of free direct speech here enables her to 'become' a teacher for a moment and the stylised teacher's voice transforms the conversational frame, in Goffman's sense, from 'winding up Kieran' to 'doing maths'. While changing the frame in this way may be partly motivated by an anxiety to hide the off-task nature of their conversation, or a desire on Nicole's part to bring in an adult before the argument gets too out of hand, it also rekeys the interaction between the children, enabling Nicole to claim a new dominant position (through her teacher's voice) within the conversation. Whether Kieran accepts the joke or is inhibited by Mrs. Kilbride's approach is unclear, but in any case he does not respond.

As I mentioned in Chapter 1, children often present and reflect on their own attributes, or desired attributes, through a contrast with another child's behaviour. Here Nicole's identity as a brave person is being constructed dialogically through contrasting the reconstruction of her courageous refusal to be intimidated by Michelle with Kieran crying and hiding behind the table on his first day at school. Kieran, on the other hand, has to defend himself against a negative identification by Nicole, and resist his positioning by her as weak and fearful. In this kind of way, reconstructed dialogue and the various connections and relations it invokes mediate children's ongoing negotiations between the ways they are identified by others and their emerging internal sense of self.

Evaluation in projected speech and reported thought

In the examples so far, the reported speech is based, however loosely, on dialogue from previously experienced events. Children however, like adults, also report hypothetical and unvoiced speech. In the next example below, Geoffrey is hanging around at the edge of a group of more dominant and physically mature children: Terry, Darren, his girl-friend Sherri, her friend Sarah. The conversation occurs while they are standing in line in the school corridor. Darren has just pretended to give Sherri a love bite. Sarah and Geoffrey use grammatical and prosodic cues, and actions, to convey irony through a reported voice.

Table 4.9

Sherri	*(laughing)* My mum thinks I've been in fights again!
Sarah	What do your mum go? *(higher pitch)* 'Who gave you a big bruise?' *(laughter)*
Terry	I'll give her a double bruise, aha!
Darren	I gave her one on the arm
Geoffrey	Oi, you could never give someone a love bite on the arm, could you, could you? You can't!
Sherri	You can, if you've got a T-shirt on
Geoffrey	Yea I mean, look, *(faster pace)* it's really exciting look, let's get down to there, next time it'll be your finger! *(noise of kissing)*.

Both Sarah and Geoffrey set up their reported speech ('What do your mum go?', 'Yes, I mean, look'), and adopt a particular tone to convey the naivety of the voice. Sarah pitches the mother's voice high, as if she were addressing a young child, and Geoffrey puts on a faster paced, enthusiastic voice to show just how ridiculous such enthusiasm would be. He is trying to explain to Sherri that he was not asking whether it is physically possible to give someone a love bite on their arm, but whether it is 'done', that is, sexy. As with Sarah's double-voiced portrayal of Sherri's mother, we are aware of Geoffrey's authorial voice mocking his own exaggerated behaviour in his hypothetical speech. (The styling of the voices is obviously clearer on the audiotape than on paper). Geoffrey's use of free direct speech enables him to momentarily take on another identity, as it were, of a naive kisser, who is simultaneously represented as ridiculous through his use of prosody and loud kissing noises.

Reporting other people's and one's own thoughts, as well as their speech, is a common technique both in written narratives and in ordinary conversation.[9] The children in my study used reported thought, or told me what they had felt like saying, to convey personal experiences which came across as particularly intense and emotional. It was as if they needed to somehow put an inner emotional state into words because this was such an important part of their memory of the event. The next examples come from the interviews.

Table 4.10

a.

Terry: Sometimes when I go home dinners and my mum's always out, and I feel like just going 'Right, I'm leaving!'

b.

Karlie: I was all dressed up in this lovely feathered suit and my hair like this and I come walking into this great big hall where, and there was millions and absolute millions of people in there and this thing was only a little round small thing and we thought 'Oh God, how you going to dance on that?', really panicking.

Here, the reported thoughts convey an inner state which is intimately related to the evaluation of an external event. Terry is describing his anger and frustration with his mother who is always out at lunchtime if he goes home for dinner and Karlie is conveying her panic, and her sense that all the dance troupe are feeling the same, when faced with the huge audience and tiny stage. The audience of the reported voice is complex; it is partly the speakers themselves (they are talking to themselves in the reported speech), partly by implication other people (Terry's mother and the other members of Karlie's dance troupe, indicated by her use of 'we' and possibly the ambiguous 'you'), partly myself, and partly the friend sitting with them in the interview. In one sense children's talk to others is always also talk to themselves; they hear and react to themselves responding in particular ways. In another sense inner talk to themselves is also always talk with others; Terry feels like saying 'Right, I'm leaving!' to his mother and Karlie is asking other members of her dance troupe, internally, 'Oh God, how you going to dance on that?'

As I pointed out in Chapter 1, both Volosinov and Bakhtin, like Vygotsky, suggest that consciousness is organised in the form of inner dialogues. As Bakhtin puts it: 'To think about someone is to talk to them'. Individual thought processes involve responding to voices heard in previous conversations, in the light of the relationships and contexts which they invoke. This is illustrated particularly clearly in the final extract in this chapter, also from the interview with Karlie and Nicole. Karlie has explained that she sometimes goes to visit her father in prison and I asked her what this was like. Karlie answers me by representing her feelings at the prison as a kind of inner dialogue, which involves invoking her own voice as if she were talking first to herself, and then to her father.

Table 4.11

Karlie	It's like – it's just loads and loads of bars. So you think 'What's my dad doing in here, he didn't do nothing' because he got accused by chopping someone's hand off so – and it weren't true – and you get in there, and you're seeing him, and you think 'Come with us, come with us, you can't stay in here cause it's not true really, is it?' so you think 'You can come with us now, you can get out', but it's just not true.

I have marked what I interpret as direct reported speech in Karlie's account, but I found it difficult to make out exactly where one voice ends and another starts, or to identify precise audiences. Sometimes she seems to be addressing herself, sometimes her father, sometimes myself and sometimes previous voices she has heard. It is difficult to know, for example, to whom her final 'it's just not true' is addressed, and whether this refers to the crime of which her father is accused of or to the possibility of taking him home with her, or to both. The fragmented nature of the dialogue invoked in Karlie's response to my question would suggest that her talk here is close to inner speech, where dialogues we have had and those which we might have with other people feed into our internal thought processes. This utterance then has its own internal business: Karlie is struggling to come to terms with her father's imprisonment, and positioning herself in relation to the differing accounts of his guilt which she has heard people give. She is also, at the level of my interview conversation with her, constructing the voices in the representation of her inner dialogue in order to convey a particular presentation of herself, and her father, to Nicole and myself.

Conclusion

In this chapter I have begun to examine how children use reported voices to produce meaning. I have suggested they can invoke and stand in, as it were, for people and scenarios and also refer to and index speech genres associated with particular kinds of social practices, like swapping or fights. Reproduced voices and snatches of dialogue are enormously powerful ways of recreating and commenting on experience and drawing the listener in. Their use is also always evaluative, involving some kind of judgement on the people, relationships and events which are being represented. I have argued that evaluation is a particularly significant aspect of children's meaning-making. Through evaluation they appropriate and reproduce the beliefs and values of their social world, inserting themselves into practices and genres. But evaluation also expresses and reflects a child's individual experience and positioning, and their personal efforts to understand other people and themselves. In this sense the evaluative functions of reported voices play an important role within the processes of both socialisation and identification.

All the examples in this chapter can be seen to have some kind of evaluative function. Miss Potts is positively represented as strict and funny, Mr. Sinclair negatively as soft and inconsistent, Darren's mother as inconsistent and prone to exaggeration, Mrs. Kilbride's scolding is nasty. A sense of the positive or negative quality of the child's relationship with the reported person is also simultaneously conveyed. In the other examples, Julie demonstrates her current expertise in swapping through her explanation to me in contrast with her initial naivety and uses a report of the ritual formula to prove to Ellie that a swap took place. She reports an enhanced version of David's speech to model a closer engagement and Melissa and Nicole invoke Kieran's crying on his first day at school, in contrast to Nicole's behaviour on her first day at the Warehouse, as proof of his cowardice. Geoffrey's ironic production of an enthusiastic kisser, and Terry's and Karlie's expression of their own feelings illustrate how evaluation is also a centrally important part of meaning in projected speech and reported thought.

Evaluation is conveyed, firstly, through the speaker's use of grammatical, prosodic and nonverbal cues. In general, children used directly reported or free direct speech to allow a considerable amount of the evaluative perspective through into the reporting context, for instance when Julie is conveying Miss Potts' funniness (Table 4.2), Nicole takes on Mrs. Kilbride's voice to chastise Kieran (Table 4.8), or Terry wants to convey the force of his feelings about his mother being out (Table 4.10). Prosodic and non-verbal cues can be equally important, to reproduce Miss Potts' self-parody and Mr. Sinclair's gruff voice, the force of Darren's mother's exaggeration or to parody a mother's naivety and inappropriate kissing. On the other hand, indirect reported speech is used when children need to distance themselves from the evaluative perspective of the reported voice, for instance Josie's mother's comments that she is a baby and Mrs. Kilbride's negative judgement of Kim in Table 4.3. In Table 4.11, Karlie's stream of consciousness reporting is grammatically ambivalent, blending her thoughts at the prison with her thoughts now, in the interview, as she remembers her experience.

Evaluation of reproduced speech is also accomplished through dialogic relationships in the conversation where it is reported and through the links it invokes with various aspects of the children's social context. Michelle's reproduction of the boy's niceness in a conversation about other people's nastiness, the juxtaposition of Mr. Sinclair's strictness and softness, Kim and Michelle's repositioning of Mrs. Kilbride's reported voice and Darren's alignment of his mother's and his own exaggeration with Martie's, are all part of the dialogical production of the meaning of the reported voice, in relation to shared knowledge about the significance of choosing TV channels, what makes a good teacher and what counts as admirable and despicable behaviour within the children's social world. Any single instance of dialogue always has the potential for different evaluative accenting. For instance, in the discussion about exaggerating, Darren could have been quoting his mother to demonstrate what an inventive and entertaining storyteller she is. 'I whacked my head and all blood was coming out!' might then provide an example of how exciting his mother's accounts can be (and maybe, indeed, there is also a sense of this alongside his presentation of her tendency to exaggeration). My interpretation of the particular meaning of a reported voice is based not only on cues within the current dialogue, but also on its links with the recurring patterns of children's preoccupations, issues and questions which emerged across the data I collected, and with the social practices I documented through my ethnographic research.

While reported speech and thought can powerfully and economically invoke people, relationships, feelings and events for the children, the range of ways in which this speech can be nuanced (grammatically, prosodically and non-verbally, dialogically and through contextualisation) enables children to question and reflect on other people's and their own actions and on significant events within their social world. This questioning and reflection contributes to children's growing knowledge and understanding of people, relationships and events and to their developing moral judgement and sense of themselves as a unique person. How this is done in further ways through the more extended dialogues children reproduced in their anecdotes and narratives is the subject of the next two chapters.

5
Articulating Dialogue: Agency and Gender in Children's Anecdotes

'... we dream in narrative, daydream in narrative, remember, anticipate, hope, despair, believe, doubt, plan, revise, criticise, gossip, learn, hate and love by narrative'.

(Hardy, 1968, p. 5)

Julie   Right, the other day when my mum went to go and hit me, right, my next door neighbour was coming in and my mum went like that *(swipes in the air)* and I ducked and my next door neighbour went *(higher pitch)* 'Aaaagh', she's only five, and my mum went 'phew!', she went 'Oh sorry, Michelle!'
David   Did your mum hit you?
Julie   No, I ran, straight away. I ran all the way down to the bottom street and back.

I did not set out to study the narratives in children's conversations, but they cropped up persistently throughout the data in a way which could not be ignored. The 10–12 year-olds I recorded used narratives to explore ideas, explain, argue, entertain, pursue relationships and present themselves as particular kinds of people. Their stories ranged from fleeting anecdotes to lengthier, clearly framed accounts. Some were told by one speaker, some collaboratively, some were contested and broken off while other stories emerged piecemeal through the course of a conversation. In this chapter, I shall focus on the brief anecdotes that children told each other in the continuous recordings of talk across the school day, looking particularly at the narrator's use of reported voices and presentation of self. In Chapter 6, I shall look at the longer stories children told in the course of their interviews, which provided a more extended space for the exploration of moral issues. Questions about personal agency and gender identification run through both chapters.

Representing experience and exploring the self

Scholars have long seen narrative as a fundamentally important way of structuring and interpreting experience. Bruner (1986, 1990), for instance, argues that stories enable us to account for our actions and the events we experience and to develop a sense of how we relate to others around us and of our own place within our social world. Centrally important to this process is the fact that people do not just simply relate their experience in stories, but also, explicitly and implicitly within the telling, interpret and comment on this experience. Dangerous or embarrassing moments may be embellished for effect, particular lines of action presented as morally justified, and the actions of others censored. Narratives, like the reported voices discussed in the last chapter, interpret and evaluate experience rather than simply recording it. In the children's case, the commentary and evaluation in anecdotes and stories are part of their ongoing collaborative exploration of their social world. Evaluative points are not always clear-cut, but are often provisional, dialogised within conversation and in relation to wider experience and returned to again and again in different ways.

Narratives also provide particularly clear opportunities for presentations of the self.[1] In stories about the narrator, the temporal continuity of events provides a time frame against which a sustained 'self' is represented, both for the audience and, reflexively, for the narrator themselves. In the anecdote above, for instance, Julie represents herself as skilfully managing to avoid a slap from her mother, thus saying something about her own relationships in the social world and about other people's reactions to her. Narrators show themselves confronting problems and challenges and dealing with moral issues, being kind, courageous, cunning, and resourceful. Even when the narrators themselves do not appear in the story, their accounts of other people and their actions also say something about themselves, through the ways in which others are represented and evaluated. For the children I recorded, stories provided an arena where they could present themselves as agentive, affecting others around them and their environment. As narrators, they framed the evaluative viewpoint when revisiting an event in an anecdote and cast their own role, and the roles of others, from this perspective. Often at the beck and call of teachers and parents in their ongoing daily experience, in their stories children became, however fleetingly, powerful central characters.

These two important uses of narrative, to evaluate experience and present the self, place story-telling at the centre of the double-sided process of socialisation and identification. Children learn to use narrative as a symbolic resource to recount and, through the telling, collaboratively reflect on ordinary and out of the ordinary experiences. They also learn what counts as 'tellable', both in terms of topic and in the way it is represented. Experience has to be processed and reproduced in particular socially accepted ways in order for it to become recognisable as a story for an audience in a particular context. In addition, the interest and response of the audience are vital to confirm the experience being related and the narrative self being presented. In the case of the children I recorded, listeners had a powerful role in creating space for the narration and collaborating with the narrator, often offering prompts which pushed the narrative further in a particular direction. An audience could corroborate the point of the story, challenge it, add to it, subvert it or ignore it. Thus individual experiences expressed in stories become, through interactive narration and cultural expectations about tellability, socially forged.[2]

In addition to telling their own stories, children at the brink of moving into adolescence are also becoming increasingly interested in the stories told by other children. Acting as sounding boards for each other's interpretations and evaluations of events, they vicariously explore other children's experiences, learning and rehearsing possible strategies for dealing with dilemmas they themselves are having to confront or which they might have to deal with in the future: how to stand up to a parent, how to court a girlfriend or boyfriend, how to react to an injustice, how to cope with violence. 10–12-year olds use stories to explore different ways of being a teenager as opposed to being a child, to try out and respond to new gendered identities and new kinds of relationships with adults and with each other, and to question and take up value positions on moral issues. The explorations, questions and issues addressed in these stories are pursued within and across conversations, in the context of children's gradually emerging sense of a clearer independent sense of self.

Three levels of narrative meaning

As I listened to the tapes of children's talk, I came to see their stories as providing a kind of discursive space which momentarily suspends the ongoing conversation in order to explore an idea or question more fully in relation to their own experience, before the conversation moves on. Narrative meaning is created simultaneously on three levels: through the words of the story, through the way in which it functions dialogically and interactionally at a particular point in a conversation, and through the contextual links it makes with children's past experience.

First, the textual structure of narrative provides an organised discursive space for exploring experience. Often introduced by an *abstract*, which sets out the main themes or point of the story, Labov (1972) showed that narratives in conversation then provide an *orientation* (a description of who, where and when). This is followed by the *complicating action*, which usually consists of a series of events related in temporal order. Stories then explain what finally happened, or the *resolution*. In addition, there may be a *coda* which links the story back into the ongoing conversation. This recounting of events accomplishes what Labov calls the *referential function* of the narrative, in other words the selection and representation of experience in temporally sequenced clauses. In spontaneous talk, there is often structural ambivalence, especially at the boundaries with other speaker's turns. Thus, Julie's anecdote at the beginning of the chapter is structured in approximately the following way:

Table 5.1

Julie	Right, the other day when my mum went to go and hit me,	Abstract/Orientation
	right, my next door neighbour was coming in	Orientation (cont.)
	and my mum went like that *(swipes in the air)* and I ducked and my next door neighbour went *(higher pitch)* 'Aaaagh',	Complicating action
	She's only five,	Evaluation (external)
	and my mum went 'phew!' she went 'Oh sorry, Michelle!'	Resolution (1) *or* continuing complicating action
David	Did your mum hit you?	
Julie	No, I ran, straight away. I ran all the way down to the bottom street and back.	Resolution (2) *and/or* Coda

As often happens in rapid conversation, 'Right, the other day when my mum went to go and hit me' serves both as the abstract (this is what the story is going to be about) and the first part of the orientation, which continues in 'right, my next door neighbour was coming in'. We now know when the story takes place ('the other day'), that it happened somewhere near an entrance ('my next door neighbour was coming in') and we have been introduced to the three main characters: Julie, her mother and the neighbour. The complicating action then includes a number of events related in sequential order: 'and my mum went like that *(swipes in the air)* and I ducked and my next door neighbour went '"Aaaagh"'. Julie then provides what could be a resolution: 'and my mum went "phew!" she went "Oh sorry, Michelle!"' This does not entirely satisfy David and his question 'Did your mum hit you?' prompts Julie's response 'No, I ran, straight away. I ran all the way down to the bottom street and back'. This final comment could be seen as a Coda linking the story back to the point in the conversation where it started. On the other hand, if we treat the story as dynamically produced between Julie and David, then David's question could be seen as eliciting a more satisfactory resolution which then retrospectively recasts Julie's early ending 'and my mum went "phew!" she went "Oh sorry, Michelle!"' as part of the ongoing complicating action. In this way narratives are collaboratively, not individually, produced, through the expectations about tellability and the structural interventions of the audience as well as through what is initially produced by the narrator.

In addition to its referential function, Labov argues that stories always have an evaluative function, which he defines as the significance of the events for the speaker and the whole point of narrating them in a story.[3] For instance, when the men in Labov's research told stories about how they had survived a near-death experience, they used a variety of ways within the telling to emphasise just how serious the danger had been, and how resourceful they were in avoiding it. The ways in which they did this contributed to the narrative evaluative function. Julie's dramatic account, of how her mother went to hit her and caught the next door neighbour Michelle by mistake, functions as an entertaining joke and it also presents Julie as cunning and resourceful, evading adult discipline. The skilful timing of Julie's aside 'she was only five', which provides the playful twist undercutting the initial implication that her mother had hit (or almost hit) an adult neighbour, is important to the successful performance of the joke and an example of what Labov calls *external evaluation*. (In the children's accounts, adults hitting adults always had far graver consequences than adults hitting children). Evaluation may also be *embedded* within a comment by a character who might, for instance, say something about the danger faced by the narrator to emphasise the point of the story. In Julie's story, her mother's 'Oh sorry, Michelle!' which moves the action on, is also an embedded evaluative comment on her mother's mistake, marking it as reprehensible. Finally, evaluation may be *internally* conveyed, through the use of intensifiers (gestures, sound effects, quantifiers, repetition) and comparisons, which add emphasis and build up suspense. Julie's 'aaagh' and 'phew' (intensifiers conveying fear and shock through characters' voices) function as both internal and embedded evaluation.

In order to fully understand the evaluative functions of a story, we also need to look at the second level of narrative meaning to see how it is established dialogically through the telling, as Julie's story above is, within the context of a particular performance. The audience is always involved in establishing the evaluative function of a narrative through their response, for instance what they attend to with most interest, whether they accept or question the account presented and whether they accept the story as worth telling and the narrator as having the right to tell it.[4] When, in answer to David's question 'Did your mum hit you?' Julie provides a new resolution: 'No, I ran, straight away. I ran all the way down to the bottom street and back', David's involvement and his expectations of what the story is going to be about help not only to shape the referential function, as I discussed above, but also the evaluative function, in providing the prompt for Julie to present her successful escape. Interactive aspects of story telling are particularly visible in the anecdotes from children's ongoing conversations, where the links stories make with previous conversational points can be traced and the collaborative production of evaluation is often clearly evident.

In interpersonal terms, narratives can be used to express friendship and foster closeness with others or to exclude them, to construct positions and alignments within families and friendship groups.[5] Julie's anecdote, for instance, is part of an ongoing project to catch David's interest. Over the three days during which I was taping her, she persistently tried to engage his attention, dropping hints about the possibility of him becoming her boyfriend and quizzing other girls about who they were 'going out with' (see Tables 2.7 and 4.7). And Julie is not only speaking to David when she tells the anecdote about her mother's misplaced slap. There are a number of other children nearby who, as in Table 4.7, fall somewhere between an official and unofficial audience. The story presents Julie as quick-thinking, assertive and an entertaining raconteur to these other children as well, and she may also, as I suggested in the pickpocketing game, be publicly demonstrating her interest in David. The evaluative function of Julie's story emerges within this particular interactive context.

Stories, then, create meaning through their internal structural coherence as a recreated scenario seen from a particular evaluative perspective, produced dialogically at a specific interactional moment. At the third level of narrative meaning, the significance of the story emerges through the links it makes with children's past experience and with the contexts of their lives. A story performance provides a licence for entertainment through a certain amount of exaggeration (often presenting the narrator as powerful), but in my data the scenarios children created, however much embroidered, always implied a strong link with previous encounters and conversations. As we saw in the last chapter, one of the most economical and powerful ways of invoking experience from other contexts, and evaluating it, is through reported speech. It is not surprising, then, that most of the children's stories contained a considerable amount of reconstructed speech and that the crux of the complicating action, where audience engagement is most vital, was almost always animated through the direct reproduction of voices. These are often referred to in the present tense (e.g. 'I says ... he goes ...'), creating immediacy and drawing listeners more deeply into the crucial point of the story.[6]

Indexicalisation and dialogic relationships

In order to explore children's narrative orchestration of voices in more detail, and the links these voices invoke, I shall focus on anecdotes told by Julie and by Martie and Darren.[7] These children's narratives have many of the structural, dialogical and evaluative features which I found in the children's story-telling more generally (see Chapter 6), but they also convey a distinctive individual flavour of the narrator's interactive story-telling style and personal interests and preoccupations.

Julie

Earlier the same day before telling the story at the beginning of the chapter about her mother's misplaced slap, Julie told another story about an argument with her mother to Kirsty and Sharon, as they sat together finishing off some work. This is the anecdote that I introduced in Chapter 1, which was sparked off by the girls' anxiety about the amount of swearing on the tapes I was recording:

Table 5.2

Julie	Children aren't meant to swear
Kirsty	If people swear at them, they can swear back *(brief pause)*
Julie	I swore at my mum the other day because she started,[8] she hit me
Kirsty	What did you do?
Julie	I swore at my mum, I says 'I'm packing my cases and I don't care what you say' and she goes 'Ooh?' and *(I go)* 'yea!'. I'm really cheeky to my mother.

Julie's anecdote starts with a conflated abstract and orientation 'I swore at my mum the other day because she started, she hit me'. After the invitation from Kirsty to tell the rest of the story, she moves quickly into the complicating action: 'I swore at my mum, I says "I'm packing my cases and I don't care what you say" and she goes "Ooh?" and *(I go)* "yea!"' Julie finishes with an external evaluative comment 'I'm really cheeky to my mother', which also functions as a resolution and/or coda, linking the anecdote back to the question of whether or when children are 'meant to' swear.

Julie uses reported dialogue to call up a scenario away from the here and now, quoting her own and her mother's voices. How do these voices 'stand in' for the actions she is reporting? First, the way in which Julie creates a voice indexes what Bakhtin calls a *social language*, for example the way a mother talks, or a teacher or a young child. This helps to establish recognisable characters. In the anecdote above, Julie creates an assertive, defiant voice for herself: 'I'm packing my cases and I don't care what you say' and a confrontational response from her mother: 'Ooh?' We know there is conflict between the characters and we also know something about the nature of the conflict because the invoked dialogue also indexes a particular speech genre (see Chapter 2). Just a few words are enough to conjure up the familiar experience, for Kirsty and Sharon, as they were in Julie's anecdote for David, of the genre of 'conflict with parents', where the adults are usually more powerful but where some children, like Julie, are beginning to resist their authority in quite effective ways. In this context, accounts of standing up to a parent or foiling them have a particular appeal. The voices Julie creates for her mother and 5 year-old Michelle (Table 5.1), or her mother and herself (Table 5.2), help to convey the evaluative point of the story through invoking characters within a recognisable scenario and orchestrating a particular interaction between them. The phrase 'I'm packing my cases' also accomplishes indexical work, both within Julie's account to Kirsty and, if it was actually used, within the original exchange. Invoking a recognisable formulaic phrase associated with social breakdown and leaving home highlights the extreme provocation which resulted in Julie 'swearing'.

In addition to the action within the anecdote, there is also Julie's subsequent evaluative comment: 'I'm really cheeky to my mother'. Listening to the tape a number of times, I still found it impossible to decide whether 'I'm really cheeky' should be interpreted as the appropriation of an adult negative evaluation, or as a defiant boasting which is part of the positive feisty image Julie is creating, or as a mixture of both. The defiant interpretation is not exactly in line with either of Julie or Kirsty's original positions, but more of a moving on in Julie's presentation of herself. Both compliant and defiant interpretations, however, in commenting on what happened in the anecdote, also provide a response to Julie's own original comment 'Children shouldn't swear'. We can represent the two evaluative positions which are explored in this exchange, and the possible third position (depending on the interpretation of 'I'm really cheeky'), as follows:

Table 5.3

Evaluative position (1): compliance	Evaluative position (2): reasoned response	Evaluative position (3): defiance
Children aren't meant to swear	If people swear at them, then they can swear back	
I'm really cheeky to my mother (interpreted as compliant)	I swore at my Mum... because she...hit me	I'm really cheeky to my mother (interpreted as defiant).

The relationships between these differences are explored in the course of a few minutes of dialogue, through interconnected layers which also set up links and connections, in a third level of narrative meaning, with the children's shared past conversational experience and their more general social context. As well as exploring when it is appropriate to swear, for anyone who has been around Julie for any length of time this anecdote falls into the recognisable genre of picaresque stories she tells about herself and her mother. The theme of Julie's relationship with her mother is related to the more general issue for these older children of their changing relationships with adults who get in the way of what they want to do and are no longer seen as unquestionable authorities. In terms of this intergenerational struggle, the anecdote invokes links with other stories Julie has told her friends, both about her mother and about standing up to adults generally. The two themes, relationships with adults and when it is appropriate to swear (which adults are allowed to do but children may not be), are brought together in an anecdote which Kirsty and Sharon will hear and interpret not just as a turn in their current conversation, but also in terms of the links it invokes with other anecdotes with similar themes.

The contrast between Julie's representation of her own voice, and her ambivalent comment on this as narrator, nicely illustrates the way in which the children I recorded used dialogue within anecdotes to explore their transitional status between childhood and adolescence and to try out particular presentations of themselves. Julie often presented herself in anecdotes as feisty and assertive (see also her accounts of being sent to the head teacher in Table 2.6 and of pickpocketing David in Table 4.7 and swapping with Ellie in Table 4.6). But she could also present another side of herself, and take up an evaluative stance which has echoes in the talk of many of the girls in my study. In addition to the grammatical production of the voices in the next anecdote as direct reported speech, the use of prosodic features is important, as it was in the anecdotes discussed above, to hold the attention of the audience and to create a particular kind of voice for evaluative purposes. Julie and Kirsty were working together in class and another child had just asked to borrow Julie's rubber (eraser):

Table 5.4

Julie	Right, this morning, right, my sister- my mum got my sister this little dressing table, right, and my sister didn't like it and she says *(high-pitched baby voice)* 'Julie, you got a rubber?' and I go 'yea' and I go 'yea' and she goes 'Can I bowwow it?' and I goes 'What for?' She goes 'I just want to bowwow it' and I go 'Alright, here you are' and she goes 'errrrr' like that *(makes rubbing out movement)*. I found my rubber, it was about that big – I ain't got it any more, it's absolutely disappeared. I go 'Where's my rubber?' She goes 'Don' know, but I can't wub my desk out!'
Kirsty	Ah, isn't that sweet!

Julie's story starts with the orientating information 'Right, this morning, right, my sister – my mum got my sister this little dressing table, right', with 'Right' signalling that she has something to tell and the deictic 'this' which follows signalling a switch away from the time and place of the current conversation into the context of the story. 'My sister didn't like it' could be seen as the abstract conveying what the story is going to be about, and also the beginning of the complicating action. Julie then switches into the present tense and uses dialogue to develop the complication. The punch line and resolution 'Don' know, but I can't wub my desk out!' is also given in direct reported speech. The naive baby voice which is so central to the evaluative point of the story is represented using a higher pitch and the substitution of 'w' for 'r' to index the immature speech of a young child. Julie's sister's words are particularly clearly 'double voiced'; we can simultaneously hear what her sister is saying, and also Julie's voice behind this, constructing and animating the dialogue in particular ways (Bakhtin, 1981). The double voicing itself, conveying the metamessage *here am I, producing this cute voice for you* is an important pleasurable part of the story performance for both Julie and Kirsty, regardless of its precise referential accuracy.

In addition to indexing the language of a young child through the voice she creates, Julie also conveys a particular evaluative perspective towards her sister. Her tone produces the young child's voice as vulnerable and endearing, rather than, for example, stupid and annoying, and Julie creates a kindly cooperative voice for her own responses within the anecdote. Kirsty picks up and confirms this positive interpretation of the little sister's behaviour ('Ah, isn't that sweet!') and her response suggests an evaluative function which links in with a recurring stance in other talk which I recorded among the girls. A couple of days previously when Julie produced a small model dog to swap at playtime she announced 'Me got this little dog to swap'. This use of baby talk seemed intended to convey the cuteness and vulnerability of the dog (hence increasing its swapping value) and her audience responded by exclaiming about the dog's 'sweetness' and offering to 'look after it'. In the data, the use by some girls of expressions and voices which invite listeners to take on this kind of nurturing role invariably obtained an enthusiastic response. The girls' use of this nurturing discourse illustrates its powerful role, indexing what Connell *et al.* (1982) refer to as an 'emphasised femininity', the symbolically powerful marking of particular ways of being a woman, within their community.

Julie's anecdote is successful, therefore, not just because of its immediate entertainment value, but also because it plugs into this powerful speech genre of exclaiming and doting over cute, small, vulnerable objects or beings. For Julie and her friends, a particular kind of nurturing social activity, involving, for instance, little sisters or toys, is associated with being a girl and this is indexed through the positively evaluated higher-pitched baby talk and confirmed through exclamations like 'Ah, isn't that sweet!' Significantly, I did not find any instances of this kind of talk among the boys, and find it hard to imagine any of them talking in this way, without a hefty dose of double-voiced irony.[9]

As I discussed in Chapter 3, an important dimension of children's socialisation, and also of their emerging sense of self, is the way in which they try out and take on particular aspects of gender identity. The linguistic features of reproduced voices in children's stories index social meanings (stances, social acts, and social activities) and these in turn help to index gender. So, while Julie's representation of her dialogue with her little sister indexes the social languages for the particular characters (sweet funny little child, kind elder sister) and the speech genre of informal sibling interaction at home, it also indexes a stance and social acts for Julie which, in this community, are associated with being a girl. This indexing works within each of the three dialogic levels: the production and articulation of the voices within the anecdote, Kirsty's response confirming the evaluative perspective and the intertextual links between the stance in this anecdote and the echoing of stances in other talk among the girls about small vulnerable beings and objects. The process of gender identification through indexicalisation in anecdotes is further explored in the discussion of the boys' anecdotes in the next section below.

Darren and Martie

Narratives from children's conversations during the school day, like Julie's above, are usually brief and punchy. Often told within the context of fast moving exchanges and a competitive jostling for conversational space (especially among the boys), stories have to immediately grab and hold the audience's attention, and strategies involving the listener (like the attention catching 'right' and the appellation 'man') are strongly marked. As we saw in Chapter 3, more dominant boys like Martie and Darren often tended to throw in points of information or rudimentary anecdotes in a rapid quick fire exchange until one gained the floor for a more extended turn. Frequently, the audience for the boys' stories extended beyond their own group to other children in the class: girls whom they want to impress or other boys hanging around the fringes of the group, like Geoffrey and Philip.

The first example below in Table 5.5 comes from talk in the boys' changing room where they had placed a small cassette recorder on a bench. Around eight boys are getting ready to swim and Martie and Darren collaborate, in a competitive kind of way, to produce an anec- dote together. (This extract comes a few moments before Martie and Darren's conversation about G-force, in Table 3.8).

Table 5.5

Martie	Who was here when we went with Miss, Miss Russell?
Darren	Me, I was
Boys	I was, I was
Martie	Em did you, em, what about the way Keith dived?
Boys	Yea
Darren	What about Scott, man
Martie	Right Scott was, Scott was going *(exaggerated enthusiasm)* 'I'm cool, man, I'm going to dive', right, and he is standing
Darren	/And he goes to the edge, right, yea, and he just goes splat. There's the white line, he just goes bang on his tummy, come out and he had all red marks all over him, man. That was well bad
Martie	/Er you know when we first had to dive in, me and him scraped our tummies – you said you did ...

Here, although Martie initially introduces the subject of Keith's dive, Darren takes the floor from him with the abstract 'What about Scott, man'. Martie concedes to the change of topic and attempts to recap- ture the floor with the orientation 'Right Scott was, Scott was going *(exaggerated enthusiasm)* "I'm cool, man, I'm going to dive", right, and he is standing', but Darren cuts in and retakes the floor for the compli- cation (unusually, not using reported dialogue) 'And he goes to the edge, right, yea, and he just goes splat. There's the white line, he just goes bang on his tummy, come out' and the resolution 'he had all red marks all over him, man'. Darren then adds a final external evaluative remark 'That was well bad'.

The anecdote, constructed in a way which reflects Martie and Darren's ongoing jostling for centre stage in the group, recalls a strik- ing shared experience sparked off by the immediate setting. Telling the anecdote also provides a space to explore a recurring theme for boys' talk in the public arena, of who can successfully accomplish the most daring feats of physical courage and prowess. Here this theme is presented not as a direct personal boast, but through the ridiculing of an opponent. The voice Martie constructs for Scott, 'I'm cool, man. I'm going to dive', is an example of the kind of stylised dialogue chil- dren use to index a particular kind of stance (like Julie's 'I'm packing my cases' and Terry's 'Come on you c.u.n.t.' and all that). Here, the stance invoked is 'showing off'. Through the exaggerated enthusiasm in Martie's reproduction of Scott's voice we can clearly hear Martie's irony behind Scott's boast, signalling Martie's evaluative purpose. This double-voicing sets the scene for Scott's subsequent humiliating downfall.

Earlier, during the fifteen minute coach journey to their once weekly swimming lesson, the children's talk had ranged over various journeys they had made with their families outside school. While the themes of their stories again linked with the conversational context (a coach journey), these narratives also provided a space to explore various other issues as well. Darren and Martie are swapping their experiences of aeroplane travel with other children sitting nearby.

Table 5.6

Martie	Do you like getting off the seat?
Darren	No
Martie	I love getting off the seat. I was sitting in the middle of the floor and reading a book and the hostess come
Darren	/I did that once
Martie	/And the hostess come, and she said, she was, she was REALLY nice if you know what I mean, and as she came past she had this trolley with all the dinners on it and she went *(high pitched 'neep neep' horn sound, laughter)* and all I done is, I went *(low pitched sound of car engine)* and I moved to the side as she went past *(groan)*. Her legs, man *(groan, short pause)*. I was going to eat the dinners, man
Boy	Chicken
Darren	/And you can leave what you want.

As is common in the children's stories, the complicating action after the orientation 'I was sitting in the middle of the floor and reading a book and the hostess come' is constructed through a kind of dialogue, non-verbal in this case, between the airhostess's high pitched imitation of a car horn, and Martie's own deep throated engine noise. Martie's external evaluative comment 'she was, she was REALLY nice if you know what I mean' underlines one point of the story – the attractions of the air-hostess.

Martie's story is successful here partly because, like Julie's story about the eraser, it plugs into a powerful gendered discourse, this time a male discourse about fancying attractive females. But this is mixed in with more childish pleasures. Like the other 10–12 year-olds in the recordings, Martie moved easily back and forth between the worlds of childhood and adolescence, depending on the context and his purposes. His account nicely illustrates the ambivalence which this dual identity creates, where a boy can play on the floor like a child but can also look up an airhostess's skirts and admire her legs. Physical attractions are discussed in the same breath as the aeroplane meals and a child's delight that you do not have to eat all the food on your plate. The dialogue between the horn and the engine noise, as Martie presents it with his suggestive deep-throated purr, is similarly ambivalent and can be interpreted either as a child's game or as a flirtatious joke. The comment 'I was going to eat the dinners, man' which could be either a coda or the start of a new story again shifts the interest, away from the hostess's legs and onto what she has on her trolley. When Martie holds the alternative interpretative frames of child play/adolescent flirting, as Julie did when she asked David about playing after school (Table 2.7), this allows him the possibility of switching frames to save face and to offer alternative points of engagement for his audience.

When Martie introduces sexual innuendo into the above account, he positions himself firmly as a heterosexual male, inviting the listener into his perspective ('her legs, man ...'). As well as presenting an active gendered position for himself (Martie is the one doing the fancying), this stance also positions his audience along gendered lines. The boys are invited to collude with the gendered perspective of the narrator: 'she was <u>really</u> nice if you know what I mean'. This in-group *we're all boys together who fancy attractive women* statement in effect excludes the girls, who became passive spectators. Martie's orientation to what Connell *et al.* (1982, 1995) would see as a hegemonic heterosexual masculinity is accepted unproblematically by both the girls and boys in his audience, suggesting that this is a relatively untroubled identity (at a discursive level) for the children.

Darren, as we have seen, often presented himself as tough, knowing, canny and actively heterosexual in more public settings in the classroom. A final anecdote from him (below) is constructed almost entirely through reported speech. Like Julie in her story about swearing at her mother, Darren manipulates a number of different discursive layers in conveying the story's evaluative function and in presenting himself within it. Darren tells this anecdote to other children who are milling around in the queue next to him in the school playground, as they all wait to go in to lunch. At this point, one child has just sworn at another.

Table 5.7

Martie	I said that to a real man and he went, he went 'dick head' *(and I went)* 'of course I am!'*(laughter)* And he goes 'erm!' *(growling and laughter)*
Darren	This man called me a fucking bastard, right, I go 'back to you', he goes 'come here', I go 'come on, then' and he's got about size ten trainers and he chased me, right, and then when he got, he catched me, right, like that, and he goes 'who's fucking saying?' And I goes 'fuck off', I says 'fuck off' and he goes, he goes, 'Do you want a fight?' I go *(falsetto voice)* 'not tonight, darling' and he goes 'piss off!' *(laughter)*.

After the orientation and framing 'This man called me a fucking bastard, right', Darren uses reported dialogue to tell his story and to display his own courage and defiance in standing up to an aggressive adult. The external evaluative aside 'and he's got about size ten trainers' emphasises the man's size and therefore by implication, Darren's bravery. But Darren does not only create voices for himself and the man. He also, at the point in the story when things are getting really alarming, portrays himself as taking on a different voice again: ('not tonight, darling'). The falsetto pitch caricatures the rejection of sexual advances and the metamessage of this double-voicing conveys a joke, through playfully signalling a switch of frame from 'escalating fight' to 'lovers' standoff'. The voice and phrase invoke a stance, with associated relationships, in the same way as Julie's 'I'm packing my bags'. In Darren's case, calling up this particular speech genre (and the associated ambivalent sexual position identity) changes the relationship between himself and the man in a way which uses humour to defuse the situation and signals a kind of submission while still maintaining face.

Within the anecdote, then, voices are used to index, first, the social language and speech genre of a man and a boy starting a fight and secondly, the nested speech genre invoked by Darren's falsetto voice. At the interactional level between children, Darren is responding to Martie and competing with him for the attention of other children. He mirrors the content and the evaluative point of Martie's rather minimalist anecdote, thus confirming their alliance,[10] but also decisively caps it, with a much more arresting story. Darren's anecdote is more developed; the man is more frightening, and the turnaround at the end more dramatic and ingenious. The voices Darren creates within his anecdote also contribute towards this interactional aim. As well as providing a turn in the immediate conversation, the anecdote also contributes to the recurring theme in the boys' talk concerning their toughness and canniness, which are important aspects of the way they present themselves to each other. And Darren's anecdote also echoes the concern in Julie's about how far adult authority can and should be contested.

Martie and Darren's anecdotes, like Julie's, open up the possibility for constructing meanings through the relationships between the different dialogic layers within the anecdote, the current conversation, and in relation to children's broader experience. The capacity of a few seconds of reported dialogue (even the orientation in Darren's anecdote 'This man called me a fucking bastard, right' is indirect reported speech), for discursive work around issues and identities is enormously amplified through the way in which this reported speech invokes links with themes and relationships in the ongoing conversation and intertextual connections with other conversations and stories.

Conclusion

I have suggested that the textual structure of narrative offers children an organised discursive space within which they can present, explore and reflect on various aspects of their experience and identity. Within anecdotes, the voices children invoke and the dialogues they orchestrate convey what happens, particularly at the crux of the story, through indexing particular social languages and speech genres which in their turn index recognisable scenarios. In relation to these scenarios, the characters' utterances also index actions and stances. They are always double-voiced, often prosodically marked to reflect the narrator's intention behind them, and are articulated within dialogues to make particular evaluative points. Within the context of the anecdote, a character's voice may also invoke a different speech genre again, which contributes an additional nuance of meaning, for example Julie's 'I'm packing my bags' and Darren's 'Not tonight, darling'.

As part of ongoing conversation, the anecdotes are intensely dialogic, that is, orientated towards listeners and also towards previous conversational turns. At the textual level, in addition to interactional markers (the use of interrogatives, 'right', the boys' solidarity term 'man'), the opening and closing sections of the anecdotes in particular are structured in relation to the conversational context. The abstract and orientation sections are sometimes conflated and at the end of stories, near the boundaries with the next speaker's turn, there is frequently structural and evaluative ambiguity, for instance when David asks for another resolution to Julie's story about the misplaced slap (Table 5.1), the evaluative ambivalence in Julie's anecdote about swearing at her mother (Table 5.2), the blending into further talk about scraped tummies at the swimming pool (Table 5.5) and about the talk about dinners at the end of Martie's anecdote about the airhostess (stories often produce more stories). The dialogising of meaning within an anecdote is shown particularly clearly in Julie's account of swearing at her mother, where she reconfigures the two evaluative positions expressed in the previous exchange, within the structure and evaluation of her anecdote. Children's use of reported voices, as well as being centrally important in fusing the narrated and narrating event, is crucial to the evaluative message, far more important than Labov's account of embedded evaluation would suggest.

Many anecdotes are collaboratively constructed: children prompt narrators to produce more satisfactory resolutions, thereby retrospectively creating a longer complicating action as David does in the anecdote about the misplaced slap (Table 5.1), they corroborate an evaluative point as Kirsty does in exclaiming over the behaviour of Julie's little sister (Table 5.4) and they produce different bits of the narrative structure and chains of responsive anecdotes like Darren and Martie (Table 5.7). In addition to this responsive and participatory role for listeners, I have argued that stories are by their very nature collaborative because their performance depends on an audience who accept them as 'tellable' and who are prepared to listen. Children recount individual experience from their own point of view, representing their own role in events and recreating their own voice in particular ways. Their narratives often convey a strong sense of children's personal agency, a way of reflecting with hindsight on their own role in events which at the time might have felt less within their control. But they do all this in socially acceptable ways, representing others and themselves and evaluating actions and events in terms of shared beliefs and values which their audience can recognise and relate to. The narration of anecdotes in this sense enables children to tackle the meaning of personal experience and moral judgements in relation to the responses of other children, as well as from their own point of view, as part of their active involvement in their own socialisation into a particular community.

Anecdotes have an interactional function within the context where they are produced, for instance to attract another child's attention, express friendship or compete for social dominance and they are often sparked off by something in the immediate environment: a scuffle among children, a child wanting to borrow an eraser, an imminent swimming lesson, travel in the school coach. Rather more significantly, they set up intertextual connections with other contexts and other conversations. The dialogue in an anecdote creates an additional conversational layer within which a particular theme can be explored in more depth, often through exploring the relationship between different evaluative perspectives invoked by different voices.

While stories might appear to present a coherent 'self', if only momentarily, they are in fact more like a snapshot of a particular moment within a continuing process of social construction of the self, both within the story and through its interactive performance. One theme which runs through the stories is the taking on and trying out of new gender identities and how children present themselves as a girl or a boy moving into their teenage years in relation to the dominant representations of femininity, masculinity and sexuality in their community. Within the anecdotes, gender is indexed through characters' voices (including the narrator's representation of their own voice) and the orchestration of a dialogue which invokes particular stances, actions and activities within recognisable scenarios. The anecdotes I have discussed illustrate, in the case of Darren and Martie, an orientation towards the assertive heterosexuality, toughness, canniness and social dominance which characterised what appeared to be a dominant representation of masculinity in the children's environment. Julie, on the other hand, expressed the strong nurturing stance towards small vulnerable cute beings or objects, combined with a kind of feisty assertion towards other children and certain adults which was typical of the 'emphasised femininity' within this group of working class girls.

These rather stereotypical representations of gender are, however, only one aspect (albeit a powerful one) of the influences on children's own gender identification. While public spaces seemed to offer the more powerful boys opportunities for taking central stage and expressing dominant discourses about masculinity, a rather different story emerges in the next chapter where I discuss children's narratives in the interviews. In this more private, leisurely context, both girls and boys expressed a wider range of gender positionings in the course of telling longer narratives. These interview narratives reveal some more about the children's identification processes and about their struggles with the moral dilemmas which they encounter in their personal experience.

6
Narrative Reflections and Moral Complexities

> We come to define ourselves as we narratively grapple with our own and others' ambiguous emotions and events. As a result, narrative constructions of uncertainty as well as certainty play an important part in configuring selves.
>
> (Ochs and Capps, 2001, p. 290)

Michelle   My mum says best not to, cause he might come round and say 'You've been getting at MY daughter to make me not touch you' but he said from now on he won't lay a hand on her, but that's a lie my mum said.

In this chapter, I look at the longer narratives children produced in the course of their conversations with me in my interviews with friendship pairs. Children used these narratives to present and reflect on themselves and their experience and they also had the time and space in the interviews to explore questions that concerned them, at some length. Building on the discussion about reported voices and narrative in Chapters 4 and 5 and focussing again on the three levels of narrative meaning (textual, interactional and contextual), I shall look in particular at the moral issues which were centrally important to many of the stories told by the children within the interview context. A story functions as a memorable shared resource for further meaning-making and the moral issues it raised were often explored later in the conversation following the narrative, rearticulated through reported voices. This exploration of moral positions is crucial to children's working out of their own moral code and identity as a person and is also intricately tied up with learning about the social practices, beliefs and values which constitute their social world.

As I explained in Chapter 1, the initial purpose of the interviews in my research was to gather additional contextual information about the topics which cropped up in the continuous recordings, for instance swapping, boyfriends and girlfriends, clubs, expectations about friendship, relationships with adults. I wanted to get more of a sense of children's social lives and to find out about their uses of literacy and their other interests outside school. Starting initially with individual interviews, I then acquiesced with Karlie's request to bring Nicole with her and found that talking with two friends together produced a more relaxed and egalitarian atmosphere. At times, for instance, children interrupted me, or ignored a question from me to carry on discussing an issue between themselves. This combination of two friends became the pattern for the remainder of the interviews within which children talked at length about their lives, spontaneously producing many narratives in the course of relating their personal experience.

As well as enabling me to collect valuable contextual information, the interviews became another context within which to study their use of language, including their orchestration of reported voices inside and outside stories. The narratives tended to be longer and the conversations more leisurely, offering many opportunities to examine the interactive nature of the production of the stories and the roles played both by the friend, and by myself, in their referential and evaluative functions. The children's talk often included 'duetting' (see Chapter 3), where children collaboratively presented an account to me, and friends frequently corroborated each other's stories, thus warranting their authenticity. Although we had to hold the interviews squashed behind shelves of stationery in the corner of the school store room, the interstitial nature of this physical space was perhaps consistent with the children's practice of colonising the margins within territory occupied and organised by adults. The combination of two friends and an attentive adult in this corner which was tucked away from the hustle and bustle of life in the rest of the school seemed to facilitate quite extended personal reflections in which I myself, as interviewer, played an important part.

Articulating moral stances

Secrets and lies

Let's look first at how all three participants in the interview (i.e. both friends and myself) were involved in producing and responding to a story. In the example below, I had just asked Nicole who else lived at her house and Karlie mentioned that Nicole's sister, Terri, had recently had a baby.

Table 6.1 (a)

1	Janet	So does your sister live quite near you?
	Nicole	She lives with us
	Karlie	Cause she's only quite young
	Nicole	She's young, she's sixteen
5	Janet	Ah right
	Karlie	She did the best thing about it, though, didn't she, Nicole?
	Nicole	She didn't tell a soul, no-one, that she was pregnant
	Karlie	Until she was due, when she got into hospital, then she told them
	Nicole	On Saturday night she had pains in her stomach, and come the
10		following Sunday my mum was at work and my sister come to the
		pub and my aunt Ella was in it and my sister went in there and said
		'I've got pains in my stomach!', so my aunt Ella went and got my
		mum, and took her to the hospital, and my mum asked her if she
		was due on and she said 'No, I've just come off' and when they got
15		her to hospital they said 'Take her to Maternity!' My mum was crying.

In lines 2–4 Nicole and Karlie duet to answer my question about where Terri lives. The story is introduced by Karlie's evaluation 'She did the best thing about it'. Now set up for the narration, Nicole herself provides the orientation (lines 9–11), followed closely by the complicating action, which culminates in the dramatic 'Take her to maternity!' Finally, Nicole's external evaluative comment 'My mum was crying' emphasises the shocking nature of what happened.

The fluency with which Nicole told this story and the phrase 'come the following Sunday' suggest that she has heard or told it before – it is the only story I collected which shows such signs of rehearsal. My own immediate response (see below) picked up on what for me was the most extraordinary aspect of the story, the mother's apparent ignorance about her daughter's pregnancy. My repeated questions about this may have prompted Karlie's quoting of her Dad (line 25 in Table 6.1 (b) below):

Table 6.1 (b)

	Janet	Your mum didn't realise she was pregnant?
	Nicole	No. And my mum slept with her when she was ill!
	Janet	And didn't it show?
	Nicole	It was all round the back
20	Janet	Is she a big girl anyway?
	Nicole	Yea, she is really big, in't she?
	Karlie	Hm
	Janet	So your mum didn't know?
	Nicole	No
25	Karlie	/My dad said she did, Terri did the best thing about it. Her sister's
		Terri

Table 6.1 (b) – *continued*

	Nicole	Or if she did tell, as she's so young, she weren't allowed to have him
	Janet	Oh I see
	Nicole	My mum was glad she was due, then
30	Janet	So she was shocked when she found out and then
	Nicole	/Yea, took her a week to get over the shock! My dad was even crying. My dad!
	Janet	Is he okay now?
	Nicole	Yea, he loves him. He feeds him, he changes the baby's bum!
35		*(surprised tone)* My dad changes the baby's bum! *(giggle)*
	Karlie	My aunt's pregnant, because me and Nicole are becoming cousins soon
	Janet	Are you? How come?
	Karlie	Because
40	Nicole	/My uncle's getting married to her aunt and they're having a baby.

The additional information Nicole gives in line 17 'and my mum slept with her when she was ill' (and still didn't notice that she was pregnant) emphasises the extraordinary nature of the events. Listening to the tape I can hear the incredulity in my repeated questioning (lines 16–23), and Karlie's comment 'My dad said she did, Terri did the best thing about it' in line 25 may have been a way of countering this by supporting and warranting her friend's story. We also learn in line 25 that the evaluation Karlie initially presented in line 6 as her own 'She did the best thing about it, though, didn't she, Nicole?' is also what her father had said. Although I cannot provide incontrovertible proof, the ways in which I could trace children reproducing adult voices in the data (see Chapter 7) strongly suggest that Karlie has reproduced her father's voice in line 6, appropriating his moral perspective as her own. She then acknowledges the source of this judgement in line 25, adding her father's authoritative weight to this stance in response to my repeated questioning of Nicole. In developmental terms, this appropriation of an authoritative voice seems to be part of the process of internalising a moral viewpoint (of course, some appropriated voices may be rejected at a later stage). It is interesting to consider at what stage we would consider this perspective to be securely Karlie's own; or indeed how far moral positions are ever really individually held.

As in the anecdotes analysed in the last chapter, the instances of reported speech inside Nicole's story each play a vital role in unfolding the plot. 'I've got pains in my stomach!' (line 12) articulates the problem and sets off the train of events, 'No, I've just come off' (line 14) (i.e. just finished menstruating) adds to the deepening mystery and suspense, and 'Take her up to Maternity!' (line 15) reveals the dramatic outcome. The urgency of the voices draws the listener in, heightening the suspense and confronting them with the contradiction between Terri's apparent lack of pregnancy symptoms, ('I've just come off') and the verdict of the hospital ('Take her to Maternity!'), the contradiction which I immediately picked up in my initial response. The dynamic opposition between Terri's voice and the voice of the hospital staff is central to the point of the story, creating the impact of a dramatic event which is unusual and 'tellable'.

However, the contradiction between these two voices within the story is also framed by the overall evaluative slant given by Karlie's comment that Terri 'did the best thing about it'. From this point of view, Terri's response 'I've just come off' could be interpreted as part of the concealment of her pregnancy, which the girls see as sensible and admirable because otherwise 'as she's so young, she weren't allowed to have him' (line 27). While the relationship between the reproduced voices within the story provides the dynamic that drives it forwards, the additional relationship between these voices and comments by Karlie and Nicole in the conversation around the story (some of which were prompted by my responses) are central to the evaluative point the girls are making about the wisdom of Terri's concealment.

In addition to the apparently conflicting voices within the story, there are contrasting stances presented in the conversation at this point: my incredulity versus Karlie's support and warranting of the story. There are also contrasting stances within the girls' community: Karlie's father's approval of the concealment as opposed to the authorities who wouldn't have allowed Terri to have the baby if her pregnancy had been revealed. Over time, we also hear, Nicole's parents' shock has changed into pleasure. Nicole continues to comment on her parents' happiness and involvement with the baby in the conversation following the story, in this way emphasising and elaborating the argument that Terri did 'the best thing'. The criss-crossing dialogic relationships here between voices representing stances within the narrative, positions expressed by myself and Karlie, and the evaluative positions children reported from within their broader community, are part of the moral landscape within which the meaning of the story is socially forged.

Righteous violence

Nicole's narrative has signs of being a retold story,[1] but its evaluative function is recreated, dialogically, within the context of the interview.

On other occasions, where a narrative was not fully formed, children would still use reproduced voices to convey the evaluative point of what they were trying to say. Terry, for instance, told me a much more raw and confusing story about a fight outside his house the previous evening, in the context of my interview with him and Keith. Either the recent nature of the experience, or Terry's less developed narrative skills, or perhaps because he and Keith were not as close friends as Nicole and Karlie and not as relaxed with myself, led to a much more fragmented account. Keith had been talking about his interest in model aeroplanes and Terry about his work with an adult friend repairing cars. Terry told me he had an older brother and sister and I asked if his brother was also interested in cars. He responded 'Not that much. My sister's more interested in fighting and bunking *(i.e. skipping school)*', and went on to say 'They had a fight last night in the Court' (the part of the estate where he lived), and that all of his kitchen windows and front door had been smashed.

Table 6.2 (a)

Terry	When they came back to do the windows there was ten of them. I was going, 'Rick, you're dead, you're all dead, come out here'. Cause they had, you know the new baseball bats with the metal tips?
Keith	Yea
Terry	They were just trying to cause trouble and that's how the fight started again 'Come on you c.u.n.t.' and all that lot, and then they hit my dad on the back of the head. Ruby knew they were going to do it. Ruby run in her house, got a blade, 'I'm gonna kill them, I'm gonna shove this blade so far down their throat'.

The reproduced voices here play an important part in portraying the violence in Terry's story, especially forcefully in the free direct speech ('Come on you c.u.n.t.') where characters speak, as it were, directly to myself and Keith. Even within this direct representation, however, Terry conveys sensitivity to the interview context in his spelling out of the word 'c.u.n.t' (he would hardly have spelled it out in the original event). In this way he can demonstrate his knowledge and use of a sexual taboo word, strengthening the depiction of the violence in his account, while still maintaining 'politeness' to myself.

A fuller story began to emerge over the next fifteen minutes. Terry explained that the fight started because his sister had been wrongly accused of stealing someone's walkman tape recorder. I found it hard to follow the temporal sequence of who had done what to whom, as he switched rapidly between different parts of the action:

Table 6.2 (b)

Janet	What was your mum doing all this time?
Terry	She was in the shower, she run downstairs. She run downstairs and said, 'Oi, what the heck, heck's going on?' and my dad come running downstairs and he goes 'Get your silly little brother and go' and he turned round to walk in and he, Carl went, bang, on my dad's back, so Louise turned round and hit 'im and that's how it all started, my dad turned round, grabbed him and threw 'im on the floor and then pinned 'im down, the police got there but he wriggled out …

In the future, this rather disjointed explanation may turn into a more clearly crafted account. But in the interview it felt as if Terry had seized the first possible moment to talk about events that had happened only the previous night and which he was still trying to process. His recent experience has not yet settled into the kind of well-worn narrative structure Nicole produced in Table 6.1. In fact, the confusion in Terry's account from the lack of a clear story structure demonstrates just how much we rely on the narrative genre to interpret people's accounts of their experience,[2] and how effectively it fulfils its referential function. However, the evaluative message is already coming through clearly in Terry's emphasis on the danger of the situation: 'there were ten of them' (i.e. against Terry, his father and sister), 'they had, you know the new baseball bats with the metal tips?', and especially through the violence portrayed in the reported speech: '"Rick, you're dead, you're all dead, come out here" … "Come on you c.u.n.t" … "I'm gonna kill them, I'm gonna shove this blade so far down their throat"'. There is a kind of respect and pride behind Terry's portrayal of his family's toughness as righteous, a spirited self-defence against a wrongful attack. Within this evaluative framing the aggressive, macho voice Terry gives himself: 'Rick, you're dead, you're all dead, come out here', emerges as virtuous, justified in relation to the violence directed against his family and vindicated by the eventual police arrest of some of the attackers.

Although the story of the fight does not emerge directly from a theme in the previous conversation, Terry still manages to make a link to a question from myself through his response about his sister's interest in fighting, which then enables him to embark on his account. After talking for some time about the fight, we then moved back to talking about model planes and repairing cars and Terry's story was left hanging, as it were, raw and somewhat incoherent in its own terms and not referred back to again by either boy, at least within the interview. Perhaps because of the way Terry presents the topic, or the boys' lack of close friendship, or the lack of enough rapport with myself, Terry and Keith did not do the collaborative warranting that happened between Nicole and Karlie. The complex dialogic expression of different moral stances which we saw in Table 6.1 is replaced by a monologic statement about meeting violence with violence. The fight story, however, did invoke links with the more general theme of courage and toughness in boys' stories, demonstrated for example in Martie and Darren's anecdotes in Chapter 6. It also links with a theme running through Terry's accounts and self-presentation, an orientation towards a more adult identity expressed here through fighting alongside his father and through his descriptions of repairing cars with a 'mate' in his early twenties (see also Chapter 8).

Beleaguered positions

The evaluative points in Nicole's story come across as currently fairly settled within the girls' community: the drama is over, Nicole's parents are happy with the outcome and Karlie's father has expressed his approval of Terri's action. And in Terry's story, the heroes and villains are fairly clearly identifiable and the moral positions non-negotiable. Often, however, the evaluation in children's narratives is less certain. This uncertainty may indeed be part of the reason for telling a story in the first place, in order to test out my own and their friend's responses. As Ochs and Capps (2001) point out in the quotation at the head of the chapter, narratives do not necessarily present experience and selves unequivocally, but also provide a space for grappling with ambiguity and uncertainty.

Unjust punishment

As I explained in Chapter 3, the interview was a context which encouraged cooperative talk between the friendships pairs of boys as well as girls. Simon and Sam, for instance, collaborated closely in a story about why Simon had been 'grounded'.[3] I had just asked the boys if they played together after school:

Table 6.3 (a)

Sam	At the moment he's been grounded for a month. He's still grounded
Janet	Why have you been grounded?
Simon	Ah, cause of a boy
Janet	What did you do?
Simon	I bought some Lego off my friend, right, and his mum, he told his mum he let me lend it and em his mum writ a letter saying can he have it back, right, so he got it back and I asked for my money back and he didn't give me it, so I asked him again and he nicked it out of his mum's purse
Sam	He *(Simon)* got grounded for it, though.

Often in the interviews a child would offer a piece of information, like Sam explaining in the first turn above that Simon was grounded (or Karlie's comment: 'She did the best thing about it, though, didn't she, Nicole?') which could serve as an invitation to their friend for further explanation, or as an invitation to myself to ask the question which would prompt the story. In this way Karlie and Sam are expressing their closeness to their friend by demonstrating knowledge about important events in their life as well as cueing them to speak. Sam here provides a possible opening 'he's been grounded for a month', and what could be a resolution or coda for Simon's story: 'He *(Simon)* got grounded for it, though'. The final 'though', here, is important to the evaluative message of the story, signalling the sense of injustice which is the point of telling it. This became clearer when I questioned Simon further about what had happened. After a discussion about what grounding means and the various prohibitions it can include, the boys together provided a more explicit explanation of the evaluative point of the story. Mr. Perry is the boys' head teacher at Lakeside:

Table 6.3 (b)

1	Janet	So is that say to be grounded for a month, is that quite a severe ...?
	Simon	Em. I'm not going to do it again
	Janet	So what was she particularly cross about?
	Sam	The police coming round, I think. If the police never come round,
5		and the head teacher, I think he'd only be grounded for about a week
	Janet	What had you done that was so wrong?
	Simon	I kept on asking him to give me my money
	Sam	Yea, and cause it was his *(the other boy's)* fault for nicking the money
10		and it got all put onto Simon, so really he *(Simon)* never done nothing

Table 6.3 (b) – *continued*

	Simon	But he's *(the other boy)* the one who done it and Mr. Perry goes, em he should have been punished as well. He should, he should have been the one who was punished, got punished
15	Sam	He was lucky that Mr. Perry didn't do him.[4] He *(Mr. Perry)* said he can't do nothing cause it was out of school time.

When I questioned him, Simon's first two responses 'I'm not going to do it again' (line 2) and 'I kept on asking him to give me my money' (line 8) seem to imply an acceptance of his punishment. These responses also, however, had the effect of cueing Sam to exclaim about how unjustly Simon had been treated. Simon's response in line 8: 'I kept on asking him to give me my money', with its subtle choice of the possessive pronoun 'my' which signalled his own valid right to the money, had Sam practically jumping out of his seat to vindicate his friend in lines 9–11: 'Yea, and cause it was his *(the other boy's)* fault for nicking the money and it got all put onto Simon, so really he *(Simon)* never done nothing'. Only then, Simon confirms Sam's comment about the culpability of the other boy in line 12 'But he's the one who done it', thus explicitly expressing his own innocence. He immediately strengthens this evaluation by reporting what his headteacher had said: 'Mr. Perry goes, em he should have been punished as well. He should, he should have been the one who was punished, got punished.'

Like Karlie, Simon strengthens his own moral position through invoking an authoritative voice, but in his case in not quite such a straightforward way. Although there is an initial reporting clause 'Mr. Perry goes', Simon's voice quality does not change to signal he is actually reproducing his head teacher's voice and the last sentence above in particular 'He should, he should have been the one who was punished, got punished' could be either a continuation of what Mr. Perry said, or a merging back into Simon's voice. This ambiguity actually further strengthens Simon's claims about his own innocence. It enables him to back up his position (Mr. Perry is both an authority figure and lacks the boys' vested interest), without having to assume full personal responsibility for proclaiming it.[5] Simon's presentation of himself to me in the interview is thus skilfully deflected so that, when it comes down to his word against the other boy's, Simon makes sure his case is warranted both by Sam, and by the reported authoritative voice of their headmaster. Indeed, Simon's responses were also effective in invoking indignant feelings in myself about his treatment. The evaluative point, that Simon has been unjustly blamed and punished, emerges as much through the responses which he evokes in his listeners as in what he explicitly recounts himself.

Simon's story and the additional evaluative comments about Mr. Perry are constructed mainly around represented speech acts and indirect speech: 'he told his mum ... his mum writ a letter ... I asked for my money back ... I asked him again ...'. Rather than being focussed around one specific event, with the complicating action expressed in direct speech, the evaluative point concerning the injustice of Simon's punishment emerges through a number of events spread over time – the original purchase of the Lego, the boy's lie to his mother, her letter, Simon's returning of the Lego and request for his money, the boy's stealing from his mother's purse, the involvement of the police and Mr. Perry's comments. Simon distances himself from what he is reporting, through his use of reported speech acts. Like Kim in Table 4.3, he is presenting a situation where he has been seen as culpable by adults, and producing their voices (or the voice of the other boy) directly would give immediacy to their evaluative viewpoint which would reflect negatively on himself. Significantly, the only direct reporting clause 'Mr. Perry goes' is followed by comments which provide a positive evaluation of Simon's position in a mixture of direct and indirect reporting within free indirect discourse, where Mr. Perry and Simon's evaluative stances can be blended. Finally, the more distanced nature of speech act reporting is consistent with Simon's deflected style of self presentation and his projection of the responsibility for more specific, committed position statements onto Sam and Mr. Perry.

In Sam and Simon's interview this story became a focal point which is referred back to on a number of occasions. It serves as a shared semiotic resource, its evaluative messages revisited and amplified and Simon's own moral position strengthened, through subsequent comments. For instance, shortly after the exchanges transcribed above, Sam showed me some miniature cars which he has got from Simon and Simon remarked: 'He *(Sam)* bought them off me but I'm not the sort of person who wants to get them back'. The phrase 'get them back' echoes the similar phrase in the story he told earlier about the Lego: 'his mum writ a letter saying can he have it back, right, so he got it back'. Through this dialogic echo, Simon implicitly contrasts his own behaviour with the boy in his first story who is, by inference, 'the sort of person who wants to get them back'. Again, the phrase in the Lego story 'he told his mum' is echoed about twenty minutes later in the interview when Simon explains how another boy, Alan, stole things from the shed which Simon and Sam were turning into a club house with shelves to exhibit all the animal bones they had found in the fields: 'The other day he *(Alan)* nicked two, a hammer, my two torches, my Sherwood stickers, there was this tray with four pockets in, he nicked my wallet, my wood and I went round his house, got the stuff and I wouldn't even tell his mum.' In this mini-narrative (with its own orientation, complication, resolution and evaluation), Simon is again presenting himself as a particular kind of person through contrasting his own actions (represented this time through the speech act 'I wouldn't even tell his mum'), indirectly, with those of the boy in the Lego story, who 'told his mum'. The point of Simon's story about Alan's theft emerges *in relation to* the earlier story about the Lego.

Telling kindness

Evaluative points were often echoed and revisited in stories told by different friends in the same conversation. Like Sam and Simon, Lee and Geoffrey were close friends. They talked extensively to me about their interest in animals and birds and Lee had just told a lengthy and complicated account about a local stray black cat adopted by his family when Geoffrey offered the following story of his own:

Table 6.4

Geoff	There was this black stray cat who started coming into our garden for two nights
Lee	Is it really scruffy?
Geoff	Yea, and it didn't have no collar. It had no collar, and it had white bits at the paws, right on the paws and it had little white under there, and every night when it came into our garden we thought 'Oh, we got no food for it, all we got is dog food', cause we've only got a dog, and I said to my mum 'Mum, do you want me to go to the shops or will it be closed?' and she said 'I think it'll be closed, it's nine o'clock!' *(laughter)*
Janet	So what did you do?
Geoff	I thought 'Em, do cats like bread?' cause I had a few sandwiches, and my mum said 'That one might, you never know', so I gave it a bit of bread and it eat a bit, it eat a bit, only a little bit
Lee	Yea and my Uncle Edward and my Auntie Jennie and the others give my mum a cockatiel ...

Geoffrey's use of deixis in '<u>this</u> black stray cat' signals a switch away from the here and now of the interview to the context of the black stray cat and Lee's question 'Is it really scruffy?' invites Geoffrey to tell the story and also helps to shape the content of his orientation section, which concentrates wholly on the appearance of the cat (including the lack of collar suggesting it might be a stray) so that the boys can determine whether Geoffrey's cat is the same as the stray Lee had been previously telling us about. The complicating action is as usual conveyed mainly through direct reported dialogue and in this case reported thought ('we thought "Oh, we got no food for it, all we got is dog food"'). The narrative initially finishes with Lee and my laughter confirming the joke about Geoffrey's lack of sense of time in his mother's comment: 'I think it'll be closed, it's nine o'clock!' This would suggest that the cat goes hungry. However, in response to my question 'So what did you do?' (prompted by my expectation of a different kind of resolution), Geoffrey provides a continuation of the complicating action, and a new resolution 'so I gave it a bit of bread and it eat a bit, it eat a bit, only a little bit'. As when David asked Julie 'Did your Mum hit you?' (Table 5.1), my intervention invites a further extension and development of both the referential and evaluative functions of the story (producing Geoffrey's explanation about the final helping of the cat). Presentations which feel incomplete to the listener can ensure their greater involvement, as in the case of David and myself. On other occasions, of course, the audience may not be sufficiently interested to ask for more. In the example above, my question produces what feels to me like a much more satisfying resolution, with its final striking three-part rhythmic repetition 'it eat a bit, it eat a bit, only a little bit'.

Twelve minutes later in the interview, this theme of responding to animals in distress is taken up again by Lee. I have included the remarks which occurred just before and after Lee's story:

Table 6.5

Geoff	Since I started drawing birds, like in Miss Clark's class I had to draw that parrot, right the big parrot about that big
Lee	/I drew the man, didn't I?
Geoff	Since I drew that, whenever I started getting bored, I went upstairs, got my paper, and drew a couple of birds, tiny ones. I used, whenever I went over me uncle's house, I used to take a couple of pieces of paper and some felts like and draw all these birds parrot

Table 6.5 – *continued*

Lee	/Yesterday I was on, I was walking with my mum, we walked past this bush, and there was this nest and it was fallen down on the floor, and I goes 'Mum look, there's a nest on the floor', and I goes 'Mum can I go and have a look at it?' and I went over there and there was four baby chicks in it, little chicks, I think they were willow warbler and my mum said 'Climb up and put them back in the tree', so and I had some bread, eaten some bread, so I fed it bits of bread, cause she had to go to the phone, and em she waited and I put it back up in the tree and its mum's with it now. Yea, cause someone, someone had pulled the nest down, out of the tree
Geoff	I know this kid called Richie Binns who knocked a nest down ⌈ on purpose
Lee	⌊ They'd probably be dead by now
Geoff	/three little birds in there, one of them got thrown in my court and got squashed, one of them got dumped in a bush and that got squashed, and one got run over
Janet	Aah, that's a shame
Geoff	And I spent all that time putting worms and that in the nest, put it up in the tree, Richie Binns knocked it back down again. That's, then, that's when they got squashed.

Lee's story seems to be sparked off by Geoffrey's comments about drawing birds, but it is also a strong statement about their shared moral perspective. The story about the birds' nest almost exactly mirrors the structure and evaluative message of Geoffrey's earlier story about the stray cat. In both cases the complicating action section *(C)* starts with a problem described in dialogue, followed by a polite request to Mum who then offers helpful advice. In both resolutions *(R)* Lee/Geoffrey give the animal or bird some bread. Lee's moral alignment with his friend is thus expressed through the parallel structure of his story, right through to the three part list at the end, as demonstrated in the following table.

Table 6.6

This black stray cat	This nest	
we thought 'Oh, we got no food for it, all we got is dog food'	I goes 'Mum look, there's a nest on the floor'	*(C)* *problem*
'Mum, do you want me to go to the shops or will it be closed?'	'Mum, can I go and have a look at it?'	*request*
my mum said 'That one might, you never know'	my mum said 'Climb up and put them back in the tree'	*advice*
so I gave it a bit of bread and it eat a bit, it eat a bit, only a little bit	and I had some bread, eaten some bread, so I fed it bits of bread.	*(R)* *giving bread*

Lee's strong mirroring of a story told by Geoffrey twelve minutes earlier is in itself an evaluative comment expressing an alignment with his perspective (how to respond to creatures in distress, how to express gentleness) and an affirmation of their friendship.[6]

In order to convey their own evaluative perspective, Lee and Geoffrey construct gently-spoken, polite, caring voices which seem consistent with the kinds of selves they are portraying. The management of these voices is also an important part of the evaluative function of the story and of contrasting their own behaviour with that of other children. After Lee has expressed his alignment with Geoffrey in his story about the bird's nest, Geoffrey reconfirms their shared perspective in his comments which follow (he also has put a nest back in the tree) and contrasts both their behaviour with that of Richie Binns, who pulls nests out. Putting the nest back is a practical response to the situation and also a moral response, redressing the thoughtless cruelty of others. Accounts of other children's thoughtlessness and cruelty continue to be explored as the conversation continues:

Table 6.7

Lee	The ones *(birds)* I found yesterday are probably dead by now cause this girl I know called Ellie goes to George Bell *(name of school)* she'll probably nick them, cause she loves birds
Geoff	I know someone called Alan Horton, whenever he sees a bird's nest he climbs up the tree and goes *(gruff voice)* 'There's eggs in it' and takes the whole bird's nest into his shed, gets the eggs and smashes them with a hammer.

Lee and Geoffrey again express a shared moral position, implicitly contrasting their own rescuing of birds with, first, Ellie whom Lee implies couldn't care for them properly and, secondly, Alan Horton[7] who smashes up nests. While Geoffrey's animation of Alan Horton involves a switch in focalisation which enables him to explore this different, more violent version of masculinity, albeit only for a few seconds, he is also clearly positioning himself as different from Alan and similar to Lee.

In the same way as Simon who, in the face of injustice, continues to reemphasise his own integrity in the conversation following the story about the Lego, Lee and Geoffrey continue to contrast their own actions with those of other children, suggesting a need for further confirmation and reassurance that their own evaluative position is indeed justified. It may be that they are talking about aspects of themselves which do not fit easily into the dominant conceptions of masculinity expressed by boys like Martie, Darren and Terry. Interestingly, Lee and Geoffrey present their kindness and nurturing as a way of solving a problem, that is, saving baby birds from certain death. Different from Richie Binns and Alan Horton, they also distance themselves from Ellie, who 'loves birds' but won't be able to keep them alive. Lee and Geoffrey's nurturing is practical and knowledgeable: birds are identified as willow warblers, nests are replaced, and chicks are fed with bread and worms. In this sense, their talk contrasts with the *Ah, isn't it sweet* discourse of some of the girls, which I discussed in Chapter 5.

Both pairs of friends (Sam and Simon and Lee and Geoffrey) are expressing beleaguered evaluative positions, as it were. In the example in Table 6.3, both boys believe Simon has been unjustly blamed but he is still grounded and in Tables 6.5–6.7 Lee and Geoffrey both want to help baby birds but complain about other children who knock down nests and smash eggs. There is a slight lack of confidence in the children's presentation of themselves, expressed through the deflection of responsibility for defending their position on to others, repeated expression of alignments with each other and repeated contrasts with other children. Lee and Geoffrey, in the high value they place on nurturing and caring for small vulnerable creatures, may be presenting a less symbolically dominant kind of masculinity and therefore need to do more discursive work in order to back up their position. Excessive justifications, comparisons and contrasts suggest some kind of 'identity trouble'.

Divided loyalties

In addition to sometimes having to defend their own viewpoint against those of (often more powerful) others, children also sometimes found themselves in a difficult moral position when they became caught between two opposing camps. This might occur, for example, in a fall-out between friends where a third friend is pressured to take sides. The most powerful stories about competing loyalties that children told me, however, were about conflict between parents and their own role within the family dynamics. As in many of the stories more generally, the child narrators portrayed themselves as exercising a considerable amount of personal agency, in this case often mediating between parents and having the power to avert disastrous outcomes. In the final two examples in this chapter, I examine how children try to make sense of their parents' behaviour, articulating and exploring their parents' conflict and their own evaluative position through the representation of voices in their stories and through the dialogic relationships across different levels of narrative meaning.

Selling Tiny

In my interview with Karen and her friend Helen, Karen had been telling me about all the animals she used to have at home, 'three different houses ago', as she put it. At various times, she explained, the family had kept parrots, cockatiels, budgies, ferrets, rabbits, cats, hamsters, guinea-pigs and thirty-six dogs. Karen explained that they moved house because her parents split up and divorced, but then got back together again, although they had not legally re-married. The conversation moved back to the family pets, and I asked Karen if both her parents liked animals.

Table 6.8

Janet	Are they both keen on animals?
Karen	Well my dad isn't that keen, my mum is. We used to have this little dog like this called Tiny and my dad sold her. Well we were going to try and get rid of some of our dogs, one day a man come and he said, he *(dad)* was showing him all the other dogs and he didn't show him Tiny and he goes, 'Who lives in that kennel there?' and he *(dad)* goes, 'Oh, that's my wife's dog, Tiny' and he took one look at her and he said, 'I'll have her, yes', he goes, 'I want her' and my dad goes, 'Er, alright'. So he sold it. Just before the man went I went into my house and I goes, 'Mum, Dad's sold Tiny!' and she just burst into tears and so I come running up going, 'Dad, if you sell Tiny Mum will never talk to you ever again!' He goes, 'Sorry, you can't sell *(buy)* that' and I took off, rushed into the house with Tiny and my mum just, her face, she was crying her eyes out, as soon as she saw her, she goes, 'Give me her here now!' and when he come in she goes, 'You horrible thing, I never, told you I'd never sell Tiny as long as I live!' And then
Helen	/As long as it's lived as well
Karen	And then my dad let one of the dogs out, well he let Tiny out and he thought this other dog would be playful with her, and she killed it.

I first analysed this as one story with two possible different resolutions, either at 'So he sold it.' or at 'You horrible thing, I never, told you I'd never sell Tiny as long as I live!' I finally came to the conclusion, however, that in terms of narrative structure Karen actually provides two linked stories. At the beginning, her use of 'this' signals a switch away from the here and now of the interview to focus on the context of the story about the dog, and her phrase 'like this' was accompanied by holding up her hands to show just how small Tiny actually was, bringing a sense of the little animal physically into the room. Karen had just explained to me about her family's large number of dogs, so she passes quickly over the orientating section of the story into the complication, expressed through directly reported voices representing a man who wants to buy Tiny and Karen's dad's final agreement. The resolution to this first narrative is 'So he sold it'. However, there is then a new orientation 'Just before the man went I went into my house' with complicating action again presented through directly reported speech. The drama is intensified through the build-up of emotive verbs (burst into tears, running, took off, rushed, crying) and the accumulation of clauses 'my mum just, her face, she was crying her eyes out, as soon as she saw her, she goes' which increases the suspense by delaying the point where Karen's mother finally realises that Tiny has not been sold. Her mother's final comment 'You horrible thing, I never, told you I'd never sell Tiny as long as I live!' conveys the intensity of her attachment to Tiny and also something of her feelings towards her husband.

The narrative comprising the first half of the story, about Karen's father's interaction with the dog-buyer, is told rapidly in a fairly flat tone with slightly gruff voices for the men. From the point where Karen rushes into the house to tell her mother what is happening, however, the characters' voices become more and more dramatic and agitated on the tape. The hysterical, tearful voice Karen creates for her mother contrasts with her father's gruff, matter of fact voice earlier. Karen's construction of these voices is central to her portrayal of her mother's devastation at the sale of Tiny, and her father's thoughtlessness. However, the way in which Karen creates her mother's voice, with the exaggerated anguish which comes through clearly on the tape, conveys a slight distance between her own evaluation of events and her mother's. The listener hears, behind Karen's mother's hysteria, Karen the narrator sympathising, but slightly detached. After all, in the story Karen's father does not initially show Tiny to the dog-buyer and it is only when he is put on the spot that he agrees to sell the dog. Immediately Karen explains her mother's feelings, her father revokes the sale. And, in the brief sequel prompted by Helen, Karen's father appears to be responsible for Tiny's subsequent death through ignorance rather than intention: 'he thought this other dog would be playful with her'. We can understand Karen's mother's point of view, but the clear double-voicing suggests that Karen is not unreservedly aligning herself with her mother but also seems to be suggesting that her father is not entirely blameworthy.

Because of where it occurs in the conversation, this story can be read at a number of different levels. In answer to my immediate question, it demonstrates that Karen's Dad is less keen on animals than her mother. He is prepared to sell his wife's dog to the man and 'so he sold it' provides an apparent resolution to the first story. Then, in the second story her father's lack of personal feeling for the animals is contrasted with her mother's emotional attachment to Tiny. But these two linked stories are also about the relationship between Karen's parents and Karen's role in the family, explored through the 'Tiny' incident. The voices which Karen creates for her parents and the words she puts into their mouths are therefore not just a device for increasing dramatic involvement and conveying their different approach to the animals, but are also vital to a second evaluative function. Taking on her father's voice and then her mother's provides a way for Karen to explore, albeit briefly, her father's perspective and her mother's feelings, as well as commenting on them through the way in which she presents the voices. The story thus links back with comments she made earlier in the interview about her parents' divorce and subsequent reconciliation and on this level it is about the misunderstandings and dynamics of her parents' relationship.

In relation to this issue the evaluation is more uncertain. Is her father stupid, uncaring, or malicious? Is Karen's mother badly treated by her father, or unreasonably hysterical? The ending of Karen's second linked story is also ambivalent, resolving Tiny's fate (for the moment) but also vividly conveying the emotional distance between her parents. Following the account about Tiny, Karen told another story about a dog aged fifteen that had survived three strokes but was badly injured falling from an upstairs window and had to be put down. She commented 'even my dad was crying that day', thus somewhat softening the impression of him in 'Selling Tiny'. Rather than providing a definitive evaluative comment on an event, I would suggest that Karen's story is just one of many conversational narratives through which she visits and revisits the puzzle of her parents' relationship and of their different evaluative perspectives, and explores her own role in the family. The story's function and meaning for Karen, and probably also for Helen, are related not just to its immediate context in the interview conversation with me, but also to other conversations and other contexts where Karen has told stories with a similar theme.

Michelle's father

The final example of story-telling in the interviews comes from Michelle, whose fantasy narratives about the dragon I discussed in Chapter 2. During their interview with me, Michelle and her friend Kim directly discussed a number of moral issues and personal injustices. They talked for some time about their teacher Mrs. Kilbride, who they believed did not like them and 'can be nasty sometimes' (Table 4.3). The conversation then moved on and Michelle related a number of stories about her father's behaviour and her own role in the troubled relationship between her parents. In the first extract below, she recounts one violent incident where her father's toughness and violence are portrayed mainly through his dialogue and the reactions of the neighbours who all, even the man who considers himself 'well hard', slink back into their houses. It is only Michelle herself who, in the story she tells, has the power to protect her mother.

Table 6.9 (a)

1	Janet	Why isn't she *(Michelle's mum)* allowed boyfriends?
	Michelle	He's jealous
	Kim	/*(laugh)*
	Michelle	/you know you can get men jealous but they're allowed to
5		go with someone else but if they find out their wife's got
		someone else and they've left (........). Cause my mum – she,
		she had some boyfriends and he, he caught her out once and
		he done her really badly, smashed all the pipes in her stomach
	Janet	What, what, your dad?
10	Michelle	Cause he can be nasty when he wants to *(brief anecdote about*
		her father's rudeness to a friend of her mother) We've got a massive
		telly in our front room and all furniture we've got new and it,
		my mum run out once cause he whacked the phone right
		round her face – she just run out the back, so did I cause I'm
15		more – I love my dad, I love them both but I'm close to my
		dad, but, if he lays a hand on her I'm on my mum's side, do
		you know what I mean? So I run out with her – and em, we –
		we sat down outside the front with Ann and all that *(laughs)*
		this man thought he was well hard, the other boys called him
20		out the house, he sat out there, and when my dad come out
		and he *(dad)* goes 'You try to stick up for my wife, I'll have you
		all on, you know, beat 'em all up' *(laughs)* and all the men
		walked in their house and shut the door. So my dad goes to my
		mum 'Right, see you later, I'm going to smash your telly' and
25		he pretended to smash that he goes 'I'll see you later I'm going
		to smash your furniture in half' *(laughs)*. And my mum was
		kind of going 'If you don't get in here I will do it' and all that.
		I said 'Mum, just go in there and I'll stay with ya' so I walked in
		there with them and he didn't touch her at all
30	Kim	He won't touch her with – if Michelle's there because
	Michelle	/Yes cause I'm his favourite
	Janet	What about your brothers, do they go to stay with him?
	Michelle	No, just me, Winston said 'I'm not staying with that old "B"!'
		(laughter) But I like, I'm closest to my dad, like all girls mostly
35		are, cause my mum's closer to her dad. *(Michelle continues with*
		a story about her mother's concern for Michelle's grandfather, who is
		now old and sick).

There are cohesive ties here back to previous topics in the conversation, for example the phrase 'Cause he can be nasty when he wants to' (line 10), which serves both as an abstract and an evaluative comment, echoes the discussion of Mrs. Kilbride in Table 4.3 'she can be nasty sometimes'. After the orientation 'We've got a massive telly in our front room and all furniture we've got new' there is a lengthy complication leading to the final resolution 'so I walked in there with them and he didn't touch her at all'. As often happened with the other friendship pairs, Kim supports Michelle's perspective and warrants both her account, and the evaluation: 'He won't touch her with – if Michelle's there because' which Michelle completes: 'Yes cause I'm his favourite'. Stories told by friends are just as important a site for the exploration of values and perspectives as stories told by oneself, and they are also an opportunity for the reaffirmation of the friendship through confirming that the friends hold and express similar evaluative perspectives (like Kieran and Kevin, and Sam and Simon), and are jointly communicating these to me.

In Michelle's story, the danger and violence of the situation are given impact and immediacy through the voices she creates for her parents. Her father's three utterances; 'You try to stick up for my wife, I'll have you all on' (lines 21–22), 'Right, see you later, I'm going to smash your telly' (line 24) and 'I'll see you later I'm going to smash your furniture in half' (lines 25–26) and her mother's angry 'If you don't get in here I will do it' (27) build up the tension and suspense to make Michelle's own successful intervention all the more remarkable. The incident is strongly coloured by male violence, from Michelle's father, the neighbour who thinks he is 'well hard', and the boys who call him out, perhaps hoping for a fight. Michelle's mum is also angry, but the force of her speech is mitigated by 'kind of' (line 27). In spite of her father's violence, Michelle states twice that she is closer to him than to her mother (lines 15 and 34), and her description of how all the neighbourhood men are frightened of him suggests a certain pride. In the next extract, however, when Michelle talks further about her father's violence and explains her mother's response to the doctor's suggestion that she should take her husband to court, she aligns herself more closely with her mother.

Table 6.9 (b)

Janet	So why does why do you think your dad – em goes for your mum – he just loses his temper?
Michelle	Yea, she gets
Kim	/Yea because I suppose he gets jealous, really
Michelle	Cause he said to my mum 'It's alright me having girlfriends but you're not going to have no one in your life
Kim	/(laugh)
Michelle	/except for me' and all that sort of thing
Kim	(laugh)
Michelle	and once when she really got mad with him she said 'I want a divorce' and he, he he done his nut, he said 'I'm not divorcing you!' and he got hold of her hair and he whacked her right on the fence and the pavement and everything and she'd been getting pains in her stomach where he'd kicked her and in her head she kept going to the doctor's. But my dad can get nicked cause the doctor see all the bruises over her and he says 'Who's done this?' and he found out and it's on his records, you know they keep records, so he retyped it out again, she goes to the doctor's about crying all day with the bruises. He said that we'll go and get him done and she said 'Don't, don't' cause when he comes out here she doesn't want to do him any more cause she's really scared of him
Janet	So have you ever talked to your dad about em – that you don't like what he does to your mum?
Michelle	*(Pause)* My mum says best not to, cause he might come round and say 'You've been getting at MY daughter to make me not touch you' but he said from now on he won't lay a hand on her, but that's a lie my mum said.

Kim's first turn above 'I suppose he gets jealous' is both part of a duetted response to my question and also a confirmation of Michelle's comment earlier: '… you know you can get men jealous'. Kim is also responding to this earlier comment and, through this, supporting and authenticating Michelle's explanation. Within Michelle's two linked stories above, about her father attacking her mum and her mum going to the doctor, the action and characters are again represented mainly through dialogue – Michelle's father's voice, her mother's and the doctor's. As in Karlie's reference to her father and Simon's to Mr. Perry, Michelle uses an authoritative voice to warrant an evaluative position, in this case the doctor's view of the seriousness and the reprehensibility of Michelle's Dad's behaviour. Although the doctor's authority is backed up by institutional written practices: 'it's on his records, you know they keep records, so he retyped it out again', Michelle is fully aware of the limitations of the power of officialdom and the complexities of the situation from her mother's point of view.

Towards the end of Michelle's long turn, she moves from direct reporting of her mother's speech 'Don't don't', into a short stretch of discourse which is grammatically her own voice as narrator, but which is strongly coloured emotionally by her mother's voice. This is even clearer in the oral recording, where Michelle's voice tone echoes her mother's fear. In the comment 'cause when he comes out here she doesn't want to do him any more cause she's really scared of him' we can hear both Michelle's voice and her mother's, simultaneously. The lack of a directly connected reporting clause, the use of third person pronoun for the speaker ('she' for Michelle's mother), proximal deictics as in direct discourse ('here'), and modality markers which emanate from her mother ('doesn't want to do him'), mark this as free indirect speech.[8]

Although Michelle has explicitly said a number of times that she is closer to her dad, and she admires his power and toughness, her own narrating voice in the stories is generally aligned with her mother: 'you know you can get men jealous but they're allowed to go with someone else but if they find out their wife's got someone else', 'he can be nasty when he wants to, I'm closest to my dad, like all girls mostly are, cause my mum's closer to her dad'. Orientation to social institutions like the doctor and prison is also presented from her mother's point of view. We can in fact see these switches in focalisation happening throughout the account above, not just in the example of free indirect speech above but also through Michelle's reproduction of her parents' voices, with their two conflicting perspectives which are finally set directly next to each other in the reported speech at the close of the account: 'but he said from now on he won't lay a hand on her, but that's a lie, my mum said'. The contradiction between Michelle's statements about her closeness to her father and her focal alignment with her mother reflects the dilemma of loving both of two warring parents, whose relationship is colouring Michelle's negotiation of her own gendered identity as she moves from childhood into adolescence. While Michelle seems to position herself with her mother, she portrays herself as more powerful than her and manages to express attachment to her father and admiration of his strength without condoning his behaviour.

Conclusion

These stories do not present finished, polished selves, or fixed, final, evaluative positions. Rather, they are often constructed around conflicting perspectives and there is sometimes uncertainty about whether these have been resolved. Through presenting themselves and their experience within these stories, the children are exploring different perspectives around moral issues: how it might be 'the right thing' to conceal a teenage pregnancy, when violence can be justified and celebrated, the injustice of some adult punishments, different ways of responding to helpless and vulnerable creatures, how to deal with and understand parental discord and violence. While Nicole and Terry convey fairly consistent moral positions (which still need to be discursively justified), evaluation is more troubled within the stories about the Lego and the birds' eggs, where children repeatedly mirror their friend and contrast their own behaviour with that of others. In the story about the Lego, Simon's parents believe he deserves punishment, while Sam and the head teacher think the other boy was more to blame, and in the stories about the stray cat and the fallen bird's nest, Lee and Geoffrey contrast their own gentle behaviour with Richie Binns' and Alan Horton's destructiveness and Ellie's deadly love. Defining their own moral position can be particularly difficult for children caught between two warring parents. Karen sympathises with her mother to a certain extent but doesn't wholly condemn her father's behaviour and Michelle seems to be torn between her love and admiration for her father on the one side and her recognition that what he does is wrong and her sympathy for her mother, on the other.

In most cases I have provided parts of the conversation surrounding a story, because its evaluative function can only begin to be fully appreciated in terms of the dialogic links made in the story with voices and themes before and after. Karlie's father's approving comment about Terri's concealing of her pregnancy provides a powerful evaluative framework for Nicole's story, and Simon refers back implicitly to the Lego story when he presents himself as a particular kind of person later in our conversation. Geoffrey and Lee echo each other's stories about gentleness to animals while exploring how this contrasts with other children's behaviour and Michelle's stories about her father's behaviour to her mother echo the unjust treatment she described from her teacher earlier in the interview. I've suggested that the lack of integration of Terry's fight story into the conversation may be due to its raw, somewhat incoherent and confusing structure, or to the lack of a close friendship between himself and Keith, or to a close rapport with myself. I have also examined how I myself, as interviewer, played a significant role in the co-construction of the stories and in their referential and evaluative functions.

In relation to the moral issues they explored, many narrators bring in authority figures to substantiate the evaluative message: Karlie's father, the police in Terry's story, Simon's head teacher, Lee and Geoffrey's mothers, Michelle's mother's doctor. The limits of authority are also acknowledged, however: Mr. Perry's jurisdiction does not extend out of school time and the doctor can help to convict Michelle's father, but not protect her mother after he comes out of prison. Institutional authority is also questioned: Terri would not have been allowed to have her baby, Simon is unjustly punished by his parents, and taking Michelle's father to court might mean worse injuries for her mother later. These children live in complex moral worlds, and dilemmas about the rights and wrongs of their own and other children's actions, and of adults' treatment of them and of each other, are puzzled over and lived with rather than finally resolved.

In both the interviews and in their own ongoing conversations, children's stories present and explore various aspects of their own emerging identities and agency, often through contrasting themselves with others. In the examples I have discussed, we can see children grappling with accounts of human relationships, moral issues about care and cruelty, and their own gendered identity. Stories explore the ambiguities and inconsistencies in adult behaviour and values, and the broader regulatory functions of various social institutions. Their toughness, their new gendered identities, their changing relations with adults, are all recurring themes which are explored collaboratively by children, so that the construction of the identity of a speaking subject is very much an ongoing, negotiated process. These 'long conversations', about the recurring questions in their lives, are carried on in different contexts across days and weeks as children return again and again to the themes which are important to them, revisiting the issues in different stories and exchanges and from different perspectives. Thus the recursive and iterative process of collaborative meaning-making between children is carried on at and between three different but interrelated dialogic levels: through the dialogues they reconstruct within the stories, through the conversational exchanges from which the stories emerge, and through the ongoing long conversations about themes of particular importance to them, as they move from childhood into adolescence within this particular cultural setting.

7
Schooled Voices

> Our practical everyday speech is full of other people's words:
> with some of them we completely merge our own voice,
> forgetting whose they are; others, which we take as author-
> itative, we use to reinforce our own words; still others,
> finally, we populate with our own aspirations, alien or
> hostile to them.
>
> (Bakhtin, 1984, p. 195)

Karlie: She did the best thing about it, though, didn't she, Nicole?
Nicole: She didn't tell a soul, no-one, that she was pregnant

In Chapter 4, I showed how children use directly and indirectly
reported voices to invoke and evaluate people, relationships and
events and in Chapters 5 and 6 I looked at how reported voices can
be animated within the dialogues in children's narratives. In this
chapter I now focus on another kind of voice reproduction in children's ongoing talk, where they take on a voice and reproduce it
almost as if it were their own. I suggested in Chapter 6 that Karlie
did this when she comments on Terri's concealment of her pregnancy 'She did the best thing about it' (see quotation above). Later,
after Nicole has told the story, Karlie repeats this view, prefacing it
with 'My dad said she did'. There is initially nothing to distinguish
Karlie's voice from her father's and the only reason we know she has
taken on his voice is because she tells us. On another occasion,
Linda similarly retrospectively acknowledges her appropriation of a
phrase from Mrs. Kilbride when Mr. Sinclair, who is covering the
class in Mrs. Kilbride's absence, asks her what the contour lines
mean on a map:

Table 7.1

Linda	It would tell you that there's hills
Mr S	Shh right ⌈ so
Linda	⌊ so you'd have to put your walking boots on
Mr S	Okay, so it's my walking boots
Linda	That's what Miss said! *(laughter)*.

This kind of explicit acknowledgement of a voice source is relatively rare. On other occasions, however, there is sometimes good evidence that children are appropriating a voice (that is, reproducing it as if it were their own) and I draw on both textual and ethnographic evidence in my discussion of the examples of appropriation later below. Finally there are times when it certainly sounds, from what I know of the child, as if they are appropriating someone else's voice, perhaps from outside school, but without more data this has to remain at the level of conjecture. The purpose of this chapter is to show how, through their reproduction of other people's voices, children are agents in their own socialisation.

A number of researchers have suggested that particular ways of reporting and appropriating other people's voices (sometimes termed 'discourse representation') are developed in different spheres of human activity as a central part of institutional practices, for instance, in news reporting, advertising , social work and academic study.[1] Learning to be a successful newspaper reporter, advertiser, social worker or student involves learning particular ways of reproducing other people's voices and one's relationship to them within the associated speech genre (and breaking generic rules can count as libel or plagiarism). As I discussed in Chapter Two, educational genres are associated with the valuing of academic knowledge encoded in textbooks and mediated through teacher-student relationships and fairly tightly structured dialogue. One of the ways in which children induct themselves into educational genres is through taking on the voices of teachers and textbooks, and reproducing these voices as if they were their own, either in teacher pupil dialogue or in talk among themselves. As Bakhtin points out, 'the ideological becoming of a human being ... is the process of selectively assimilating the words of others (Bakhtin, 1981, p. 134). The associations a voice brings with it and the way in which its authority is used by a speaker contributes both to the speaker's positioning of themselves and others, and to referential and evaluative aspects of the meaning-making, in the reporting context. When listeners are told that Karlie is reproducing her father's voice and Linda Mrs. Kilbride's, this adds another layer of meaning to what has been said.

In this chapter, I start by extending the account of reported voices which I began in Chapter 4. Like Leech and Short, Volosinov and Bakhtin are interested in the relationship between the reporting and reported voice in speech which is clearly marked as belonging to someone else. They are also interested in instances of imitation and stylisation where the boundaries between the reporting and reported voices are not so clear. In addition, and most importantly for my own focus on children's development, they see the evaluative perspectives represented by the voices, and the ways in which these are managed in the reporting context, as central to the meanings which are being produced. As with reported voices which are more clearly marked as separate from the speaker's own, there are various ways of managing imitated and stylised voices which are also highly significant for children's ongoing socialisation into institutions like schooling.

A framework for understanding reproduced voices

In Chapter 4, I described Leech and Short's continuum of literary reported speech forms, which range from a narrator's representation of a speech act where the author's voice has most authority over the reported speech, through indirectly reported speech, free indirect speech and directly reported speech to free direct speech, where the character's voice is most dominant. Whereas an author orchestrates voices in line with their particular literary vision and animates them through words and punctuation on the page, however, the voices which children invoke in talk as part of their ongoing social explorations and reflection are constructed partly through prosodic and nonverbal cues, and their significance is realised within the dynamics of ongoing dialogue and through the contextual links with other conversations and contexts. In addition, the voices children produce may represent quite powerful adult forces in their lives and managing all the connotations these voices invoke, and the ways in which they may be picked up by others in the ongoing conversation, is not always straightforward. I argued in Chapter 4 that in order to understand the meanings of reported voices in the children's ongoing talk, we need to look at a combination of grammatical, prosodic and non-verbal, dialogic and contextual cues.

While Volosinov and Bakhtin, like Leech and Short, draw on literature in developing their analysis of reported speech, their goal is an overarching social theory of language rooted in the communicative practices of everyday life. They acknowledge the importance of grammatical expression, but this is only part of the story for them and other aspects of oral language, like intonation, are also highly significant. Volosinov and Bakhtin's central interest is in the relationship between the evaluative perspectives of the reporting and reported voices, and how this is managed and resolved within the reporting context. Reproduced speech contains the intentions of the original speaker together with the intentions of the speaker doing the reporting. Volosinov (1986) suggests that in *linear* reporting the voices are clearly separated, in contrast to *pictorial* reporting, where the reported speech is infiltrated by the reporting voice. The reporting mode is linked both to the nature of the voice being reported (authoritative voices tend to be reported in the linear style) and to prevailing ideological practices within a society (the linear style being associated with authoritarianism). In his study of Dostoevsky's novels, Bakhtin developed a more detailed classification of the various ways in which other voices can be represented by a speaker, ranging from clear reporting to more subtle double-voicing, where the reporting and reported voice are not so grammatically distinct. Bakhtin distinguishes between *uni-directional* double-voicing where the evaluative perspectives of the two voices are consistent (as in the case of Karlie and her father's comment on Terri's secret pregnancy) and *vari-directional* double-voicing where they are in opposition (for example in Miss Potts' imitation of the children's whining voices 'What do we do with our work?' in Table 2.5).

In order to categorise the significant kinds of linear and pictorial reporting in my data, I have drawn on Bakhtin's classification from his work on Dostoevsky.[2] Although Bakhtin spends less time on what he calls 'imitation', where a speaker merges their voice with someone else's, this turned out to be an important category within the school context. Children often repeated other people's voices, especially the teacher's, in the course of teacher-pupil dialogue, and at other times they reproduced a voice which they seemed to have taken on completely (appropriated) from someone else, or from a written text, for their own purposes. I have therefore divided imitation into 'repetition' and 'appropriation' (see below).

Different kinds of voice reproduction within the children's talk

(a) *Reporting* which, as we saw in Chapter 4, can take a direct or indirect form, giving varying amounts of prominence to the reported voice. In oral discourse speakers report something close (or not so close) to what a speaker said, in a way which fits in with their current conversational purposes. For example, when Simon quotes his head teacher 'Mr. Perry goes, em he should have been punished as well' (Table 6.3), Simon may not be quoting Mr. Perry's exact words but the phrase clearly conveys Mr. Perry's moral perspective. This reported perspective, together with Mr. Perry's authority, is used by Simon to justify his own position.

(b) *Repetition*; as we saw in Chapter 3, this is a ubiquitous feature of informal talk among friends and plays an important role in conversational coherence and in the collaborative production of meaning and relationship. The echoing of something another speaker has said has particular significance in more formally structured, asymmetrical teacher-student dialogue, as I shall discuss in more detail below.

(c) *Appropriation*, where the speaker does not simply repeat someone else but takes on the given words and makes them their own, to suit their own communicative goals. Karlie reproduces her father's words 'She did the best thing about it' and his evaluative position, but within a new context for her own intentions. Appropriation involves a merging of the child's own voice with another and was a common way in which children took on and reproduced authoritative perspectives for their own purposes.

(d) *Stylisation*, where a voice is reproduced as if it were one's own but with 'a slight shadow of objectification' (Bakhtin, 1984, p. 189). Often this is conveyed through some kind of stylistic change to signal that another voice is involved, for example a child may use a louder and more adamant tone to reproduce a teacher's instruction: 'You have to write the date'. Stylisation may be unidirectional, where the evaluative positions of the speaker and the person whose voice is being stylised are aligned (as when Melissa imitates a teacher's voice to Kieran in Table 4.8), or vari-directional when they are in opposition, as when Geoffrey ironically reproduces giving a love bite on an arm (Table 4.9). The mimicked voice not only marks what is said as reported speech, but also makes the speaker's own perspective on the reproduced voice very clear.

Bakhtin stresses that in the flow of communication such categories are overlapping and dynamic. He suggests that there is a tendency in repetition, appropriation and uni-directional stylisation to bring two voices together into one, while the tension between opposing positions in vari-directional styling (parody or irony) tends to drive the voices apart. These two contrasting tendencies produce two different kinds of statements of identity: in the first, the child is acknowledging and in some way taking on the source of authority and the evaluative perspective of the voice they are reproducing, while in the second they are defining themselves against the voice and what it stands for.

I will focus below on three sites of voice reproduction: patterns of repetition in teacher-pupil dialogue, informal peer talk and children's discreet frame switches between work and play in the classroom.

Repetition and appropriation in teacher-pupil dialogue

The more formal teacher-pupil dialogues in my data are usually tightly structured and heavily controlled by the teacher, so that the very act of taking part in them appears to express acceptance of the discursive positioning they offer, compliance with the institutional authority they encode, and commitment to the ways of talking about procedures and knowledge which the teacher is modelling.[3] Whether they are concerned with classroom management or curriculum content, these kinds of dialogues essentially entail children repeating and appropriating the teacher's voice and thus expressing commitment to her evaluative perspective. The teacher, in her turn, also picks up and rephrases what children say, as I shall discuss below. Particular token words or phrases are passed backwards and forwards across the dialogue, as pupils repeat teacher utterances, and the teacher repeats or reformulates pupil offerings.

For instance, this happens in Miss Potts' harangue about the mess in the classroom discussed in Chapter 2 (Table 2.5), where pupils were prompted to produce the phrase 'not listening' which their teacher had used many times before. Notice also how they take on her phrase 'cooperate'. In the tables below I underline words which are repeated from an utterance earlier within the table. I use broken underlining where I can identify a phrase repeated from dialogue on a previous occasion.

Table 7.2

Miss P.	What are your parents going to think, coming into a mess like this? Well they're not coming into a mess like this. Tough. You sit there and I'll clear up. And when I've finished, you can go home. OK?
Some pupils	*(uncertain)* ⎡ yea ⎣ no
	(pause while T moves round room)
Miss P.	Or are you going to cooperate?
Pupils	*(a few girls' voices)* <u>Cooperate</u>
Miss P.	I think about ten people in this room are doing clearing up. I said at the beginning that I wanted all of this work first of all put over the back. I've had five people come to me *(mimics whining voice)* 'What do we do with our work?' Which proves what?
More ps	Not listening
Pupil	<u>Not listening</u>
Miss P.	You just don't bother to <u>listen</u>. There's buckets and things all over the place, mess around, floor's a disgrace. Now there is FIVE minutes and you're not going because you've got trays out. I suggest that you get cleaned up NOW. Anybody messing around will be in trouble.

In these kinds of dialogues, the children fill in the slots left by their teacher, cued both by current discursive clues and through remembering similar exchanges in the past. In a similar way to Miss Potts' cue 'Which proves what?' Mrs. Kilbride cues her class to reproduce the instruction she had given a number of times before, to 'do something else' if the table for a particular curricular activity is already full:

Table 7.3

Mrs K.	Say that you wanted to do maths and you suddenly saw that the maths base was full. What should you do? Martie?
Martie	Do something else
Mrs K.	Do something else. And sit in a base that isn't full.

Within these strongly asymmetrical dialogues, with their very unequal distribution of speaking rights, the taking on of the teacher's voice by pupils and the taking on of pupil voices, by the teacher, accomplish rather different purposes. The children's repetition of the teacher phrases like 'co-operate', 'not listening' or 'do something else', either from the current conversation or from a previous occasion, expresses commitment (at least at the discursive level) to her evaluative perspective and to institutional roles and procedures. While some children merely go through the motions of repetition as a ritualised verbal routine, this compliance is still an important part of the production of classroom discourse because it is part of their institutional and intellectual disciplining.[4] On the teachers' side, Mrs. Kilbride's repetition of Martie's 'Do something else' signals its acceptance within the dominant genre, as does Miss Potts' reformulation of 'not listening' into 'You just don't bother to listen'. (On other occasions, repetition by the teacher of a pupil suggestion with a questioning intonation, or the repetition by the teacher, after a pupil response, of her previous question, clearly signalled her lack of acceptance of the pupil's contribution). While Miss Potts has the right in teacher-student dialogue to parody children's voices in 'What do we do with our work?' children's parodies of teacher-voices occur only in their private talk together. As in informal talk among friends (see Chapter 3), patterns of repetition in teacher-pupil dialogue help to produce coherence in topic development and interpersonal involvement at the level of individual interactions. In addition, the pattern of voice reproduction which signals commitment by the pupils on the one hand and acceptance by the teacher on the other, reflects and instantiates the asymmetrical teaching-learning relationship which underpins classroom life. In the examples above, the words 'cooperate' and 'listen' are passed back and forth between Miss Potts and her pupils in the same way as 'do something else' is passed between Mrs. Kilbride and Martie, as part of the dialogic construction of roles and practices.

The pattern of cued response and repetition I have described above is also found where children are being inducted into the genres of school subjects. For example, when the teacher is introducing and explaining a concept or procedure using a scaffolding type question and answer sequence (Edwards and Mercer, 1986), children frequently repeat the teacher's words or respond to heavily cued elicitations. In the example below, Miss Potts is endeavouring to simultaneously teach a procedure (how to write out a sum of money in a restaurant bill) with a related conceptual point (that twenty three in this context is not a whole number, but a percentage of a pound).

Table 7.4

1	Miss P.	Now twenty three pence isn't a whole pound, so what number do we put in the pounds column?
	Pupils	None
	Miss P.	Nought. Notice I've left a big space. What am I going to put next?
5	Pupil 1	Point ⌈ two
	Pupil 2	⌊ The decimal point
	Miss P.	<u>The decimal point</u>. We're not going to put the numbers,
		just the decimal point that separates the pounds, and then
		we put ⌈ two, three
10	Pupils	⌊ <u>two, three</u>
	Miss P.	Twenty three pence is point two three of a pound
		So the plaice ⌈ costs one pound fifteen
	Julie	⌊ one pound fifteen.

In this example, the pupils' voices merge with Miss Potts' in line 10 to chorus 'two, three', and in line 13, when Miss Potts returns to an earlier part of the problem, Julie anticipates what she is going to say and murmurs 'one pound fifteen' a fraction before her teacher. Miss Potts reformulates 'none' (line 3) as 'nought' (line 4) and selects and repeats 'the decimal point' (line 7) as the answer she wants. In this particularly strongly controlled example of scaffolding, the dialogue, as in the two earlier examples above, seems to merge into one voice, Miss Potts' *we* which becomes 'I' only briefly in line 4 after the unsatisfactory pupil suggestion 'none' in line 3. While Miss Potts' voice consistently dominates, however, the inclusive indexical 'we' in Table 7.4 aligns the children alongside her in a shared learning experience, in contrast to her frequent use of 'I' and 'you' in Table 7.2, where she is criticising and scolding them.

Miss Potts' reformulation of 'none' as 'nought' exemplifies a recurring feature in teacher/student dialogue where teachers pick up on students' responses to their questions and appropriate and transform their words to shift these responses into schooled frames of reference and the genres of specific subject disciplines.[5] Elsewhere in my data, Mrs. Kilbride reformulates 'beach' as 'coastline' when discussing a map with pupils. Children then reproduce terms such as 'nought' or 'coastline' when talking to teachers, in the same way as they produce 'not listening' and 'do something else'. Finally, they may use the terms appropriately in spontaneous talk among themselves. There is a subtle point at which repetition becomes appropriation, where the child takes on the voice and the genre and can reproduce them on future occasions for their own purposes. One way in which children learn to speak and write the educational genres of mathematics, geography and other subjects is through the processes of repetition and appropriation within these sorts of teaching dialogues, and through similarly scaffolded interactions with written texts.

In Vygotskian terms, the taking on of the voice of a teacher, textbook or worksheet represents a stage between the original dialogue and the internalisation of educational dialogue, which children may use later to direct their actions in the classroom and to organise curriculum knowledge. These voices are also associated with particular relationships and activities and with the validating of particular ways of talking about the world so that children are both institutionally and generically trained through participation in classroom dialogue. When children internalise voices and dialogues, they are also internalising cultural and social aspects of the institutional order and in this sense 'The history of the process of the internalisation of social speech is also the history of the socialisation of children's practical intellect' (Vygotsky, 1978, p. 27). Even where children's responses appear to be part of a 'procedural display'[6] rather than a principled engagement, these procedures are still part of the disciplining process, becoming engrained within their subjectivities so they take up particular positions in relation to school knowledge, and reproduce it in particular ways.

The three examples above show teachers and pupils repeating, reformulating and preformulating each other's voices in relation to the educational genre of relatively formal teacher-pupil classroom dialogue with its encoded constructions of knowledge, procedures, and hierarchical relationships. In the next two examples, from more informal classroom activities, teachers and a parent helper are again attempting to shift pupils into disciplinary framed subject knowledge and ways of talking. Here, however, the patterns of repeated words and phrases would suggest that, in addition to the dominant frame, children are also orientating towards alternative ways of interpreting experience and constructing knowledge. In the first example, the struggle between Mrs. Kilbride and Martie reflects a conflict between two competing schemas or frames of reference. While the words 'sunlight', 'light', 'rain' and 'raindrops' echo and re-echo across the dialogue, 'sunlight' and 'rain' are used by Martie and Karen in the context of an orientation towards common sense and relatively unformalised everyday knowledge about rainbows, while Mrs. Kilbride's use of 'light' and 'raindrops' reflects a schooled body of formalised scientific knowledge about prisms and spectrums.

Table 7.5

1	Mrs. K.	Can you tell me how a rainbow is formed?
	Martie	Em er
	Mrs. K.	a a what two things do you need to make a spectrum?
	Martie	The rain and the su.. ⌜ light
5	Mrs. K.	⌞ No, no, what two things do you need to make a spectrum?
		What have I got in my hand here?
	Martie	A ⌜ prism
	Mrs. K.	⌞ <u>Prism</u>, and what's this going ⌜ to
10	Martie	⌞ A projector
	Mrs. K.	/Yea well what ⌜ does
	Martie	⌞ <u>Light</u>
	Karen	/<u>Sunlight</u>
	Mrs. K.	<u>Light</u>
15	Martie	<u>Light</u>
	Mrs. K.	Right, so when you see a <u>rainbow</u> in the sky, which is a spectrum in the sky, yes? (yes) How, what is the <u>light</u>? Where does the <u>light</u> come from?
	Martie	<u>Sunlight</u>
20	Karen	<u>Sunlight</u>
	Mrs. K.	And where do the <u>prisms</u>
	Martie	The rain
	Mrs. K.	The <u>rain</u>drops
	Martie	<u>Drops</u>
25	Karen	<u>The raindrops</u>
	Mrs. K.	So you get hundreds and hundreds of little <u>prisms</u> which are the rain ⌜ <u>drops</u> right
	Martie	⌞ Which creates this big
	Mrs. K.	And because they're not they all join together
30		⌜ to give
	Martie	⌞ To make <u>this big rainbow</u>
	Mrs. K.	To give <u>this big rainbow</u> cause you will not get a <u>rainbow</u> in the sky if it's just raining, and you won't get a <u>rainbow</u> in the sky if it's ⌜ just sunny
35	Martie	⌞ <u>Just sunny</u>.

Although this dialogue appears more choppy and disjointed than the earlier examples above, Mrs. Kilbride uses similar discursive moves as she tries to bring together the two different frameworks of knowledge (rain + sunshine = rainbow and prism + projector = spectrum). She heavily cues the children to complete slots in lines 7, 9, 17 and 21, she selects and confirms the correct answer in line 9 by repeating 'prism', and in line 14 by repeating 'light', and in line 23 reformulates Martie's 'rain' as 'raindrops'. On their side, the children repeat her and each other in line 15, 20, 24 and 25.

The contrasting referential frameworks invoked by teachers' and pupils' use of reported and repeated voices reflect their contrasting orientations towards everyday and schooled knowledge. While Table 7.5 shows Mrs. Kilbride endeavouring to help children to elaborate and refine everyday unformalised knowledge into schooled scientific explanation, the next example shows a contrast between different conceptions of what is involved in the practice of 'reading'. The repetition and circulation of tokens in the excerpt below ('teeth', 'tentacles', 'breathes through a hole', 'eyes') invoke different reading practices entailing contrasting ways of taking and using knowledge from a library book. Mrs. Reilly (a parent helper) is encouraging Julie, Kirsty and Sharon to consult the book in relation to a snail they have collected from a scavenging expedition in the school grounds. (Between lines 18 and 23 in the extract below Julie also has a parallel conversation with a pupil who is reading a puzzle magazine and I discuss this in the next chapter).

Table 7.6

1	Julie	I'll just write 'This was drawn by bla bla bla'
	Kirsty	It's got thousands of teeth *(reads)* 'Its long tongue is covered with thousands of tiny teeth.' He's got <u>thousands of teeth</u>!
	Julie	He has, he's got <u>thousands of teeth</u>, that tiny snail has
5	Sharon	Look at its trail!
		(Miss P. approaches the group)
	Julie	Miss it's got hundreds and, it's got thousands and <u>thousands of teeth</u>
	Kirsty	/On <u>its long tongue</u>
10	Miss P.	It's got what?
	Kirsty	<u>Thousands of teeth</u>. It says here
	Mrs. R.	Those are tentacles. It's got four <u>tentacles</u>
	Julie	Yea, <u>teeth</u>, <u>teeth</u>
	Mrs. R.	*(reads)* 'to touch, feel and smell, and it breathes through the hole
15		in its side.'
	Julie	<u>teeth</u>
	Mrs. R.	So there must be a <u>hole</u> somewhere
	Julie	'eat' *(a suggestion to the pupil with the puzzle magazine)*

Table 7.6 – *continued*

20	Mrs. R.	We saw its eyes, didn't we? At the end of its tentacles, and it can only see light and dark
	Julie	*(to puzzle magazine pupil)* 'tune'
	Pupil	It can only be three letters
	Julie	/*(reads)* 'or more', <u>three letters</u> or more
	Kirsty	Miss it's got a thousand, <u>thousands of teeth</u> on its <u>tongue</u>
25	Sharon	Yes cause we went into the library. Mrs. Reilly and Kirsty went into the library to look it up
	Miss P.	What's that, the snail?
	Sharon	Yea
	Pupil	Miss, where's the sellotape?
30	Sharon	And it breathes through its side
	Kirsty	It breathes ⌐ through its side
	Sharon	⌐ It's got this little <u>hole</u>
	Kirsty	/<u>It breathes</u> through <u>a hole in its side</u>
	Mrs. R.	Mrs. Smiley *(their language teacher)* would be interested in this
35	Miss P.	Where are its eyes, then?
	Kirsty	These little things are for feeling.

In this extract, the textual voice is reproduced and used in contrasting ways by Mrs. Reilly and the children. Mrs. Reilly illustrates an approach to reading which was characteristic of how the teachers in my recordings encouraged pupils to relate to science texts. She invokes the voice of the text to encourage the girls to use this as a frame for organising how to look at the snail – to reconstruct their experience of it in the light of information from the book about its teeth, tentacles, eyes and breathing mechanism. She links direct observation with information in the text; '"it breathes through the hole in its side" … so there must be a hole somewhere'; 'We saw its eyes, didn't we? … and it can only see light and dark'. For the girls, however, the ways in which they extract and exclaim over facts about the snail's teeth and breathing, and their duetting (lines 7–9) and floor-sharing (lines 31–33), are close to informal talk among peers and their informal uses of magazines and swap cards (see Chapter 8). For instance, it is difficult to say who is responsible for the wording and conceptual content of what Kirsty and Sharon are saying in lines 31–33, the library book, the parent helper or the children themselves. The children's reporting is more pictorial (Volosinov, 1986), as they weave words and phrases from the text into their own discourse, while Mrs. Reilly's appropriated phrase from the book 'It's got four tentacles' (line 12) is followed by direct linear reporting (lines 14–15) which acknowledges the authority of the book. For Mrs. Reilly, the referential framework of the textual voice is dominant, while for the children this is interpenetrated with their own social purposes. In this relatively informal teaching context, the adults and children's invoking and repeating of voices from each other and the text suggests a mixture of schooled and informal readings. As in the contrast between the reference points in everyday knowledge and in school science in Table 7.5, there is a hybrid mix in Table 7.6 of different kinds of formalised and unformalised knowledge, and different generic practices.

Reproducing authoritative voices: appropriation and styling

It was often difficult when looking at teacher-pupil dialogue to see where repetition ends and appropriation, where children invest a repeated voice more fully with their own semantic intention, begins. In children's more informal peer talk, however, there is much more evidence of students appropriating voices from teachers and worksheets and making them their own. They then use these appropriated voices to direct their own and other students' activities and behaviour. For instance, when Mr. Sinclair announced before reading a short story to the assembled school: 'You've got to concentrate a bit more than usual', Gary whispered to the boys sitting next to him who were fidgeting: 'Shh, we've got to concentrate!' And in the French class when Martie said to Gary 'Got to get this right, Gary', Gary replied using the words which their teacher had earlier addressed to himself: 'You don't have to get it exactly, just do your best'. Again, Linda rephrases Mrs. Kilbride's instruction 'Copy it out nice and neat' to Kieran: 'Kieran, if you've drawn your thing in your book, you're allowed to copy it out'. Similarly, Tracy reformulates a worksheet instruction:

Table 7.7

Tracy	*(reading)* 'Find Scout Hall again. It is in the grid square B two. What shape shows it on the map?'
Jodie	That it? No, no
Tracy	What shape? You've got to name the shape.

These appropriated voices index institutional procedures which are used to define meaning and procedures in a child's current activity. The children's own purposes are merged with the institutional purpose they index, their orientation towards the institutional perspective often signalled through the use of modal forms like 'got to', 'have to' and 'allowed to', which are either repeated from or added to the reproduced voice. Through their intertextual orientation to the authoritative voices of teachers and worksheets, Gary, Tracy and Linda are expressing a commitment to institutional authority, framed by the modal phrases which position themselves as obedient students. This is one of the ways in which children induct each other into institutional roles and procedures, through repeating or rephrasing instructions about how you should sit still and listen in assembly, evaluate your work, or interpret worksheet questions.

An authoritative voice may also be invoked to help a child to pursue their own interpersonal goals in relation to peers. For example, Julie appeals to the many teacher exhortations in the data about making sure work is carefully, neatly and fully completed and that children should not rush their work, in order to win an argument about who has finished their writing first. The term 'finished' and the phrase 'never took your time' index teacher voices from previous occasions, and the school ground rule that rushed work does not count as properly 'finished'.

Table 7.8

Julie	We've almost finished
Pupil	So have we
Julie	You ain't <u>finished</u>
Kirsty	Some people have already <u>finished</u>!
Sharon	Yea, look, they've <u>finished</u>!
Julie	*(To student Sharon has indicated)* What's that? You never took your time on yours!

While the appropriation of authoritative voices by Gary, Linda and Tracy explicitly index the dominant institutional perspective, this perspective is also implicitly invoked in the appropriation of authoritative voices to support peer-sociable[7] goals as in Julie's use of the term 'finished'. From a Foucauldian point of view, all these uses of authoritative voices are part of the more diffuse institutional processes, through which 'power reaches into the very grain of individuals, touches their bodies and inserts itself into their actions and attitudes, their discourses, learning processes and everyday lives' (Foucault, 1980, p. 39). Implicit orientation towards institutional perspectives, as well as the explicit invoking of procedures to guide action, confirms institutional practices and discourses.

However, there are also occasions when children directly challenge the authority of a particular voice. In these cases the imported voice is strongly framed, grammatically or prosodically, and clearly separated off from the child's own. For example, Melissa uses indirect reported speech to complain to Nicole that Mrs. Kilbride has given inconsistent instructions: 'First Miss tells us you've got to do a draft, right, then she tells us we've got to do it again on the same piece of paper'. And when Gary asks Mrs. Kilbride if he can explain about a computer program in a school assembly, Darren assumes an exaggeratedly bored sounding flat intonation to mutter a parody to Gary of what he predicts will be Mrs. Kilbride's response: 'Yea and you tell about how you define it, and then how you draw it and how you, how you write it and how you look at it and how how how you (...)' Thus Darren signals his own distance from the evaluative perspective of the (preformulated) appropriated voice and his lack of commitment to school literacy practices. Tape recordings of the explicitly double-voiced parody record Darren's exaggerated boredom simultaneously with his prevoicing of Mrs. Kilbride's instructions.

Framing work and play

As other researchers have found,[8] classroom life involves the management, on a number of different levels, of switches between 'work' and 'play'. In the classrooms where I collected my data, children spent large amounts of time on worksheet or teacher-initiated tasks, sitting alongside one or more friends engaged in the same activity. Getting the work done, sometimes collaboratively, was combined with a certain amount of discreet social activity among pupils while the teacher worked her way around the individuals who were asking for her help. One of the ways in which pupils transformed a 'doing work' frame into a more playful or peer-socially orientated frame, was through the introduction of other voices, for instance starting a 'he said, she said' kind of anecdote, or often, especially in the case of the girls, by singing snatches of popular songs together, *sotto voce*. As when Julie and Nicole sang together in the girls' toilet and talked about hair and boyfriends (Table 2.1), discreet or not so discreet singing together by girls in class invoked an alternative genre, with different possibilities for expressions of identity from those available within curriculum focussed talk around classroom activities. For instance Sherri, Tina and their friends often seemed to get intense shared pleasure as they joined in with each other in humming or singing popular songs alongside completing classroom tasks and presenting themselves, in other respects, as 'good pupils'. This singing did not appear to be intended as disruptive, but seemed rather a secretive shared enjoyment of a romantic genre. The kind of collective, emotional sociability which comes from involvement in popular music was in sharp contrast to the individualistic, competitive positioning of children in terms of their intellectual abilities, within educational genres. Of course being able to join in the singing and therefore displaying familiarity with the words could be a strong in-group marker, excluding those who were less knowledgeable. Discreet singing while they were working expressed Sherri and Tina's dual orientation, towards school achievement with its associated genre and identities on the one hand, and also towards a parallel world of popular culture, with alternative models of identity, preferred relationships and authoritative knowledge on the other.[9]

In addition to shared singing where children transformed work into pleasurable sociability, the stylisation of a particular word or phrase was also sometimes used to introduce a playful element into work, or to refocus back onto work from play. In the next example Kevin and Kieran use stylised words and phrases to 'play' while they are doing a classroom activity. They are both writing answers to a worksheet called 'Finding positions'. The worksheet shows a grid plan of a zoo with drawings of different animals and buildings in the various grid squares. It gives students a list of grid references (A1, E2 etc) to which they have to match features shown on the plan and then a list of animals and buildings for which they have to find the grid references. For most of the half hour during which they worked on this worksheet, Kieran took the lead and often voiced his answers aloud to help Kevin, who initially found it difficult to understand what he was meant to do. Towards the end of the session Kevin had become more confident. In the extract below Kieran stylises the word 'wolves' which is the answer required for one of the grid references, and Kevin attempts to extend this playful frame further a few minutes later.

Table 7.9

Kieran	Have you gone to the reptiles yet, A 1?	
Kevin	No, not yet	
	(pause)	
Kieran	*(voice conveying mock fear)* 'wolves'	Kieran playful stylisation
Kevin	Toilets, you end up at the toilets on E 2!	
	(pause)	
Kieran	Reptiles. Where's the reptiles?	
Kevin	Bottom corner	
Kieran	Oh yea, A 1. That done!	

Table 7.9 – *continued*

A few minutes later:		
Kieran	Done that. *(reading)* 'Where do you find the, where do you find them, a, shop.'	
Kevin	*(vocalising his own answer)* D 3	
Kieran	Find the shop	
Kevin	*(story voice)* 'The lions'. I'm writing 'You end up dead in the lions' cage' *(giggle)*	Kevin playful stylisation
Kieran	There ain't no lions	Kieran responds in work sheet frame
Kevin	Oh, oh yea, I done that *(puts on voice again)* 'end up dead in the lions' cage!' *(giggle)*	Kevin repeats stylisation
Kieran	You would be, there.	Kieran responds in 'real life' frame

The stylisations of 'wolves' and 'end up dead in the lions' cage' invoke a playful, humorous intertext of imaginary fierce animals for the pen and paper work of the boys' worksheet activity. Children often held a playful frame for a number of minutes alongside the business of getting their work done, dipping occasionally into play and then returning to the worksheet. Such playful frames are usually fleeting and fragile, as students need to be able to revert back to 'doing work' within a few seconds, if they see the teacher heading in their direction. In this case Kevin picks up on Kieran's stylisation of 'wolves' a few minutes earlier with his own more extended suggestion 'end up dead in the lions' cage'. Kieran, however, switches back to the task frame in his answer 'There ain't no lions', meaning that, although there is a drawing of lions on the zoo plan, they don't count as a correct answer to Kevin's worksheet question. Then, when Kevin repeats his stylisation, Kieran invokes what might be called a 'real life' frame 'You would be, there'. Kevin wants to play but Kieran reverts back to a 'doing the worksheet' and then a 'real life' frame, thus cutting short the development of the playful exchange which Kevin has attempted twice to initiate. In the boys' written work, which I later copied, they produced identical correct answers, each starting with the slightly unconventional wording 'End up with', but no written suggestion, on Kevin's part, that 'You end up dead in the lions' cage'.

While students often used intertextual references (invoking a voice from a different genre) to turn work into play, they could also be used in the opposite direction, to transform an informal exchange into work. Shortly after Mrs. Reilly had read from the library book about snails' teeth, eyes and tentacles and had tried to help Julie, Kirsty and Sharon to identify these on the snail they had collected (see Table 7.6), Julie and Kirsty were sitting chatting together while Julie drew the snail. It had by this time become something of a pet, nicknamed 'Sleepy' by the girls who took turns in looking after it. Abruptly, Kirsty commented on Julie's drawing:

Table 7.10

Kirsty	Is that meant to be a snail?
Julie	Yea
Kirsty	I can't see its *(slight emphasis)* tentacles.

I cannot say categorically that Julie recognised the word 'tentacles' as an intertextual reference, but there are frequent examples in the data of children importing an authoritative voice to help pursue peer-sociable goals (as in the example of 'finished', earlier above). Using the word 'tentacles' which invokes two authoritative voices (the library book and Mrs. Reilly), potentially gives considerable force to Kirsty's comment. It also brings with it generic connotations of the earlier interaction, when the parent helper encouraged the girls to examine the snail through the eyes of the library book, as it were, and to view it in terms of technical details about teeth, eyes and tentacles. This intertextual reference indexes a schooled genre which constructs what the snail is through the lens of an authoritative text. The 'looking after Sleepy' frame is transformed into the 'doing work for a school display' frame, which Kirsty uses to authorise her criticism of Julie's drawing. Speakers often use an appropriated voice to invoke a new frame within which they can be more powerfully positioned. Thus Kirsty, whose relationship with Julie was ambivalent and often competitive, uses an intertextual reference to attempt to undermine Julie's work. Alongside their interpersonal effects, transformed frames highlight different aspects of the participants' identities. Kevin attempts to foreground his identity as Kieran's playmate, rather than the identity of struggling student. And in importing the frame of the library book activity into a context where the girls are casually chatting, Kirsty highlights Julie's identity as a 'pupil' who therefore will have to answer to school criteria in the evaluation of her drawing. This strategic use of intertextual references is so apparently automatic in children's talk that the cognitive processing involved must happen at a relatively unconscious level, suggesting that the use of reproduced voices to make evaluative meanings is an integral part of these children's thought and language.

Conclusion

In all kinds of voice reproduction, the nature and authority of the voice, the content of what is reported and the associations which a voice brings with it are all central to meaning-making in the reporting context. So too is the management of the voice by children who may use a range of discursive strategies which I have categorised as reporting, repetition, appropriation and stylisation. Like researchers looking at other institutional contexts, I have found different patterns of voice reproduction which are closely connected with the production of institutional genres. The authoritative texts which tended to frame social behaviour and set reference points for what counts as worthwhile knowledge, within the classrooms I observed, are the teacher's voice and the authorised written text (textbook, library book or worksheet). In the more formally structured teacher-student dialogue, there was a kind of hierarchy of intertextual relationships with the written text at the top, the teachers in the middle and the children at the bottom. The teacher quoted, explained and took on the voice of written text (i.e. appropriating downwards), and repeated and rephrased student responses to shift students into school discourses (i.e. appropriating upwards). Students, on the other hand, tended to directly repeat key words or phrases from the teacher in class discussion, or to take on her voice as it were in filling in the gaps she created for student 'responses' in her explanatory and directing monologues. This repetition and entering into the teacher's voice by the children, and the selection and reformulation of pupil utterances by the teacher, reflects and confirms their asymmetric roles in relation to the production of school knowledge and procedures.

Through taking part in this kind of classroom discourse, children learn how to talk about school knowledge and how to be a student. On some occasions, in less formal teacher-pupil talk which falls somewhere between the genre of strongly controlled teacher-pupil dialogue and the more inwardly persuasive discourse of pupils' informal talk, patterns of repeated words and phrases suggest that the teacher and pupils are orientating towards different knowledge schemas, or different conceptions of activities like reading. In these cases, the patterns of repetition show a struggle between alternative points of reference, with teachers attempting to shift children into a framework of schooled genres and procedures.

In informal talk among themselves the pupils used a wider range of more pictorial reporting strategies, where the evaluative perspectives of the voices they take on are mingled in with their own purposes, which include the completion of classroom tasks and also the pursuing of private peer-sociable goals. They appropriated authoritative voices from teachers, textbooks and worksheets and used these to guide their own and other children's attention and activity. When children use appropriated voices in personal rivalries and arguments, these still reflect the speaker's orientation towards schooled sources of authority, which is often used to support a personal position. This institutional orientation also frequently underpins students' criticisms of individual teacher's actions, for example Melissa's complaint about Mrs. Kilbride's unclear instructions. Occasionally children contested a voice and its institutional provenance more directly, for example in Darren's parody of Mrs. Kilbride's instructions for producing work to display in assembly. In these cases children clearly (grammatically or prosodically) mark their distance from the evaluative perspective of the voice they are reproducing.

I have emphasised that the hierarchical patterning of intertextual referencing through voice reproduction is important in both academic and institutional disciplining. Referential, interpersonal and evaluative meanings are intertwined within children's talk, where appropriation and styling of authoritative voices serve to instantiate institutional practices, relationships and identities, as well as to scaffold students' engagement in classroom tasks and learning. Children also use voice appropriation and stylisation to switch between work and play and a switch in frame always opens up possibilities for a change in relationships and foregrounded aspects of identity. Children's use of voices is strategic and evaluative in terms of their own individual goals, and it also functions ideologically because the sources of authority invoked by children to pursue individual goals are embedded within the institutional practices and genres of schools and classrooms. Thus children become involved as active agents in the institutional forging of schooled knowledge and identities.

8
Official and Unofficial Literacies

> What it is to be a person, to be moral and to be human in specific cultural contexts is frequently signified by the kind of literacy practices in which a person is engaged.
>
> (Street, 1994, p. 141)

Our rules of our club

1 No smoking.
2 No useing and you must always use your manors.
3 No swearing.
4 No going off.
(...)

Why a chapter on literacy in a book about children's talk? First, a large amount of the talk I recorded was closely connected with written texts. The classroom lives of the children I studied revolved around reading and writing and their interactions with print were nearly always mediated through talk. Teachers set up how reading and writing tasks should be done through talk and children often negotiated these tasks through talk amongst themselves. Apart from the official curriculum, what might be termed unofficial literacy activities were also strongly infiltrated with oral language. Without in any way denying the importance of children's cognitive and technical skills in interpreting print and images and in producing their own texts, I was strongly struck by the very social nature of the development, application and assessment of these skills and by the important role of dialogue in assigning value and significance to various texts, official and unofficial, in different contexts throughout the school. Understanding what was going on in the talk I recorded, therefore, entailed understanding its role in the literacy activities which filled children's days and served to organise time and space in the classroom.

From two theoretical points of view, talk can be seen as an integral part of learning to read and write. From a Vygotskian perspective, dialogue around texts extends individual children's capacity to establish their meaning (in culturally shaped ways), beyond what the children could have managed on their own. Thus teachers 'scaffolded'[1] pupils' interactions with texts through talk, frequently quoting and mediating the voice of the text. It was also clear in my recordings that texts were being collaboratively interpreted in children's informal talk among themselves, although not through the initiation-response-feedback structures which typified teacher-pupil interactions. Talk is an important part of decoding texts, whether official or unofficial, helping to establish their meaning and significance, and how they should be read. Indeed, following Vygotsky's argument that intermental activity stimulates and feeds into individual development (Vygotsky, 1978), the interpretations of texts negotiated in children's talk may well be ahead of and leading their individual comprehension.[2]

My second theoretical justification for seeing talk as closely intertwined with literacy in the classroom comes from the ethnography of communication tradition[3] and its more recent reworking within New Literacy Studies.[4] Ethnographers of communication in the 1970s and 80s argued that reading and writing should be studied as culturally shaped communicative practices. This ethnographic approach to researching literacy emphasises the importance of talk around texts in establishing what texts mean in a particular cultural context and how they are used to achieve particular social purposes. Heath (1983) defined a *literacy event* as 'any action sequence, involving one or more persons, in which the production and/or comprehension of print plays a role'. Building on this work and broadening Heath's definition of literacy to include images and electronic texts as well as print, the more recent New Literacy Studies draws also on poststructuralist theorists, especially Foucault and Bourdieu, to highlight the ideological nature of literacy and the implicit values and beliefs which underpin the everyday use of texts.[5] Key analytic concepts in New Literacy Studies are *literacy event* (see above) and *literacy practice* which is a more abstract concept including both recurring patterns of activity and talk around texts and also the beliefs and values associated with them (Street, 1984). So, for instance, the talk connected with the school library book on snails in Chapter 7 could be seen as a literacy event. It is an observable, recordable activity. On the other hand, the ways in which teachers encourage pupils to use science texts as lenses through which to perceive and understand real world phenomena like snails (or rainbows) is a literacy practice. Literacy practices, with their inbuilt assumptions about textual sources for authoritative knowledge, shape literacy events and the relationships and identities which they entail. As with children's talk, their use of literacy signifies the kind of person they are, both through inducting them into particular kinds of cultural practices and knowledge, and through offering the opportunity for individual choice and acts of identification.

I started off examining the relationship between talk and literacy by focussing on literacy events in the data, looking at how the talk involved in these shaped how the reading and writing was done. However, as I moved away from the 'tableau' notion of context (see Chapter 1), towards a more dynamic, processual conception of children's meaning-making, I often found it difficult to precisely define the scope and boundaries of literacy events and began more and more to think in terms of literacy activities and to focus on what children did and said when producing, interpreting or referring to texts of different kinds. Children's literacy activities are underpinned by educational literacy practices, that is, beliefs and values about the authority and value of different kinds of texts in school and about how educational texts should be interpreted and produced.

Once I started looking at literacy in the classroom, I needed to find a way of conceptualising its central role in organising children's activity and in producing schooled knowledge. Bakhtin's conception of 'authoritative discourse', which transmits the knowledge of teachers, textbooks, the law, religion and so on captures some sense of the power of official texts in school, but does not address how this transmission actually works. To understand the strong institutional structuring of children's literacy practices in the classroom, I also draw on Foucault's ideas about the role of institutions like education to 'discipline' people into powerful macro level complexes of values, forms of knowledge and beliefs (discourses) which define how they should think and act. The literacy practices children learn in school are at the heart of their production as educated people, establishing the authority of particular bodies of formalised knowledge and producing children as particular kinds of readers and writers.[6] As I shall describe below, I found that the children's official literacy activities acted as an organising framework for managing and regulating time and space in the classroom, and constituted the main material resources and outcomes within interactions between teachers and pupils. In addition, official literacy practices exerted a powerful influence over children's unofficial activities, where literacy was also used to organise and regulate activities, relationships and knowledge.

I shall start by looking at the role of official literacy in organising classroom life, its close association with institutional power and the emphasis in talk around official literacy activities on procedure and product. In the second section, I focus on one extended example of Kevin and Kieran's work on a mathematics exercise, showing how, as in the talk around the book on snails (Table 7.6), there is a hybrid mixture of different kinds of activity going on. This includes interactions which might be dismissed as irrelevant or even disruptive to Kevin and Kieran's 'real work', but which are actually crucial to their moving from incompetence to competence and managing to complete the worksheet. I then look at unofficial literacy activities going on in the classroom, which are orientated towards non-school identities and knowledge and, finally, I examine the children's uses of writing for personal non-curriculum purposes, both inside and outside school, and at its different kind of regulating role here within family and peer relationships and the construction of self. There has been something of an ideological divide in research on literacy and education between those focussing on reading and writing in the classroom, who see children's non-school literacy practices as less relevant to academic learning and those researching children and adults' literacy outside the school, who often see classroom literacy as narrow and oppressive (Hull and Schultz, 2002). In this chapter I argue that 'classroom literacy' is a lot more hybrid than this opposition in the research literature would suggest. While life in the classrooms I recorded was dominated by official school literacy, children were also involved in a range of unofficial practices. In their ongoing classroom activity the authoritative discourse of schooling, with its official texts, practices, and schooled identities was interpenetrated by the more inwardly persuasive discourse of other parts of children's lives and experience, and their relationships and identities outside the curriculum.

Official literacy: power, procedure and product

While power is clearly continually exercised and negotiated in teacher-pupil talk, and in talk among pupils, for example where a speaker transforms a conversational frame to reposition themselves more advantageously (e.g. Tables 2.6, 3.7, 4.8, 7.10) school literacy crystallises powerful complexes of knowledge, activity and relationship particularly clearly, articulated through the use of textbooks and worksheets, and in children's productions of text. Foucault (1979, 1980) argues that education is an important institution for the production of what counts as 'truth' in a society and for identifying the legitimate ways of acquiring it. Children's engagement in classroom activity, for Foucault, fundamentally changes them as people, 'disciplining' them into particular kinds of behaviour, postures, beliefs and subjectivities. He suggests that disciplining in powerful institutions like education is done through allocating subjects to 'functional sites' designated according to a particular way of managing knowledge, time and activity within an institutional space. In their serialisation and segmentation of time, Foucault argues, institutions try to fill it up completely, so that there will be no opportunity for unaccountable or unofficial activity.

Thus, in Camdean there were different 'functional sites' (classrooms) for managing 'knowledge' (different curriculum subjects) and in Lakeside three separate 'functional sites' (tables) in the classroom were designated for work corresponding to each of three curriculum areas: mathematics, science and English and humanities. In each school the day was divided into working sessions which children spent using the appropriate textbook or worksheets, and these sessions accomplished the institutional serialisation and segmentation of time. There was no unaccountable time in the official schedule: children not working on allotted worksheet tasks were told they were 'wasting time' and teachers often admonished individuals about how little time they had left to get their work finished. This kind of surveillance was internalised by the children, who frequently checked their own progress against others: 'Are you still only on "Contours 1"? I've nearly finished "Contours 2"'. They also, in Lakeside, were responsible for keeping their own Activity Record Sheet, which was checked weekly by Mrs. Kilbride. In this kind of way, Foucault suggests, power becomes multi-circuited, rather than simply top-down: 'power reaches into the very grain of individuals, touches their bodies and inserts itself into their actions and attitudes, their discourses, learning processes and everyday lives' (Foucault, 1980, p. 39). We saw this same kind of internalisation of institutional power in children's reproduction of authoritative school voices as an evaluative reference point for peer-sociable activity, for instance in Simon's appeal to his head teacher's authority over the Lego money (Table 6.3) and Kirsty's use of the library book term 'tentacles' to criticise Julie's picture of the snail (Table 7.10).

Foucault argues that institutions also discipline subjects through controlling their use of objects or equipment and their movement. In Lakeside, where the children ostensibly had more choice in deciding which session in the day they wanted to spend on each of the three curriculum areas, their use of space and objects was in fact highly regulated. The worksheet activities managed pupils' movements by placing them in a particular area of the classroom and stipulating which other areas they could move into, for example the 'wet area' outside in the landing if an activity involved painting or sticking, or the 'quiet room' for an experiment with the overhead projector. Once Mrs. Kilbride knew which worksheet a pupil was working on she could quickly spot any unauthorised movement. Any additional movement by children around the class had to be justified in terms of locating and finding the tools and materials they needed: paper, rulers, scissors and so on. Enacting the reading and writing activities stipulated by the worksheets in line with school procedural conventions carried children through time and space in a way that enabled them to be controlled, ranked and classified (largely through the 'writing up' of their work) and also served to define and authenticate particular ways of 'reading', and particular ways of displaying knowledge through writing (Street and Street, 1991).

A large proportion of talk in the classroom, both between teacher and pupils and also among the pupils themselves, was about procedures: how to organise work, how to carry out activities and how to produce the piece of text that each worksheet demanded. Teachers laid emphasis on correct procedures, and the production of a satisfactory textual product. This quotation from Miss Potts was typical:

Miss P.   What we'll be looking at is not only that you've collected everything, but the people, the group who do the best display of work. So you need to write each heading on your piece of paper, you need to stick labels on by each thing, so we know what it is. We'd like to put some up on the wall.

Miss Potts' emphasis on labels and headings is reproduced within talk between the teacher and individual pupils around specific texts, where children are taught how to label the parts of a snail, or coastlines, or contour lines. Teachers also often shifted pupils towards the more literate uses of language which were associated with particular subject areas, modelling their use, together with how children should 'read' the worksheet, through talk. For instance, when Mrs. Kilbride looks with Karen at the 'Contours 1' worksheet, which shows a picture of two hills and then a representation of these in a map, she tells Karen that the contour lines show 'the height' (rather than, for instance 'how high the hills are'). She goes on: 'How do you let people know height is there? Now this is what this sheet is all about'. Of course the picture of the hills is also a way of showing height, but 'this is what this sheet is all about' identifies the particular frame or lens which Karen should use to extract knowledge from the text (by focussing on the meaning of the contour lines) and the 'correct' point of view from which the worksheet should be read and interpreted. The fixity of worksheet knowledge contrasts with the dynamic, processual knowledge-making in children's talk among themselves, which I have discussed in preceding chapters.

The children were often uncertain about how to interpret written instructions, even when they had no technical problems with decoding the actual words. Understanding the worksheets involved mastery of specific classroom routines and literacy conventions, so that pupils could interpret the contextualisation cues in the text correctly, for instance connecting 'height' with the precise measurements of contour lines rather than the general impression in the picture. Learning about how to interpret questions, and the procedures for getting things done, was part of inducting and disciplining the children into the schooled literacy practices which would shape how knowledge was acquired and valued. Seeing classroom literacy and the curriculum in terms of practices, rather than in terms of decontextualised skills and competencies, helps to explain why so much talk is focussed on what needs to be labelled, how to lay out your work and what kind of terms and phrasing to use, rather than on more intellectual ideas and conceptual content.

Hybrid practices

Overall, then, official literacy activities were closely integrated with the structuring of the school day and the organisation and management of children, and the talk they involved tended to focus on procedures and products, emphasising particular fixed meanings and formats. As we have seen in previous chapters, however, within the structure of officially allocated time and activity, children also found ways of pursuing alternative purposes and of transforming time and activity in different ways. Even when they were more or less wholly focussed on completing a classroom task, the children often used a mixture of official and unofficial activity in order to get the work done. When Kevin and Kieran tackled the worksheet which was listed on their Activity Record Sheet as 'Co-ordinates Stage 4 TB 17–19', for instance, their work involved three contrasting kinds of interaction and help. Although there was none of the kind of exploratory talk which has been seen as important for collaborative learning,[7] and only a few seconds of instruction from the teacher, they managed in the course of their work to complete the written answers more or less correctly, each moving from incompetence to competency in different ways.

Even before they started on the worksheet, Kevin and Kieran have to get help in order to locate the sheet itself, since there is no worksheet actually entitled 'Co-ordinates Stage 4 TB 17–19'. They are sitting at the mathematics table opposite two older girls Tina and Louise. The boys start by discussing whether they should do the 'Coordinates' or 'Probability' worksheets and then try to work out which of the various papers on the desk the Coordinates worksheet might be. In particular, they have a problem interpreting what '17–19' means.

Table 8.1 (a)

Kieran	*(Rustle of papers)* What were them? Coordinates or Probability? How come?
Kevin	Look in your worksheet and see what page we're at, again
Kieran	Yea alright, go and get your worksheet
	(10 secs)
Kevin	*(coming back)* 17 and 19
Mrs. K.	*(to whole class)* Anybody got a Light 2 sheet?
Kevin	No, we've got to do Probability
Kieran	Or Coordinates, we ain't done that yet
Louise	This is Coordinates
Kieran	That? No it ain't. *(to Tina)* Is that Coordinates?
Tina	What?
Kieran	Is that Coordinates?
Tina	Yea
Louise	Yea, that's 17 and 18, 17 and 18, 19 here *(points to page numbers)*
Kieran	What's that?
Tina	*(exasperated)* Coordinates! That one, that one and that one
Kevin	Put it on your worksheet, anyway, Kieran
Kieran	It only says 17 and 19
Louise	It says 17 TO 19
Tina	17 TO 19
Kieran	Oh
Tina	You silly wally!
Kieran	*(imitates in high voice)* You silly wally *(he and Kevin briefly laugh)*
Kevin	We don't need this *(pushing paper away)*
Kieran	I know
Tina	Yes you do!
Kevin	No we don't
Tina	What are you going to write it down on? Your head?
Kieran	Yep
Kevin	Paper.

The worksheet Kieran and Kevin need to find for 'Coordinates' consists of three photocopied pages from a text book with the heading 'Finding positions'. Although Kevin and Kieran are not particularly friendly with Tina and Louise, the girls constitute part of the group resources into which the two younger boys can tap for help. This help is unofficial; it is not 'scaffolding' where a teacher or more able peer gives clues or asks leading questions so a child can extend their understanding, and it is given in a fairly dismissive way ('You silly wally! ... What are you going to write it down on, your head?'). But the knowledge that 'Finding positions' is the Coordinates Worksheet, and that '17–19' means pages 17, 18 and 19 rather than just pages 17 and 19 is vital for the boys to even get started on the task. Although they accept this advice, they manage to deflect the way it is positioning them by parodying and reaccenting the phrase 'You silly wally', taking the sting out of the girls' scorn.

Now that they have located the correct worksheet, the boys are still at a loss as to how to interpret the instructions. As I explained in Chapter 7, 'Finding positions' shows a grid plan of a zoo together with a list of questions asking what can be found at various positions (grid references). Each square in the grid plan contains a picture or words indicating, for example, bushes in A3 and B3, tigers in C3, reptiles in 1A and wolves in H3. Kevin says: 'Don't know what we have to do. Ask Miss'. Kieran responds 'We have to try and write it. You have to make it a grid. How to get to all the things. Look'. And he starts reading from the worksheet: 'This is a plan of the zoo'. The two boys then try to work out the answer to the first question, which asks what they would find at the grid reference C3. The correct answer is 'tigers' but Kevin thinks the answer should also include the bushes which are in fact located in A3 and B3. At this point they attract Mrs. Kilbride's attention.

Table 8.1 (b)

Kevin	Tigers ..... and bushes. Do we have to write that down?
	(to Mrs. Kilbride) Is that how you do these?
Mrs K.	What's this?
Kieran	Coordinates.
Mrs. K.	Which, where, which way do columns go?
Kieran	Downwards
Kevin	Downwards
Mrs. K.	Or upwards. Yea, okay, vertically. Right
Kieran	/Yea

Table 8.1 (b) – *continued*

Mrs. K.	The rows, which way do the rows go?
Kieran	That way, Miss
Mrs. K.	Horizontally, right
Kieran	You have to, em, find these, Miss, got to
Mrs. K.	/Right so you
Kieran	/got to see through and you go and see through so you end up
	⌈ tigers and the bushes,
Kevin	⌊ tigers and the bushes, Miss
Mrs. K.	Well, no, what is actually in this, where is the, that's the C
Kieran	And there's the 3
Mrs. K.	And the 3. So it's where they join. Actually inside that square. Where they actually join. Cause this is B 3
Kieran	So this one is tigers
Mrs. K.	And this is A 3, so you just write 'tigers'. Yea?

Once she has checked what the boys are working on, Mrs. Kilbride starts by phrasing her 'help' in terms of scaffolding-type questions ('which way do columns go?', 'which way do the rows go?') and uses the opportunity to introduce the specialist labels 'column', 'vertical', 'row' and 'horizontal'. In the same way as she rephrased pupil contributions on other occasions ('beach' into 'coastline', 'none' into 'nought'), she adds 'or upwards' to the boys 'downwards', and then reformulates both of these within the more academic term 'vertically'. In appropriating and rephrasing Kevin and Kieran's suggestions, Mrs. Kilbride is shifting them into the schooled genre and more abstract, literate conventions. When it is clear that the boys are confused about how to interpret the positions (They seem to be focussing on what could be a mini-picture, i.e. tiger + bushes, running 'C3' together with 'A3' and 'B3'), Mrs. Kilbride stops questioning them and directly explains the convention that the reference A3 refers to what is 'actually inside that square', where a letter and a number 'join', so that it is only the tigers which are 'C3'. She instructs them to 'just write "tigers"'. In this way children learn to shift their attention from reading iconic representations of tigers, or hills, to reading the abstract conventions of grid references, and contour lines.

After a brief discussion about how to spell 'coordinates', and what the date is, the boys are finally set to go. Kieran appears to have understood Mrs. Kilbride's explanation but Kevin has not, and there is a third kind of 'help' within the boys' actual work on the 'coordinates' worksheet, which Kieran offers Kevin. First, he models aloud how to do the first question and Kevin checks out how he should record his answer:

Table 8.1 (c)

Kieran	Right, let's go. Got to go C 3, so we know what that is. We end up at tigers, we end up at tigers, yea?
Kevin	Draw the square?
Kieran	No, just write it. 'End up with the tigers in C 3'.

Although Kieran understands the question, and that you do not have to draw the square, he and Kevin use the phrase 'end up with' at the beginning of each of their written answers, rather than a more appropriate literate expression. They work their way through the worksheet, with Kieran modelling aloud what he is doing for each question and Kevin listening to Kieran and responding. For example, Kieran says 'To the shop, the shop is E4' and Kevin vocalises what he is going to write: 'End up at the shop'.

Kieran appears to have no problem in simultaneously completing and voicing his own answers while also monitoring Kevin's responses, which sometimes lag a question behind. For his part, Kevin listens to Kieran's modelling of the answer to a question he is just about to get to, while also occasionally receiving feedback on the question he is currently on. Towards the end of the session Kevin is beginning to work out the answers independently and is getting more confident. For instance, in Table 8.1 (d), he correctly identifies what is in E2, and volunteers help to Kieran who is looking for the reptiles (though not using grid references to do this). Kevin's vocalising of his own (correct) answer for E2 means Kieran can still monitor his work, and let him know if he has made a mistake.

Table 8.1 (d)

Kieran	Have you gone to the reptiles yet, A1?
Kevin	No, not yet
	(30 secs)
Kieran	*(funny voice)* 'wolves'
Kevin	Toilets, you end up at the toilets on E2!
	(60 secs)
Kieran	Reptiles. Where's the reptiles?
Kevin	Bottom corner
Kieran	Oh yea, A1. That done!

At the beginning of the lesson, the boys had both been uncertain about how to tackle the questions on the worksheet, and were even unsure about which worksheet was 'Coordinates Stage 4'. Three different kinds of help each played a vital role in their activity, involving contrasting kinds of relationships and different sorts of identity positionings. In Table 8.1 (a) the boys attempted to resist their positioning by Tina as 'silly wallys' and in Table 8.1 (b) they are firmly positioned as pupils through Mrs. Kilbride's scaffolding questions, her appropriation and rephrasing of the terms they use and her authoritative teacher's explanation. Kieran struggles to play a more active part in this exchange but Mrs. Kilbride has other pupils clamouring for her attention and has to set the boys up for their work as quickly as possible. Finally, Kieran supports Kevin, and may well be consolidating his own learning, through his ongoing commentary on what he's doing and his periodic corrections of Kevin. Although Kieran's close modelling of what Kevin has to do does not fit into the conventional notion of scaffolding talk, he does seem to offer Kevin a form of 'vicarious consciousness' until Kevin can tackle the worksheet questions independently.[8] 'Finding positions' certainly involves the application of individual skills, but these are learnt and exercised through a collection of different kinds of speech genres and frames: the teasing, insulting banter with Tina and Louise, the teacher-pupil exchange involving scaffolding and shifting of pupils into school genres and finally the more relaxed, drawn-out give and take of the informal modelling, checking and play within the talk between Kieran and Kevin.

On occasion, as I suggested in Chapter 3, collaborative accomplishments could also involve disagreement and social rivalry. The work following the scavenger hunt in Camdean, for instance, involved differences of opinion between Julie and Kirsty about how items should be categorised and displayed. Pupils had been given a list of items to find, including 'A leaf, Something beautiful, Something soft, Something smooth, A small creature (be very careful)'. As they walked around the school playing field, Julie, Kirsty and Sharon made fairly amicable choices about which of a number of possible objects best represented a given item:

Table 8.2

Julie	*(reading)* 'Something soft'. Grass is soft, clovers are soft *(Kirsty holds out some thistledown)*. That's beautiful! That's really soft!
Sharon	Put one in
Kirsty	Put a few in
Julie	Yea, just in case one or two gets away.

Back in the classroom, the girls needed to recheck that they had covered every item on the list. Julie and Kirsty disagree about which items should count as 'A leaf', 'Something smooth' and 'Something soft'. In the extract below, the argument between Julie and Kirsty pushes them to invoke the implicit ground rule that there should be one and only one object to represent each of the items:

Table 8.3

Julie	*(reads)* 'A leaf'. Take that leaf. It's beautiful. No, no, not that pink one
Kirsty	Yea
Julie	No, not the pink one. No, *(frantically)* not that one, that's for something else! I think – it might be for something else – yea, that WAS for something else, 'something smooth'
Kirsty	*(emphatically)* We've got a petal
Julie	Something smooth and something soft
Sharon	Something soft
Julie	And something smooth
Kirsty	*(impatiently)* Yea, but they're both the same, aren't they?
Julie	Oh yea, so they are *(gets up)* Right you look after Sleepy *(the snail collected as 'a small creature')'*. Don't shut the door on me – something smooth.

There is a struggle here not only for leadership between Julie and Kirsty but also between everyday experience where one object can have many different qualities, and the specific literacy convention, in this classroom activity, of focussing on just one quality in each object. The convention that if a petal is 'something soft', it cannot also count as 'something smooth' is counter-intuitive, since in the everyday world a petal can be both soft and smooth and a leaf can also be beautiful. The kind of labelling and classificatory conventions being collaboratively established, which are an important part of classroom literacy practices, emerge here out of disputation produced through peer-social rivalry.

This rivalry continues to affect how Julie, Kirsty and Sharon plan the organisation of their display. Julie starts by reading out the instruction which asked them to collect 'a small creature'.

The interpretation of the instruction 'a small creature' here depends not so much on some kind of category criteria (for example whether an insect can count as a 'creature'), but on the tussle for power between Julie and Kirsty. On this occasion, when Sharon sides with Julie, Kirsty concedes, but suggests gluing Sleepy on to the page.

Table 8.4

Julie	Ah look *(reads)* 'A small creature, be very careful' cause here it is We've got to draw that, we've got to draw the snail. I've drawn
Kirsty	*(points to a dead insect on the table)* /That's our small creature
Julie	No that's what we're doing for our small creature *(points to snail)*
Sharon	He's dead, in 'e, he's dead *(looking at the greenfly)*
Mrs. R.	It's a greenfly
Kirsty	It was, but
Sharon	/That's not our creature
Julie	The snail is our creature
Kirsty	Get hold of it and glue it on
Julie:	No, you're not meant to glue the snail on, we're meant to draw a picture of it, you (...).

For Mrs. Reilly, the insect on the table may represent a species which can be usefully labelled 'It's a greenfly', but for the girls, as in deciding what counts as 'something soft', the task of matching items to the list they have been given, and the business of managing their own relationships, are closely intertwined. In many cases, a child's contributions to a classroom activity can depend as much on whom they want to socially align themselves with or distance themselves from, as on a more intellectual assessment of the task.

The literacy activities connected with the scavenger hunt also provided opportunities for the kind of behaviour and expressions which I have suggested act as a way of performing gender within talk (see Chapter 3). It was hard to imagine the boys I studied exclaiming over the thistledown: 'That's beautiful! That's really soft!' as Julie did. Linguists have found that the phrase structure 'That's lovely/soft/beautiful/pretty' is used more commonly by women than men (Holmes, 1994) and these and other expressions like 'hot' (Table 2.7) are an available resource which children can use to perform (or try out) gendered or sexualised aspects of identity. Similarly, the naming of the snail 'Sleepy' and Julie's instructions to 'look after him' exemplify the kind of nurturing behaviour which I suggested in Chapter 3 is a recurring theme in the girls' talk. In contrast to this, care and nurturing were much more likely to be expressed by the boys through knowledgeable activity (like Lee's response to the fallen bird's nest in Chapter 6). In addition to indexing a particular aspect of the speaker's identity, these kind of expressions are often also part of doing friendship, a way of saying *We share this in common, we are girls (or boys) together.*

Unofficial literacy

The hybridity of the classroom literacy activities I have described above, with their mixture of schooled practices and peer-sociable inter-action, cuts across the traditional divide in literacy research between home and school practices. Even within the official literacy-dominated framework of the school day, children's choices about how to manage their own work became peer-social choices as friends paced themselves through worksheets together, so that they could sit next to each other and work collaboratively. Mrs. Kilbride told me that the equipment children needed for literacy activities was distributed around different parts of the classroom to prevent crowding in any particular places, but this distribution also meant that children could usually find a reason for visiting any part of the room. Many pupils were adept at combining official activities like looking for a ruler or fetching paper with informal social contact. These contacts could be brief and fleeting; for example, Tom's 'All right, Kevin?' as he passed the mathematics table, much as one friend would greet another in the street, or in the school refectory. Although I almost missed this greeting when I first listened to the tape, it could have been highly significant for Kevin to be hailed by Tom, who was friendly with more dominant boys in the class like Gary and Darren.

In addition to the social contact which collecting resources could facilitate, children also initiated their own, alternative activities, sometimes sparked off by the worksheets. In a particularly dramatic example, during an official experiment with the projector and the prism (to produce a 'rainbow'), Martie showed Karen how she could look straight at the light in the projector and then close her eyes and see different colours. As they played about with the projector and prism, they found they could move the spectrum in different direc-tions, so 'it looks like a jellyfish' on the wall (Martie), or appeared in the mouth of another pupil, who pretended to eat it. They also managed to produce two spectrums simultaneously, in different parts of the room. Two boys nearby explained to Martie and Karen that the day before they had held pieces of white and black paper in turn at the same distance from the projector bulb and timed how long it took before they started to smoulder. Through this unofficial experi-ment they had concluded that black paper ignites more quickly than white. This kind of fragmentary unofficial knowledge about spec-trums and combustion, like the discussion of gravity and G-force at the swimming pool (Table 3.8), emerged at the margins of curriculum activities, drawing on scientific concepts and procedures but with only a tangential connection to official practices.

There were thus a range of literacy activities going on in the classroom, including the most tightly structured teacher-pupil interactions, looser more hybrid activity and, in addition, activities which fell completely outside the official curriculum. As well as the unofficial spectrum investigations, the talk around the school library book on snails (Table 7.6) included Julie's asides to a pupil with a puzzle magazine who was trying to make as many as possible new words out of the letters spelling 'peanut':

Table 8.5

20	Julie	'eat' *(a suggestion to the pupil with the puzzle magazine)*
	Mrs. R.	We saw its eyes, didn't we? At the end of its tentacles, and it can only see light and dark
	Julie	*(to puzzle magazine pupil)* 'tune'
	Pupil	It can only be three letters
	Julie	/*(reads)* 'or more', three letters or more.

Julie's correction 'or more' here (quoting the textual voice) is similar to Louise and Tina's correction of Kieran's reading of the Coordinates worksheet (Table 8.1(a)) 'It says "17 TO 19"'. Unofficial readings often involved the same kind of collaborative negotiation of instructions which were needed for the mathematics worksheet or the scavenging hunt list. I suggested in Chapter 7 that they could also involve the rather different kind of exclamatory style with which Julie and Kirsty announced interesting facts about snails. This exclamatory style was common where children were looking together at non-curriculum texts: bubblegum cards, old tickets, and, in the next extract, a magazine which Julie was sharing under the desk with a friend:

Table 8.6

Julie	Which picture do you like best? Who do you like best?
girl	Imagine having a princess at your birthday! Love it!
Julie	That looks like Marilyn Monroe
girl	*(in answer to Julie's first question)* That one

This kind of collaborative informal reading, where children performed friendship through the pleasures of shared fantasies and identification, went on frequently in and outside the classroom.[9] Although these readings are orientated towards knowledge and values which are in many ways antithetical to purposes and identities within schooling, the cultural discourses they invoke percolate into the classroom, through the unofficial activities which appear in the margins of children's work, under the desk, in the cloakroom (see Table 2.1) and in other relatively unregulated spaces.

In unofficial literacy activities, the relationship work around texts often appeared more provisional and unstable than the relatively fixed institutional positionings in teacher-pupil dialogues about the texts in books and worksheets. This was particularly the case where unofficial texts had been produced by pupils themselves (for example letters, notes, graffiti). Here, the meaning and significance of a text was often interpreted not only in terms of the words in the message, but also in relation to questions about who had written it, and why. When, for instance, a note was passed surreptitiously to Terry in class saying that Melissa wanted to be his girlfriend, should he interpret this as a genuine offer or a mischievous trick? Did the note come from Melissa, or a friend of hers who was playing matchmaker, or someone wanting to stir up trouble? Such questions were often the subject of intense discussion. In the next extract below, Nicole, Melissa and Ella are sitting together working on a mathematics worksheet. The text which they are talking about, however, is a piece of graffiti in the cloakroom, from where Nicole has just returned. The focus of talk is on the girls' relationships with Laura, a friend who is not present:

Table 8.7

Nicole	There was something in the girls' toilet on the mirror, it said 'Laura Clark for question mark' and I scrubbed it off with some water. It was just at the bottom of – say this is the mirror, right, the mirror, right the whole thing's the mirror and the edge of the mirror down here 'Laura Clark' smeared 'for'
Melissa	/Well why did you say me and Karlie done it?
Nicole	No, you, Karlie or Jackie done it. I just reckon it was
Melissa	Why? Well why did I get Laura?
Nicole	I know you ain't, cause we're
Ella	/It's Karlie
Melissa	If anyone's done it, it's Karlie
Nicole	I know, and Karlie's sitting on this table. Cause Karlie does write like that, doesn't she?

Although Nicole is the only one who actually saw the graffiti, her repeating of it becomes a collaborative reading. The girls do not, however, discuss its precise referential meaning. Who the question mark might signify is never explored. The focus is rather on who wrote the graffiti and why, and the implications of this for shifting relationships within the group. Nicole demonstrates her own friendship towards Laura by reporting that she immediately rubbed out the graffiti. Melissa challenges Nicole's accusation 'Why? Well why did I get Laura?' implying that her own relationship with Laura would not suggest an immediate reason for 'getting' her. Nicole immediately accepts this 'I know you ain't, cause we're', although she had previously 'just reckoned' it was either Melissa, Karlie or Jackie. As in the discussion about not talking to Kerry (Table 3.7), there is a sense here of close and painful relationship and identity work going on around who is to be included and excluded within tight yet unstable friendship groups.

The location of the graffiti, as well as its authorship, is important to its meaning. If it had been written by a close friend on the corner of Laura's rough work book cover (these covers were a mass of such graffiti, as the children termed it), then it could have been interpreted as a piece of friendly teasing. But 'smeared' on the mirror in the girls' toilet, this naming and shaming makes a potentially private relationship public in a site associated with smutty and sexual innuendo. The authorship of the text remains provisional; even the final comment 'Karlie does write like that' is ambiguous and could refer either to the style of the handwriting (which only Nicole has seen), or to its content, or to the habit of leaving graffiti in public places. There is a sense in which the text is opportunistically co-opted in the contesting of friendship boundaries between the girls. Within this context, the nature of the accusations, who makes them about whom and who defends them, may turn out to be more important than establishing the truth about the original authorship.[10]

Personal writing: identity and regulation

To get more of an overview of children's uses of literacy outside the curriculum, I asked the 32 pupils in my main research site, in their interviews, to tell me about the texts they chose to read outside school (print and media) and also how they used writing for their own non-curriculum purposes, both inside and outside school. I catalogued children's use of television, video, magazines and books, but it was their range of personal writing which I found most surprising and interesting, especially as this seemed to bear little relationship to their literacy proficiency at school. Categories of texts written by the children for personal purposes are listed in Table 8.8.

Table 8.8   Children's non-curriculum writing[11]

- personal letters (13 children)
- made up stories and rhymes (9)
- notes and graffiti in school (9)
- diaries (5)
- letters for offers in magazines, to join clubs and enter competitions (5)
- copying out popular songs (5)
- rules, and names and addresses for made up clubs (4)
- lists and charts (3)
- cartoon stories and other pictures (3).

In many ways children seemed to have 'taken hold of literacy' (Street, 1994) and used it for their own purposes. Lists, charts, letters, stories and rhymes were all genres which children were taught at school and part of their general literacy environment outside school. For instance, Terry spent a lot of time outside school repairing cars with a 'mate' in his twenties. He told me that he used a chart to record the cars he worked on, listing the names of different makes of car along the horizontal axis (e.g. Fiesta, Vauxhall) and their parts on the vertical axis (e.g. carburettor, engine), with ticks in the relevant cells to show which parts he had worked on. He was trying to expand the lists and get as many cells ticked as possible. He explained: 'It's just like a normal grid ... it's just like a register'. In explaining his grid to me, and the way in which it marked and categorised his activity, Terry was presenting a skilled, authoritative identity connected with the adult world of work, which linked also with the presentation of his role in defending his family home alongside his father (Table 6.2). It was not clear whether he had appropriated a classroom format for his chart (like the register or the worksheet 'Finding positions'), or taken the format from the car manuals which he told me he often read at home, or been taught how to record his work by his older friend. His identification of a generic connection, however, between his recording format and a format he expected I would be familiar with (the school register), showed a clear understanding of the essence of a written grid, and its potential to record, organise and plan experience.

Another boy, Gary, often drew up lists during the morning which established the positions of players for the informal football at lunchtime and these lists were used to help organise and regulate the game. I also noticed that they generated intense negotiations, around who was to be included in the teams, in which position, and who was excluded. Lists were used in other ways to mark social alliances and exclusions. Sam and Simon told me that they had made a list of the people they wanted to be members of a club they were going to have in the shed in Simon's garden, and a list of rules: 'What they're not allowed to do'. The fact that their club (like others I was told about) never developed beyond these lists of members and rules may be because organisation of activities between a larger number of children is much more difficult than the negotiation of a written list between two friends, or because the lists themselves accomplished the interpersonal and identity work which children desired. As a statement of shared allegiance to various sources of authority, the rules which children made up for imaginary clubs served both to exclude undesirable others and to express shared affinity through their highlighting of particular sources of regulation in the children's environment. Each rule pointed to, or indexed, a regulatory practice, in relation to which children signalled commitment (at a discursive level), thereby taking up a particular identity position. This positioning contributed to their habitus, that is, their individual disposition to evaluate and act on the world in particular ways (see Chapter 1).[12] The kind of bricolage of regulatory practices indexed by children's made-up rules is illustrated in Melissa and Laura's 'Our rules of our club', which they started writing one evening together at Laura's home and finished off at school the next day (spelling as in the original).

Table 8.9

Our rules of our club	
1	No smoking
2	No useing and you must always use your manors
3	No swearing
4	No going off
5	No staying in during Playtime
6	No trowing your fod at lunch time
7	allways sit with a patner
8	No calling any other member of the club names
9	No Kicking, punching, pulling hair
10	Do not lie or cheat
11	No swoping with some one outside of the club.

Melissa and Laura's list expresses different layers of authority, associated with different potential subjectivities. Rules 3, 9, 10 and the second part of Rule 2: 'you must always use your manors' index general social expectations around being 'a well-behaved girl'. 'No smoking' signs were familiar to the girls' but also had a personal significance in terms of Melissa's and Laura's intense opposition to the smoking habits of other children in the class. Rules 5 and 6 were reproductions of two school rules that Mrs. Kilbride had discussed with the class the previous week and their inclusion apparently marked an allegiance to school authority. Rules 4, 7 and 'No using' in Rule 2 relate to friendship conventions: the girls told me that 'going off' meant leaving someone without explaining why and 'using' meant falsely pretending that you wanted to be someone's friend. Sitting with a partner was important because 'you want to sit with your friends'. Finally, Rules 8 and 11 stipulated behaviour in relation to others in and outside the club, thus expressing its boundaries.

These rules expressed ideal rather than actual behaviour. The 'good girl' image they presented did not tally with my experience of Melissa in other contexts, for example when she was mercilessly teasing Kieran (Table 4.8). What was significant in terms of identification, however, was the girls' shared commitment, at a discursive level, to rules indexing certain conventional expectations of behaviour for children, in relation to community norms, school authority and the conventions of peer group friendship. 'Our rules of our club', with its repeated use of 'our', consolidated the girls' friendship and identified them as particular kinds of people through their shared choice of particular authoritative reference points. Like Julie with her alternative sources of evaluation in the class and in the girls' toilet (Table 2.1), Melissa and Laura orientated towards both adult and peer evaluative frameworks. And, as in the lists of car parts, football teams and club membership, writing served both to regulate and plan activity and interpersonal relations, and to express identity.

While two girls said they wrote reflective diaries at home and talked about this writing as filling empty time and marking when 'something happened', the use of diaries other than in a cursory noting of important dates, by either boys or girls, was relatively rare.[13] The 10–12 year-olds I studied seemed to be more interested in exploring themselves and reflecting on experience through sociable relations with others (for instance in the story telling discussed in Chapters 5 and 6), than in solitary contemplation. It is perhaps not surprising, then, that the most popular written text they talked about producing was the letter, which can be used both to extend sociability and as a dialogical expression of the self through a written relationship.[14] Many more girls than boys reported writing letters, but there was no evidence that the children themselves regarded letter writing as a gendered activity.

Personal correspondence to maintain family and other relationships was perhaps particularly important in a context where the majority of children had moved home at least once, often in connection with the break up and reconstitution of family units. 50% of the children in the class at Lakeside were not living with both their original parents (though all children lived with at least one), some were separated from brothers and sisters, and some had formed attachments in the past to people who had now moved away. Jackie, for instance, told me 'Well I normally write them (letters) to my mum because she doesn't live with us, you see, and my nan. I write to my uncle in Austria and all my cousins'. Karlie, whose father was in prison explained to me 'I write to my dad when he's so far away from me, so I let him know what's going on down here and he writes letters back and then I get cards from him at Christmas ...I write to my dad every week because he likes to get in touch with me'. Boys also corresponded with absent family relatives. Lee wrote 'letters to my dad in London and he writes back sometimes – and usually every week but mostly now every month and I've started a letter today and I'm finishing it off tonight'.

Writing was also used by children to maintain sociability over distance with people outside the family. For instance, Kim wrote to a friend of her mother's who had moved to Spain and Melissa wrote to her sister's ex-boyfriend who was in prison. A number of children also talked about writing to a child they had met when visiting relatives elsewhere, although these written relationships were usually brief. Tina explained 'I did have a pen pal' (met when visiting her aunt in another town) 'till I lost her address ... I only writ one letter'. Karlie had met her boyfriend when he was visiting his grandmother who lived in her court and said she was getting a letter from him nearly every month. Sherri met her boyfriend when she went to stay with her aunt, but 'I chucked him when I last wrote to him which was a couple of weeks ago. There's no point me going out with him when he's right over there and I'm right over here'. Some girls wrote to older teenage girls who had spent time on work experience placements in the class and one of these older teenage girls was corresponding with about six girls in the class, who had each received up to five letters from her. When I finished my research, a number of the children asked me to write to them.

In addition to its capacity to overcome physical separation and extend sociability, writing was also used as an alternative to speech, to save face and to convey emotions which might be embarrassing if expressed directly. Karlie explained how her boyfriend had first asked her out through a letter because it was 'so embarrassing' and girls reported writing letters to close friends when they wanted to apologise and make up after an argument. Finally, written communication could be used to get around classroom rules. Martie told me 'During silent reading me and Darren have chats in letters cause we can't talk' and a number of other children told me they wrote and passed jokes and puzzles in class.

Conclusion

In both the classrooms in my research, talk was an integral part of most of the literacy activities I observed, and it can be argued that talk about texts contributes directly to the development of children's reading. I have unpicked a number of ways in which children's induction into particular reading and writing practices is mediated through talk, where teachers direct their attention to the representation of fixed meanings through labels, headings, academic terms and phrases and more abstract formats. These activities are embedded within educational literacy practices which encode beliefs and values about how particular kinds of texts should be interpreted, produced and valued. Foucault's concept of institutional disciplining helps to explain the preponderance of procedural talk in connection with reading and writing, and how literacy activities are knitted into the organisation of time and space in the classroom. The literacy practices which underpin the production of formalised school knowledge also assign particular identity positions to teachers and pupils and serve to regulate children's movement, behaviour and attention across the school day.

The devolving of some of the institutional management of activity onto the children themselves (for example through the choice of activity, the personal planning of work and the Activity Record Sheet), can be seen in Foucault's terms as a further diffusion of institutional power, and a taking on by individual children of particular disciplining behaviours and genres. Close analysis of individual children's ongoing work, however, shows that 'classroom literacy' is not a monolithic activity. Completing worksheets and accomplishing other classroom tasks often involve children in a variety of communicative strategies and peer-sociable activity.

Problems are solved, knowledge is gained and competence achieved through a hybrid mix of scaffolding, modelling, collaboration, disputation and play with intellectual and peer-social processes closely intertwined. Children also find opportunities for unofficial activity within the interstices and less regulated spaces of the organised curriculum, and literacy practices and texts which are not associated with schooling, together with their associated knowledge and values, work their way into the classroom. Unofficial practices are often closely connected with peer sociability, and texts circulated and discussed among children can be used to confirm or reconfigure relationships and to express personal fantasies and desires. Rather than contrasting children's use of literacy in the classroom with their literacy practices outside school, as has often happened in past studies, I have suggested that literacy in classrooms involves a hybrid mix of official, semi-official and unofficial readings and writings, each associated with different patterns of relationship, identity and formalised or unformalised knowledge.

The propensity of written text to organise activity, relationships and knowledge is exploited by children in their non-curriculum writing. Lists and charts were used to record and plan work and games, to establish social boundaries of inclusion and exclusion and to express personal alliances and commitment. Through these practices children presented themselves as similar or different to others and defined good and bad behaviour in relation to particular authoritative points of reference. In this way literacy is an important part of habitus, or the ongoing disposition to evaluate and act on the world in particular ways. Many of the children I interviewed spoke of writing when they were bored or had nothing else to do, but they were more likely to transform this emptiness by writing a letter, than a diary. The construction of identity for the 10–12 year-olds I studied, as well as the construction of knowledge, was pursued primarily through social interaction rather than in more solitary activities.

Conclusion

This book has been about the alternative social world of children which exists in school, as it were under our very noses, and about social constructivism in action, as revealed through a close study of children's communicative practices. My analysis of what 10–12 year-old children are doing in talk is grounded, in the first instance, within their conversations among themselves, where the evaluative landscape opens up to include a wider range of authoritative voices and evaluative perspectives, and there is more space for the expression of individual agency and the exploration of personal positions. This talk between children, as well as their talk with adults, is an important site for children's acquisition of knowledge, their socialisation and their development as particular kinds of people.

I have looked at how children's collaboration in talk, their contextual and generic referencing, their reproduction of voices and uses of story and different literacies, are all part of the ongoing, dialogical processes of meaning-making. Within the various timescales of change in social life, I have focussed on the minute, moment-to-moment negotiations of meaning in children's dialogues. These micro level processes contribute to children's longer term induction into institutional practices and the social beliefs and values of their community, and are simultaneously part of the continuing construction of their individual sense of identity. Within these processes, I have particularly highlighted the often underestimated role of evaluation, as a key dimension of meaning-making.

One of the strongest effects of moving into children's perspectives on their classroom life is the realisation that the interpersonal and emotive functions of talk are centrally important in the shaping of meaning, both in peer-talk on non-curriculum matters and in talk related to classroom activities. From the speaker's point of view, collaboration in talk always has important social functions, imbued with emotion, which drive interactions and affect the construction of conceptual meaning, including its evaluative dimension. In focussing on children's negotiations in talk which is polysemic and always on the move, I have developed an analytic framework which brings together the situated insights of ethnography with the attention to textual detail in discourse analysis, drawing in particular on Bakhtinian concepts which capture the patterned, dynamic nature of communicative practice. I have replaced a discussion of text and context with a focus on contextualisation within and across speech genres, the relatively stable patterns in language use, content themes and evaluation, which emerge from social activity and are therefore also flexible and changing. Genres translate the social world into individual children's speech and induct them, through their use of language, into particular cultural practices, beliefs and values. Children also draw creatively and strategically on the generic resources of different contexts to create meaning, pursue relationships with other people and present aspects of themselves. I have suggested that speech genres provide a powerful cultural resource for children's meaning-making and at the same time place ultimate limitations on their creativity.

My focus on children's sensitivity to context and the contextualisation processes in their talk is underpinned by a contextualised approach on my own part, to the analysis of dialogue. I see a contextualised analytical approach as resting firstly on an ethnographically informed understanding of the situation in which the talk emerges, and of its referential and evaluative content. The meaning and significance of what is said, including passing intertextual references, frame switching and the mapping out of evaluative perspectives and relationships through indexicality can only be interpreted in the light of understanding about the circumstances of children's lives, and about their own reflections, feelings and perspectives. Secondly, my analytic categories have emerged out of a close attention to children's ongoing, situated communication. My analysis replaces a model of speakers and listeners with a dialogical conception of communication and I have examined how children's reproduction of voices and representations of experience are reaccented and reconfigured in ongoing conversations, and how utterances and narratives are collaboratively structured and restructured, through a network of dialogic links within and across utterances. The interweaving of voices across dialogues suggests that meaning is not located within an independent speaker's intentions, but is a more social accomplishment.

The central role of evaluation in children's meaning-making is expressed particularly through their use of reported voices, which constituted the main means of invoking other contexts away from the here and now and bringing them to bear in some way in what was happening in the present. Reproduced voices indexed stances, relationships and activities which in their turn indexed speech genres and recognisable scenarios. Authoritative voices associated with the different contexts of children's lives were reproduced to guide their action and to negotiate evaluation and identity positioning, and the voices of significant people were reproduced and orchestrated in their narratives. The central part of the book, Chapters 4–7, was concerned with building up my argument about how children reproduce these voices in different ways, in effect having a kind of inner dialogue with the voice they are reporting and expressing varying degrees of commitment to, or distancing from, the evaluative perspective it represents.

Reproduced voices were used by children to express and explore their feelings about teachers and parents, to relive moments of high emotion, and to tease and pursue relationships with other children. At a more profound level, the reproduction, articulation and reaccenting of voices helped children to explore expectations and reasons for other people's behaviour in different institutional settings across their lives and to express their own agency, desires and emerging sense of self. I have looked at how children reproduced voices as part of the representation and evaluation of people, relationships and events, and examined how evaluation is conveyed through combinations of grammatical form, prosodic and non-verbal features, the dynamics of ongoing dialogue and contextual links to other conversations and contexts. Children used more direct linear reporting where they wanted to fully convey and use the evaluative force of a reported voice and more indirect, pictorial reporting where they wanted to problematise its position and foreground their own perspective. A mixture of direct and indirect reporting (free indirect speech) was used to blend the reporting and reported voices in more ambiguous ways.

The orchestration of voices in anecdotes and longer narratives enabled children to fleetingly inhabit alternative identity positions and to represent and review the complexity of the moral issues which confronted them in their lives. Their stories included accounts of picaresque altercations with adults, an older sister's pregnancy and a younger sister's naivety, looking after lost cats and fledglings, problems between parents and fights and arguments with neighbours and other children. The articulation of voices drove both the referential and the evaluative functions of children's narratives, which were often literally and always essentially collaboratively produced. Their meaning and significance emerged dialogically, in relation to the contextual links with children's lives.

At an intricate level in the talk, there were dialogical relationships between the reported speakers in the story, and between these voices and previous and subsequent turns in the conversation. And over a longer time span, there were dialogic links between the evaluative points of the connected stories which children told across different contexts and conversations. Each story, I have suggested, contributes to a 'long conversation' which children are carrying on among themselves about persistent themes and issues emerging through their experience at this point in their lives, as they move from childhood into adolescence: the nature of their changing relationships with adults, the imperatives and expectations of friendship, the taking on of new gendered identities. Stories provided a space within which to explore these issues further and to share and exchange knowledge and ideas about how to 'be', for instance a daughter, a girl, a friend or a girlfriend, and about how to cope with and respond to the practical and emotional challenges which other children themselves might be also facing, or be faced with in the future.

In Chapters 7 and 8, I focussed in again on children's lives in the classroom. I looked at how children take on and reproduce the authoritative voices of teachers and textbooks as part of their induction into school literacy practices and schooled subjectivities. There was a hierarchy of intertextual referencing in the classroom, where teachers appropriated the voices of authoritative written texts downwards and appropriated children's voices upwards, into the teaching-learning speech genres of the classroom. I found when I started to look at the official literacy activities which were the focus of so much curriculum-focussed talk in the classroom, that I came up against a powerful fusing of more fixed conceptions of texts (with their headings, labels, academic terms and set referential meanings), formalised knowledge and institutional hierarchical power. As I described in Chapter 2, teacher-dominated dialogue in the classroom was characterised by linear referencing, backwards and forwards in time, which was part of the structured accumulation of this formalised knowledge by children as they moved through the daily, weekly and termly timetabling of their activity.

In talk among themselves, children used teacher and text book voices to organise their own and other children's activity, for peer-sociable as well as schooled purposes. In this way, and through the organisation of children's use of time and space in the classroom within the structured literacy activities, the exercise of institutional power becomes multi-circuited, as Foucault puts it, and children take an active part in their own institutionalisation into schooling. While children's lives were dominated by school literacy practices, however, I also found a lot of other kinds of literacy going on in the classroom, connected with the less formalised kinds of knowledge-making, relationships and identity which characterised children's non-curriculum talk. While school curriculum knowledge was systematically and hierarchically structured in accordance with educational principles, the broader knowledge that children were constructing together about their social worlds was much more fragmented, provisional and full of contradictions. Literacy was also used by children to order and structure their broader social experience by marking social connections and boundaries and expressing commitment to particular sources of regulation.

The dialogical and multi-voiced intricacy of children's conversations among themselves served them well in their representation and exploration of the multi-voiced and complex world of people, relationships and practices which filled their daily lives. Where children did address topics related to school knowledge, for instance questions about velocity and force, or rates of combustion, knowledge remained at a relatively fragmented and incoherent level. I did, however, find that children could accumulate a considerable amount of knowledge about a particular social activity, like smoking, through group conversations (which often included conflict as well as collaboration). There were, on the whole, very different kinds of knowledge construction going on in teacher-pupil dialogue and in dialogue among children in non-curriculum conversations. Both kinds of knowledge were important in their lives, and there was a dynamic tension between the centripetal forces of the institutional practices and knowledge on the one hand, and the centrifugal force of pupils' peer-social agendas and inwardly persuasive personal experience, on the other. This tension was often evident in the hybrid mix of talk and activity which characterised classroom life.

This book has also illustrated the diversity in terms of habitus within a white working class classroom. There were varying orientations towards adult, teenage and more childly pursuits in children's activities ranging from mending cars with older mates and fancying air-hostesses to playing with Lego and making up fairy stories, sometimes linked with the different stages of physiological development in a group of 10–12 year-olds. Children also expressed varying degrees of commitment to school practices and identities, from Sherri and Tina who sang popular songs together, sotto voce, as they completed neat pages of sums, to Kieran and Kevin who playfully stylised the words in the worksheet they were labouring over, Darren who satirised how pupils were expected to present work in assembly and Nicole who was more interested in the graffiti in the girls' toilet. Children expressed and performed their gender in different ways and expressed varying degrees of interest in girlfriends and boyfriends. They had different kinds of friendships (Darren and Martie's sparring as opposed to Sam and Simon's companionable sharing) and they talked to each other and to myself about a very wide range of activities and events outside school. The choices and alignments, the preferences and preoccupations of children like Darren, Martie, Julie, Karlie and all the rest reflected the circumstances and cultural horizons of their lives, but they also expressed a unique way of being in, acting on and evaluating their social world.

Notes

Introduction

1 Vygotsky, 1978; 1986.
2 Street, 1993.
3 While there is some controversy about whether works published under Volosinov's name were in fact written by Bakhtin, I shall refer to them by their published authorship, and use the term 'Bakhtinian' where I am drawing on ideas common to both authors.
4 Foucault, 1981.

Chapter 1   Setting the Scene

1 I draw on Bakhtin, 1981; 1984; 1986, and Volosinov, 1973; 1976.
2 The use of a radio microphone was vital for capturing spontaneous talk, and for getting around what the sociolinguist William Labov calls the observer's paradox: 'the problem of observing how people speak when they are not being observed' (Labov, 1972, p. 256). It also allowed me to record talk in contexts where my own presence would have been inappropriate.
3 I was reminded of the comment of another school ethnographer: 'I found that after about an hour I would go almost into a trance state, unable to concentrate on my fieldnotes' (McLaren, 1986, p. 111).
4 I was also influenced by Hymes' proposals for an ethnography of communication, a study of language in use situated in 'the flux and pattern of communicative events'. (Hymes, 1977 p. 5) and by Heath's 1983 ethnographic study of literacy.
5 Clifford and Marcus, 1986; Atkinson, 1990; Foley, 2002.
6 Blommaert, 1997.
7 For example Shuman, 1986; Eder and Enke, 1991; Hey, 1997; Corsaro, 1997.
8 I would have felt morally bound to seek help if children's disclosures had suggested that they were in any danger, but this did not occur.
9 Building on Malinowski's work, the American anthropologist Del Hymes, 1977, envisages the context of talk like the layers of an onion. The meaning of an individual utterance is shaped through its embedding within a *speech event* (a conversation, a political speech, a sermon), which is in its turn embedded within a *speech situation* (a party, a school lesson, a church service) within a particular *speech community*, which shares rules for conducting and interpreting speech.
10 'Any word in actual speech possesses not only theme and meaning in the referential, or content, sense of these words, but also value judgement. ... There is no such thing as a word without evaluative accent.' Volosinov, 1986, p. 103.
11 Hanks, 2001; Swann *et al.*, 2004.

12 The term 'schema' has been used to refer to people's patterned knowledge about the world, which they then use to predict the sequences of interactions and events (the 'script') in new events and experiences (Tannen and Wallat, 1993). In a similar way, children's knowledge about speech genres enables them to predict information about the themes, interaction and evaluative stances indexed by a brief reported dialogue.

13 See Hanks, 1996, and Duranti, 2001, on linguistic anthropology. Wetherell, 2005, suggests that there has been a turn towards a 'relational ontology' in social psychology over the last twenty years.

14 For example Salomon, 1993; Mercer, 2000.

15 For example, Eckert, 2000; Bucholtz, 1999; Rampton, 2004.

16 'Any utterance – the finished written utterance not excepted – makes a response to something and is calculated to be responded to in turn. It is but one link in a continuous chain of speech performances' Volosinov, 1986, p. 72.

17 Miller *et al.* 1990; 1992, explore this process of identification through comparison and contrast of oneself with others, in younger children's talk.

18 The French social theorist Pierre Bourdieu defines 'habitus' as a relatively open set of socially structured dispositions learnt in childhood and beyond, which incline people towards particular ways of acting and of perceiving and representing the world. Their habitus orientates people's actions without strictly determining them, and is reinforced or modified through experience (Bourdieu and Waquant, 1992).

Chapter 2   Context, Genre and Frames

1 Goffman, 1974, argues that in order to make sense of any interaction, participants use culturally derived interpretative frames to ascertain, at a meta-level, the nature of the interaction, for example whether it counts as a joke or a telling-off. Particular utterances, movements and gestures are then interpreted in the light of that frame. Frames can be broken or disputed, or transformed through participants 're-keying' a different interpretation of what is going on. This rekeying often serves to reposition the speaker more advantageously within an interaction.

2 In order to avoid the negative connotations of 'childish' and the implications of essential fixed attributes in 'childlike', Sealey, 2000, uses the term 'childly' to signal 'the *relational* nature of the state of being a child' (p. 9). Thus, being a child is defined in relation to being a teenager, or an adult.

3 Bakhtin, 1984, uses the term 'double-voicing' to refer to where a speaker reproduces or draws on another speaker's language, for instance repeating something they are purported to have said.

4 I don't mean to suggest a simple contrast here between oral genres at home and literate genres in the school. As has been pointed out to me, having cups of tea and doing shopping also figure in the picture books which children may read at home. The contrast is rather between the management of time, the typical activities and the kinds of people that children can be or imagine themselves to be, in these two different settings. These aspects of context are appropriated and reproduced within Michelle's two collaborative imaginative texts.

5 Edwards and Mercer, 1987, provide a detailed account of how teachers regularily invoke aspects of their shared history with pupils, both through references to what has happened in previous lessons and through teachers' reconstructions of pupils' previous talk from the current lesson, as part of the interactive construction of knowledge about curriculum and procedural groundrules by teachers and pupils in the classroom.

6 Bernstein, 1996, p. 171, describes the language of schooling as a 'vertical discourse', which is 'coherent, explicit, systematically principled structure, hierarchically organised' and associated with similarly organised forms of knowledge. In contrast, within everyday 'horizontal discourse', he suggests that knowledge is local, context dependent and multi-layered. I use the term 'linear' rather than 'vertical' to in order to emphasise the constant references to linear processes across time which were a central part of structuring discourse and knowledge in the teacher-pupil dialogues that I observed.

7 'In the very same utterance that expresses a speaker, projecting her into the world, the world is introjected into the speaker' (Hanks, 1996, p. 205).

8 Goffman, 1967, uses the term 'face work' to refer to the ways in which speakers attend to their own need to maintain a positive public self-image, while at the same time also attending to the face needs of other participants in the interaction. As well as making sure she won't herself be in danger of losing face, Julie offers David a choice of interpretative options thus, indirectly, protecting his face as well.

Chapter 3   Dialogue and Collaboration: Girls and Boys

1 In Bakhtin's later work he insists that even the most apparently monologic text (spoken or written) is in some sense a response to other texts and is simultaneously orientated towards a particular audience (Bakhtin, 1986).

2 Drawing on Vygotskian theory about the relationship between dialogue and learning, the promotion of collaborative and 'exploratory' talk has been a recurring theme in British education since the 1960s, especially in the work of the UK National Oracy Project (Norman, 1992), which influenced subsequent National Curriculum Guidance (DES/WO, 1989). See also recent educational research about talk and thinking (Mercer, 2000).

3 Swann and Graddol, 1995; Cameron, 2000. See also Swann, 2003.

4 See, for example, Lakoff, 1975; Tannen, 1990; Coates 1986; 1994.

5 Cameron, 1997, p. 49, contrasts the traditional sociolinguistic assumption that 'people talk the way they do because of who they (already) are', with what she terms the postmodernist approach that 'people are who they are because of (among other things) the way they talk'.

6 Tannen, 1989, sees repetition like this as a ubiquitous and creative aspect of conversation. She points out that repetition is economical in terms of mental energy because the speaker does not have to think up new words and phrases, it creates interpersonal involvement between speakers through expressing alignment and it also helps to create coherence at the level of meaning through building up the collaborative expression of a shared world.

7 Shuman, 1986; Goodwin, 1990; Hey, 1997.

8 Labov, 1972, shows how stories in conversation often start with a brief abstract, then set the scene, recount complicating action and provide a res-

olution. The structure of children's narratives and their evaluative functions are explored in detail in Chapters 5 and 6.

9 Coates, 1994; 1996, suggests that this departure from what Sacks, Schegloff and Jefferson, 1974, define as the normal rules of turn taking in English (one at a time and no overlap), is a 'positive politeness' strategy, which women use to signal closeness and intimacy.

10 Sheldon, 1997, challenges the characterisation of girls' talk as more collaborative and boys as more conflictual, and discusses the ways in which both girls and boys express conflict in talk.

11 I use the term 'floor' to refer to the interactional space occupied by speakers (Swann *et al.*, 2004).

12 Similarly, Hewitt, 1997, uses data from group talk among boys to show that competitiveness, at another level, can also be part of collaboration. He suggests that 'cooperation' has often functioned more as a moral term than an analytical one, and that not enough attention has been paid to the various different ways in which it can be accomplished.

13 Thorne, 1993, Hey, 1997, and Eckert and McConnell-Ginet, 2003, all discuss the key role of heterosexuality as a metaphor around which children begin to organise their social relations as they move towards their teens.

Chapter 4   Reported Voices and Evaluation

1 I follow other linguistic researchers (for example, Tannen, 1989; McCarthy, 1998; Myers, 2004) in using the term 'reported' where there is a clear grammatical indication that children are referring to the words of another speaker, or to their own words on an alternative occasion. These words can be directly reported (she said '...') or indirectly reported (she said that ....). The term 'reported' is in fact something of a misnomer because reported speech is often rephrased and always recontextualised (Tannen, 1989). In this chapter I begin to examine how transformations of reported speech contribute to children's meaning-making.

2 For example, see Tannen, 1989; Buttny and Williams, 2000; Myers, 2004.

3 Skinner *et al.*, 2001, illustrate the evaluative functions of represented voices particularly clearly in their Bakhtinian analysis of a narrative told by a 16 year-old Nepali, Hari. The juxtaposition and orchestration of voices within Hari's account shows that he does not simply internalise the authoritative discourse about caste distinctions in his community, but problematises it in the light of more recent discourses about modernisation through education, which give him a potentially more powerful position.

4 As linguists, Leech and Short, 1981, refer to deictic grammatical expressions of space and time. For linguistic anthropologists, deixis is included within the larger category of indexicality.

5 Leech and Short, 1981; Toolan, 2001.

6 McCarthy, 1998; Gunther, 1999; Myers, 2004.

7 Opie and Opie, 1959, record a number of traditional sayings to clinch swapping transactions from various parts of Britain, in some cases dating back to the nineteenth century. Many involve touching black, leather, wood or iron to seal a transaction. Another version of the rhyme used in Camdean was 'Touch black, can't swap back'. This was usually accompanied by the child

touching their shoe, even when this was not black. Shoes are of course often made of leather, and in the nineteenth century children's boots would have had an iron heel. 'Black Jack' originally referred to the devil.

8　I have included this as a kind of reported speech because Melissa reports a vocal communication conveying feelings which functions here in the same way as similarly reported words.

9　For literary examples see Leech and Short, 1981; Short, 1996. Tannen, 1989, and Myers, 2004, discuss examples from adult speech.

Chapter 5　Articulating Dialogue: Agency and Gender in Children's Anecdotes

1　See for example Schriffrin, 1996; Ochs and Capps, 2001; Wortham, 2001; De Fina, 2004.

2　Ochs and Capp, 2001.

3　While 'evaluation' has a specialised meaning in the context of Labov's narrative theory, this is also in line with the Bakhtinian argument that all uses of language are evaluative, always conveying a situated point of view and some kind of interpretative slant on whatever is represented.

4　Bauman, 1984; Shuman, 1986; Cortazzi and Jin, 2000; Ochs and Capps, 2001.

5　For example see Shuman, 1986; Goodwin, 1990; Schiffrin, 1996; Coates, 1996; Norrick, 1997; Evaldsson, 2002.

6　Wolfson, 1982, suggests that when narrators switch from past to present tense, the switch itself grabs the audience's attention.

7　Julie, Martie and Darren all wore the radio microphone for part of my research, so I have access to continual recordings of each of their conversations over at least three days.

8　'She started' in children's talk implied 'started to have a go at me', that is, complain, criticise, scold. The term could be used with reference to either adults or children's talk or behaviour. For instance, adults might warn their recalcitrant child 'Don't start!'

9　Connell *et al.*, 1982, suggest that this conception of 'emphasised femininity' complements the symbolically powerful version of masculinity which dominates other forms of masculinity and femininity within a society.

10　Goodwin, 1990; Coates, 1996.

Chapter 6　Narrative Reflections and Moral Complexities

1　Norrick, 1997, shows how familiar stories get retold in families to express and confirm shared values and to build rapport and shared identity.

2　However, story-telling styles vary across different social groups. Michaels, 1981, contrasts children's use of 'topic-centred' and 'topic-associating' narrative styles in a school 'sharing time'.

3　When children were grounded by their parents, as a punishment, they were usually not allowed to leave their home and were sometimes also forbidden to have sweets or to watch television.

4　A teacher or other authority figure 'doing' someone means giving them a severe telling off or other punishment. Used in other contexts, it can also imply a physical assault.

5 cf Hill and Irvine, 1992.
6 Goodwin, 1990; Coates, 1996.
7 This is the same Alan who stole from Sam and Simon's shed (see earlier). As he did not attend the schools in my study I did not meet this boy, but he seemed to be an important local figure in a number of children's lives.
8 Toolan, 2001, suggests free indirect discourse is an important strategy for temporary alignment, in words, value and perspective, of the narrator with a character. Often emotive, it conveys the internal perspective of a particular character, thus constituting a switch in focalisation.

Chapter 7   Schooled Voices

1 For discussion of the role of discourse representation in news reporting see Bell, 1996, in social work see Hall *et al.*, 1999, and in academic study see Baynham, 1999. Scollon, 2003, shows how discourse representation in three different communities of practice (academics, journalists and advertisers) serves to establish different positions and sets of relationships between authors, texts and readers or viewers in each case.
2 Bakhtin's typology of voice reproduction (Bakhtin, 1984) has also been used to analyse students' written and spoken language by Kamberelis and Scott, 1992; Scollon *et al.*, 1998; Rampton, 2005a.
3 cf Sola and Bennett, 1985.
4 Foucault, 1980; Luke, 1992; 1996.
5 Wertsch, 1991; Mercer, 1995.
6 Bloome, 1992.
7 I have borrowed this term from Ben Rampton.
8 Lytra, 2003.
9 See Rampton, 2005b, for a detailed account of the dynamics of singing in a secondary school classroom.

Chapter 8   Official and Unofficial Literacies

1 Bruner, 1985, pp. 24–5, uses the term 'scaffolding' to describe how a child may be helped to extend through his/her zone of proximal development, i.e. 'the distance between the actual developmental level as determined by independent problem solving and the level of potential development as determined through problem solving under adult guidance or in collaboration with more capable peers' (Vygotsky, 1978, p. 86). Bruner suggests that the adult or more capable peer provides the child with a vicarious form of consciousness until they can internalise the external knowledge from this scaffolding and convert it into a tool for independent use. See also Cole, 1985; Edwards and Mercer, 1987; Maybin *et al.*, 1992.
2 Maybin and Moss, 1993.
3 For example see Hymes, 1977; Basso, 1989; Szwed, 1981; Heath, 1983.
4 See Street, 1984, 1993; Gee, 1990; Barton, 1994; Baynham, 1995.
5 Street has pointed out that the taken-for-granted western educational definition of literacy as a neutral set of technical skills and competencies is just one (highly powerful) conception of reading and writing. Drawing on anthropological evidence, he argues that the meaning and significance of

literacy, and its power, emerges through the social practices surrounding its
use in different cultural contexts.

6   Luke, 1992; 1996.

7   Mercer, 2000.

8   See note 1 above.

9   See also Moss, 1996; 2000, on boys' informal collaborative reading.

10 See also Shuman, 1986; Goodwin, 1990.

11 When I did this research in the early 1990s, only a few children in the class
reported having computers at home. Livingstone and Bober, 2004, in a
national survey of 1,511 nine to nineteen year-olds and their families found
that 61% of working class young people in this age group had accessed the
internet at home and 53% of all 9–11 year-olds surveyed had a mobile
phone. It would be interesting to know how far phone texting and computer mediated literacies may be supplanting the pen and paper activities
I found among 10–12 year-olds, and whether these have led to new
patterns of sociability and identity construction within this age group.

12 Scollon and Scollon, 2003, discuss how regulatory signs in the environment
index particular discourses of authority and how people's responses to these
signs, in their turn, index aspects of their habitus.

13 Diary-writing has been particularly associated with teenage girls' reflections
on the self (see Camitta, 1993).

14 See Altman, 1982; Basso 1989; Barton and Hall, 2000; Jolly, 2006
forthcoming.

References

Atkinson, P. (1990) *The ethnographic imagination: textual constructions of reality*. London: Routledge.

Altman, J. (1982) *Epistolarity: approaches to a form*. Columbus: Ohio State University Press.

Bakhtin, M. ([1929]1984) *Problems of Dostoevsky's poetics*. ed. and translated by C. Emerson. Minneapolis: University of Minnesota Press.

Bakhtin, M. ([1935]1981) 'Discourse in the novel', in *The Dialogic Imagination: Four essays by M.M. Bakhtin*, ed. M. Holquist, trans. C. Emerson and M. Holquist. Austin, Texas: University of Texas Press.

Bakhtin, M. ([1953]1986) 'The problem of speech genres', in C. Emerson and M. Holquist (eds) *Speech genres and other late essays*, trans. V.W. Mc Gee. Austin, Texas: University of Texas Press.

Barton, D. (1994) *Literacy: an introduction to the ecology of written language*. Oxford: Blackwell.

Barton, D. and Hall, N. (2000) *Letter writing as a social practice*. Amsterdam: John Benjamins.

Basso, K. (1989) 'The ethnography of writing', in R. Bauman and J. Sherzer *Explorations in the ethnography of speaking: Second Edition*. Cambridge: Cambridge University Press.

Bauman, R. and Sherzer, J. (eds) (1989) 'Introduction to the second edition', in *Explorations in the ethnography of speaking: Second Edition*. Cambridge: Cambridge University Press.

Bauman, R. (1984) *Story, performance and event*. Cambridge: Cambridge University Press.

Baynham, M. (1995) *Literacy practices*. London: Longman.

Baynham, M. (1999) 'Double-voicing and the scholarly "I": On incorporating the words of others in academic discourse', *Text*, 19(4): 485–504.

Bell, A. (1996) 'Text, time and technology in news English', in S. Goodman and D. Graddol (eds) *Redesigning English: new texts, new identities*. London: Routledge.

Bernstein, B. (1996) *Pedagogy, symbolic control and identity: theory, research, critique*. London: Taylor and Francis.

Blommaert, J. (1997) *Workshopping: professional vision, practices and critique in discourse analysis*. Ghent: Academia Press.

Bloome, D. (1992) 'Reading as a social process in a Middle School classroom', in D. Bloome (ed.) *Literacy and schooling*. Norwood: Ablex.

Bourdieu, P. and Waquant, J.D. (1992) *An invitation to reflexive sociology*. Cambridge, Polity Press in association with Blackwell Publishers.

Bruner, J. (1985) 'Vygotsky: a historical and cultural perspective', in J. Wertsch (ed.) *Culture, communication and cognition: Vygotskian perspectives*. Cambridge: Cambridge: University Press.

Bruner, J. (1986) *Actual minds, possible worlds*. Cambridge MA: Harvard University Press.

Bruner, J. (1990) *Acts of meaning*. Cambridge, MA: Harvard University Press.

Bucholtz, M. (1999) 'Why be normal? Language and identity practices in a community of nerd girls', *Language in society*, 28(2): 191–211.

Buttny, R. and Williams, P.L. (2000) 'Demanding respect: the uses of reported speech in discursive constructions of interracial contact', *Discourse and Society*, 11(1): 109–133.

Cameron, D. (1997) 'Performing gender identity: young men's talk and the construction of heterosexuality', in S. Johnson and U.H. Meinhof (eds) *Language and Masculinity*. Oxford: Blackwell Publishers.

Cameron, D. (2000) *Good to talk? Living and working in a communication culture*. London and Thousand Oaks, CA: Sage Publications.

Camitta, M. (1993) 'Vernacular writing: varieties of literacy among Philadelphia High School students', in B. Street (ed.) *Cross-cultural approaches to literacy*. Cambridge: Cambridge University Press.

Clifford, J. and Marcus, G. (eds) (1986) *Writing culture: the poetics and politics of ethnography*. Berkley: University of California Press.

Coates, J. (1986) *Women, men and language*. London: Longman.

Coates, J. (1994) 'No gap, lots of overlap', in D. Graddol, J. Maybin and B. Stierer (eds) *Researching language and literacy in social context*. Clevedon: Multilingual Matters.

Coates, J. (1996) *Women talk: conversation between women friends*. Oxford: Blackwell Publishers.

Cole, M. (1985) 'The zone of proximal development: where culture and cognition create each other', in J. Wertsch (ed.) *Culture, communication and cognition: Vygotskian perspectives*. Cambridge: Cambridge University Press.

Connell, R.W., Dean, J., Ashenden, S.K. and Dowsett, G.W. (1982) *Making the difference: schools, families and social division*. London: Allen and Unwin.

Connell, R.W. (1995) *Masculinity*. London: Polity.

Corsaro, W.A. (1997) *The sociology of childhood*. California: Pine Forge Press.

Cortazzi, M. and Jin, L. (2000) 'Evaluating evaluation in narrative', in S. Hunston and G. Thompson (eds) *Evaluation in text*. Oxford: Oxford University Press.

De Fina, A. (2004) *Identity in narrative: a study of immigrant discourse*. Amsterdam: John Benjamins.

Department of Education and Science and the Welsh Office (DES/WO) (1989) *English for ages 5–16: Proposals of the Secretary of State for Education and Science and the Secretary of State for Wales (the Cox report)*. London: Department for Education and Science and the Welsh Office.

Duranti, A. (2001) 'Linguistic anthropology: history, ideas and issues', in A. Duranti (ed.) *Linguistic anthropology: a Reader*. Oxford: Blackwell Publishers.

Eckert, P. (2000) *Linguistic variation as social practice*. Oxford: Blackwell Publishers.

Eckert. P. and McConnell-Ginet, S. (2003) *Language and gender*. Cambridge: Cambridge University Press.

Eder, D. and Enke, J.L. (1991) 'The structure of gossip- opportunities and constraints on collective expression among adolescents', *American Sociological Review*, 56(4): 494–508.

Edwards, D. and Mercer, N. (1987) *Common Knowledge: the development of understanding in the classroom*. London: Methuen.

Evaldsson, A. (2002) 'Boys' gossip telling: staging identities and indexing (unacceptable) masculine behaviour', *Text*, 22(2): 199–226.

Falk, J. (1980) 'The conversational duet', *Proceedings of the 6th annual meeting of the Berkley Linguistics society*, Vol. 6, pp. 507–14.

Foley, D. (2002) 'Critical ethnography: the reflexive turn', *Qualitative studies in education*, 15(5): 469–490.

Foucault, M. (1979) *Discipline and punish*. (A. Sheridan trans.) New York: Harper.

Foucault, M. (ed. Colin Gordan) (1980) *Power/knowledge: selected interviews and other writings 1972–9*. London: Harvester Press.

Foucault, M. (1981) 'The order of discourse', in R. Young (ed.) *Untying the text: a post-structuralist reader*. London: Routledge and Kegan Paul.

Gee, J. (1990) *Social linguistics and literacies: ideology in discourses*, London: Falmer Press.

Goffman, E. (1967) 'On face-work: an analysis of ritual elements in social interaction', in *Interaction ritual*. Harmondsworth: Penguin.

Goffman, E. (1969) *The presentation of self in everyday life*. London: Penguin.

Goffman, E. (1974) *Frame analysis*. Harmondsworth: Penguin.

Goffman, E. (1981) 'Footing', in *Forms of talk*. Oxford: Basil Blackwell.

Goodwin, M.H. (1990) *He-said-she-said: talk as social organisation among black children*. Bloomington: Indiana University Press.

Green, J. and Bloome, D. (1995) 'Ethnography and ethnographers of and in education: a situated perspective', in J. Flood, S. Heath, D. Alvermann and D. Lapp (eds) *A handbook for literacy educators*. New York: Macmillan.

Gunther, S. (1999) 'Polyphony and the "layering of voices" in reported dialogues: An analysis of the use of prosodic devices in everyday reported speech', *Journal of Pragmatics*, 31(5): 685–708.

Hall, C. Sarangi, S. and Slembrouck, S. (1999) 'Speech representation and the categorisation of the client in social work discourse', *Text*, 19(4): 539–570.

Hammersley, M. (1990) *Reading ethnographic research*. Harlow: Longman.

Hanks, W. F. (2001) 'Indexicality', in A. Duranti (ed.) *Key terms in language and culture*. Oxford: Blackwell.

Hanks, W.F. (1996) *Language and communicative practices*. Boulder, Colorado: Westview Press.

Hardy, B. (1968) 'Towards a poetics of fiction', *Novel*, 2: 5–14.

Heath, S.B. (1983) *Ways with words*. Cambridge: Cambridge University Press.

Hewitt, R. (1997) '"Box-out" and "taxing"', in S. Johnson and U. Meinhoff (eds) *Language and masculinity*. Oxford: Blackwell Publishers.

Hey, V. (1997) *The company she keeps*. Buckingham: Open University Press.

Hill, J. and Irvine, J. (1992) 'Introduction', in J. Hill and J. Irvine (eds) *Responsibility and evidence in oral discourse*. Cambridge: Cambridge University Press.

Holmes, J. (1994) 'The role of compliments in female-male interaction', in J. Sunderland (ed.) *Exploring gender: questions and implications for English language education*. London: Prentice Hall.

Hull, L. and Schultz, K. (2002) *School's out! Bridging out-of-school literacies with classroom practice*. New York: Teacher's College Press.

Hymes, D. (1977) *Foundations in sociolinguistics: an ethnographic approach*. London: Tavistock.

Jakobson, J. (1960) 'Closing statement: linguistics and poetics', in T.A. Sebeok (ed.) *Style in language.* Cambridge, MA: M.I.T. Press.

Jenkins, R. (1996) *Social identity.* London: Routledge.

Jolly, M. (2006 forthcoming) 'Sincerely yours: everyday letters and the art of written relationship', in J. Maybin and J. Swann (eds) *The Art of English: everyday creativity.* Basingstoke, Hants: Palgrave Macmillan.

Kamberelis, G. and Scott, K.D. (1992) 'Other people's voices', *Linguistics and Education,* 4(3–4): 359–403.

Labov, W. (1972) *Language in the inner city.* Philadelphia: University of Philadelphia Press.

Lakoff, R. (1975) *Language and women's place.* New York: Harper and Row.

Leech, G. and Short, M. (1981) *Style in fiction.* London: Longman.

Leont'ev, A.N. (1981) *Problems of the Development of Mind.* Moscow: Progress Publishers.

Livingstone, S. and Bober, M. (2004) *UK Children go online: surveying the experiences of young people and their parents.* ESRC. http://www.children-go-online.net.

Luke, A. (1992) 'The body literate: discourse and inscription in early literacy training', *Linguistics and education,* 4: 107–29.

Luke, A. (1996) 'Genres of power? Literacy education and the production of capital', in R. Hasan and G. Williams (eds) *Literacy in society. Applied linguistics and language study series.* London: Longman.

Lytra, V. (2003) *Constructing play frames and social identities: the case of a linguistically and culturally mixed peer group in an Athenian primary school.* Unpublished PhD Thesis, King's College London.

Malinowski, B. (1923) 'The problem of meaning in prinitive languages', in C.K. Ogden and M.A. Richards *The meaning of meaning.* London: Kegan Paul, Trench, Trubner.

Malinowski, B. (1935) *Coral gardens and their magic.* London: Allen and Unwin.

Markova, I. (1993) 'Acts in discourse: from monological speech acts to dialogical inter-acts', *Journal for the theory of social behaviour,* 23(2): 173–95.

Maybin, J., Mercer, N. and Stierer, B. (1992) '"Scaffolding" learning in the classroom', in K. Norman (ed.)

Maybin, J. and Moss, G. (1993) 'Talk about texts: reading as a social event', *Journal of research in reading,* 16(2): 138–47.

Maybin, J. (1994) 'Children's voices: talk, knowledge and identity', in D. Graddol, J. Maybin and B. Stierer (eds) *Researching language and literacy in context,* Clevedon, Multilingual Matters: 131–150. Reprinted in Cheshire, J. and Trudgill, P. (eds) (1998) *The sociolinguistics reader: Vol 2: Gender and discourse,* London: Edward Arnold: 278–94.

Maybin, J. (1999) 'Framing and evaluation in 10–12 year old school children's use of appropriated speech, in relation to their induction into educational procedures and practices', *TEXT,* 19(4): 459–84.

Maybin, J. (2002) 'What's the hottest part of the Sun? Page 3! Children's exploration of adolescent gender identities through informal talk', in J. Sunderland and L. Litosseliti (eds) *Discourse analysis and gender identities.* Amsterdam: Benjamins.

McCarthy, M. (1998) *Spoken language and applied linguistics.* Cambridge: Cambridge University Press.

McLaren, P. (1986) *Schooling as ritual performance.* London: Routledge and Kegan Paul.

Mercer, N. (1995) *The guided construction of knowledge: talk amongst teachers and learners*. Clevedon: Multilingual Matters.

Mercer, N. (2000) *Words and minds: how we use language to think together*. London: Routledge.

Michaels, S. (1981) '"Sharing time": children's narrative styles and differential access to literacy', *Language in Society*, 10: 423–42.

Miller, P.J., Potts, R., Fung, H., Hoogstra, L., Mintz, J. (1990) 'Narrative practices and the social construction of self in childhood', *American Ethnologist*, 17: 292–311.

Miller, P.J., Mintz, Hoogstra, R., Fung, H., L., J. Potts (1992) 'The narrated self: young children's construction of self in relation to others in conversational stories of personal experience', *Merrill-Palmer Quarterly*, 38: 45–67.

Moss, G. (1996) *Negotiated literacies: how children enact what counts as reading in different social settings*. Unpublished PhD thesis, The Open University.

Moss, G. (2000) 'Informal literacies and pedagogic discourse', *Linguistics and Education*, 11(1): 46–64.

Myers, G. (2004) *Matters of opinion*, Cambridge: Cambridge University Press.

Norman, K. (ed.) (1992) *Thinking voices: the work of the National Oracy Project*. London: Hodder and Stoughton.

Norrick, N.R. (1997) 'Twice-told tales: collaborative narration of familiar stories', *Language in Society*, 26: 199–220.

Ochs, E. (1992) 'Indexing gender', in A. Duranti and C. Goodwin (eds) *Rethinking context*. Cambridge: Cambridge University Press.

Ochs, E. and Capps, L. (2001) *Living narrative: creating lives in everyday storytelling*. Havard: Harvard University Press.

Opie, I. and Opie P. (1959) *The lore and language of school children*. Oxford: Oxford University Press.

Rampton, B., Tusting, K., Maybin, J., Barwell, R., Creese, A. and Lytra, V. (2004) 'UK Linguistic Ethnography: a discussion paper', http://www.lancs.ac.uk/fss/organisations/lingethn/

Rampton, B. (Second edition) (2005a) *Crossing: language and ethnicity among adolescents*. Manchester: St. Jerome Press.

Rampton, B. (2005b) *Language in late modernity: interaction in an urban school*. Cambridge: Cambridge University Press.

Sacks, H., Schegloff, E. and Jefferson, G. (1974) 'A simplest systematics for the organisation of turn-taking in conversation'. *Language*, 50(4): 696–735.

Salomon, G. (ed.) (1993) *Distributed cognitions: psychological and educational considerations*. Cambridge: Cambridge University Press.

Schiffrin, D. (1996) 'Narrative as self-portrait: sociolinguistic constructions of identity', *Language in Society*, 25: 167–203.

Scollon, R., Tsang, W. K., Li, D., Yung, V. and Jones, R. (1998) 'Voice, appropriation and discourse representation in a student writing task', *Linguistics and Education*, 9(3): 227–50.

Scollon, R. and Scollon, S.W. (2003) *Discourses in place: language in the material world*. London and New York: Routledge.

Scollon, R. (2003) 'Intertextuality across communities of practice', in C.L. Moder and A. Martinovic-Zic (eds) *Discourse across language and cultures*. Amsterdam: John Benjamins.

Sealey, A. (2000) *Childly language: children, language and the social world.* London: Longman/Pearson Educational.

Sheldon, A. (1997) 'Talking power: girls, gender enculturation and discourse', in R. Wodak (ed.) *Gender and discourse.* London: Sage.

Short, M. (1996) *Exploring the language of poems, plays and prose.* London: Longman.

Shuman, A. (1986) *Storytelling rights: the uses of oral and written texts among urban adolescents.* Cambridge: Cambridge University Press.

Skinner, D., Valsiner, J. and Holland, D. (2001) 'Discerning the dialogical self: a theoretical and methodological examination of a Nepali Adolescent's Narrative', Forum: Qualitative Social Research [on-line Journal **2b** (3). Available at: http://www.qualitative-research.net/fqs-texte/3-01/3-01skinneretal-e.htm: accessed 7.01.05.

Sola, M. and Bennett, A. (1985) 'The struggle for voice: narrative, literacy and consciousness in an East Harlem School', *Journal of Education,* 167(1).

Steedman, C. (1982) *The tidy house.* London: Virago,

Street, B. (1984) *Literacy in theory and practice.* Cambridge: Cambridge University Press.

Street, B. and Street, J. (1991) 'The schooling of literacy', in D. Barton and R. Ivanic (eds) *Writing in the community.* London: Sage.

Street, B. (1993) 'Culture is a verb: anthropological aspects of language and cultural process', in D. Graddol, L. Thompson and M. Byram (eds) *Language and culture: British studies in applied linguistics,* 7. Clevedon: Multilingual Matters.

Street, B. (1994) 'Cross-cultural perspectives on literacy', in J. Maybin (ed.) *Language and literacy in social practice.* Clevedon: Multilingual Matters.

Swann, J. and Graddol, D. (1995) 'The feminisation of classroom discourse?', in S. Mills (ed.) *Language and gender: interdisciplinary perspectives.* London: Longman.

Swann, J. (2003) 'Schooled language: language and gender in educational settings', in J. Holmes and M. Meyerhoff (eds) *The handbook of language and gender.* Oxford: Blackwell Publishing.

Swann, J., Deumert, A., Lillis, T. and Mesthrie, R. (eds) (2004) *A dictionary of sociolinguistics.* Edinburgh: Edinburgh University Press.

Szwed, J.F. (1981) 'The ethnography of literacy', in M.F. Whiteman (ed.) *Writing: the nature, development and teaching of written communication,* part 1 Hillsdale, N.J.: Erlbaum.

Tannen, D. (1989) *Talking voices: repetition, dialogue and imagery in conversational discourse.* Cambridge: Cambridge University Press.

Tannen, D. (1990) *You just don't understand!* New York: Morrow.

Tannen, D. and Wallat, C. (1993) 'Interactive frames and knowledge schemas in interaction: examples from a medical examination/interview', in D. Tannen (ed.) *Framing in discourse.* New York: Oxford University Press.

Thorne, B. (1993) *Gender play: girls and boys in school.* Buckingham: Open University Press.

Toolan, M.J. (2001) *Narrative: a critical linguistic introduction.* Second edition. London: Routledge.

Volosinov, V.N. ([1929]1973) *Marxism and the philosophy of language.* trans. L. Matejka and I.R. Titunik. Cambridge, MA: Harvard University Press.

Volosinov, V.N. ([1927]1976) 'Discourse in life and discourse in art', in *Freudianism: a Marxist critique* trans. I.R. Titunik, ed. I.R. Titunik and N.H. Bruss. New York: Academic Press.

Vygotsky, L. ([1920s–30s]1978) *Mind in society: the development of higher psychological processes* ed. M. Cole et al., Cambridge, MA: Harvard University Press.

Vygotsky, L. ([1934]1986) *Thought and Language*. Cambridge, MA: MIT Press.

Wertsch, J. (1991) *Voices of the mind*. London: Harvester Wheatsheaf.

Wetherell, M., Phoenix, A. and Hollway, W. (2005) 'Identities, relationality and the psychosocial: different journeys to the same place'. Inaugural Lecture, The Open University.

Wolfson, N. (1982) *CHP: the conversational historical present in American English narrative*. Dordrecht, Holland and Cinnaminson, USA: Foris.

Wortham, S. (2001) *Narratives in action: a strategy for research and analysis*. New York: Teachers College Press.

Index